UNION WOMEN

Social Movements, Protest, and Contention

Series Editor   Bert Klandermans, Free University, Amsterdam

Associate Editors Ron R. Aminzade, University of Minnesota
David S. Meyer, University of California, Irvine
Verta A. Taylor, University of California, Santa Barbara

For more books in the series, see page viii.

UNION WOMEN

Forging Feminism in the United Steelworkers of America

Mary Margaret Fonow

Social Movements, Protest, and Contention
Volume 17

University of Minnesota Press
Minneapolis • London

Published by the University of Minnesota Press
111 Third Avenue South, Suite 290
Minneapolis, MN 55401-2520
http://www.upress.umn.edu

Library of Congress Cataloging-in-Publication Data

Fonow, Mary Margaret, 1949–
    Union women : forging feminism in the United Steelworkers of America /
Mary Margaret Fonow.
        p.   cm. — (Social movements, protest, and contention ; v. 17)
Includes bibliographical references and index.
    ISBN 0-8166-3882-9 (HC : alk. paper) — ISBN 0-8166-3883-7 (pbk. :
alk. paper)
    1. Women labor union members—United States—History.   2. Women
iron and steel workers—United States—History.   3. Feminism—United
States—History.   4. United Steelworkers of America—History.   I. Title.
II. Series.
HD6079.2.U5 F655 2003
331.4'781691'0973—dc21   2002152593

Printed in the United States of America on acid-free paper

The University of Minnesota is an equal-opportunity educator and employer.

12 11 10 09 08 07 06 05 04 03   10 9 8 7 6 5 4 3 2 1

For Sharon Stiller, Sue Milling, and Cecelia (Sissy) Humienny,
and in solidarity with all the "Women of Steel"
of the past, present, and future

Contents

Social Movements, Protest, and Contention (continued)

Acknowledgments

A project of this scope and magnitude would not have been possible without the friendship, support, and talent of many individuals and the cooperation of various institutions and organizations—particularly the United Steelworkers of America and The Ohio State University. I am deeply appreciative of the support I have received from my family, friends, colleagues, and students. My partner, Cory Dillon, was with me every step of the way, offering encouragement, brilliant editorial assistance, and an abundance of good humor. I wrote most of this book while my son, Ben, was at Earlham College meeting his own intellectual challenges, and I thank him for the wonderful hours of conversation and the music we shared during his years as an undergraduate. And I thank my mother, Mary Fonow, for her support, love, and encouragement.

So many kind and smart people have read and responded to my work over the years that I cannot even begin to express my gratitude. I owe a special thanks to Verta Taylor, who played a key role in helping me to develop an analytic framework that could handle such a large amount of original material. Karen Beckwith, who shares my theoretical interest in how labor movements become gendered, was important to the book's development. Judith Cook and David MacKenzie read the entire manuscript and provided crucial advice as I was nearing its completion. Old friends like Laurel Richardson and Leila Rupp were there from the beginning with encouragement and insight. Along the way I made new friends, like Jack Metzgar, who was incredibly generous with his time and talent. I am also indebted to my friends and colleagues from The Ohio State University who read and commented on various portions of the manuscript: Cindy Burack, Susan Hartmann, Sally Kitch, Valerie Lee, Cathy Rakowski, Stephanie Shaw, and Ara Wilson.

Colleagues and friends at other universities have also participated in the creation of this book. I received invaluable feedback from discussants at professional meetings and from manuscript reviewers, and for this I would like to thank Linda Blum, Robert Bruno, Nancy Campbell, Cynthia Deitch, Bonnie Thortonbill, Myra Marx Ferree, Nancy Gabin, Robin Leidner, Jane Melnick, Ruth Milkman, Ronnie Steinberg, Eileen Willenborg, Martha Wharton, and Nancy Whittier. I am also grateful to Ruth Needleman, James B. Stewart, and Judy Stepan-Norris, who generously shared their works in progress with me, and to Jim Lane, who shared his wonderful oral history interviews with the women in the District 31 Women's Caucus.

Thanks also to Stephen McShane of the Calumet Regional Archive and Denise Conklin of the Penn State Labor Archive, who provided important help locating documents and records. A special thanks to women's studies librarians Linda Krikos and Virginia Reynolds at The Ohio State University and to Carrie Mullen and Julie DuSablon from the University of Minnesota Press.

Over the years I have had the good fortune to work with many skilled research assistants, including Lu Zhang, Jen Kiper, Ditmar Coffield, Jelena Batinic, Nancy Mortell, Eva Mutandi, Elora Chowdhury, Aimee Sisco, Jessica Turner-Crim, and Angel DeChant. A special thanks to Norma Juarbe-Franceschini, who translated the Frente Auténtico del Trabajo documents from Spanish to English, and to Lu Bailey, who skillfully managed *Reading Women's Lives* and gave me time to concentrate on writing this book. Also a special thanks to Karen Earnhardt-Martinez, who supervised the *Women of Steel* telephone survey and provided statistical analysis, and to Oona Besman and Susan Lantz, who collected the data.

Many steelworkers past and present have been especially gracious with their time, talent, and energy. Sharon Stiller, Sue Milling, and Sissy Humienny all provided ideas, information, analysis, and good cheer. I am indebted to Roberta Wood (who gave me many original documents of the District 31 Women's Caucus), Dorreen Carey, Nancy Lessin, Colette Murphy, Marsha Zakowski, Leo Gerard, Lawrence McBrearty, Michael Lewis, Marlene Gow, Fern Valen, Santo Santoro, Denise Saiter, and Steffi Domike for their valuable insights and to Lisa Blanchette and Gerald Dickey for access to the wonderful union photographs.

Finally, I am grateful to the funding and research release time I have received from the Department of Women's Studies, the College of Humanities, and the Survey Research Center at The Ohio State University. Without their confidence and material support this project would not have been possible.

1

Union Feminism, Social Movements, and Gender

I don't think feminist is a four-letter word. I'm very proud to be one. It means a lot of things. I think mainly it means to me that I'm going to stand up for what I believe in and fight for what I believe in.

—Sandy Sutton

I think I am [a feminist]. If I know what feminism means, I think I am. I think. I don't understand how you cannot be a feminist. How you can raise daughters and not be a feminist?

—Loretta Tyler

Sandy Sutton and Loretta Tyler, presidents of their union locals, share a similar understanding of feminism—for them it means equality between the sexes, fairness, and action. Both evoke the movement for women's rights and hold themselves accountable for changing things. Loretta is the president of a predominantly male amalgamated local and has been a member of the United Steelworkers of America (USWA) since 1976. She became active in the union when she filed a grievance for the right to be a forklift operator. A successful outcome convinced her of the value of the union, and she has been active ever since. Loretta worked her way into the presidency of her local by virtue of her performance in a series of other positions—trustee, steward, member of the grievance committee, and recording secretary. Loretta was caught off guard when I asked her if she considered herself a feminist and had to think for a minute before she said, "How could you not be?"[1]

For Loretta, an African American, feminism is just one of a number of tacit assumptions about social justice that informs her political consciousness along with her commitment to civil rights and her labor activism.

Sandy, who is white, also worked her way up to the presidency of an office-and-technical local that was organized in the wake of a campaign to prevent outsourcing at a large steel mill.[2] She is proud to call herself a feminist, but she is also aware that feminism is a part of her identity she might be called upon to defend. During our interview, it was my turn to be caught off guard when Sandy compared being a feminist to being a Lutheran. She told me that feminism "has a lot of connotations that any more are not real positive. It's kind of like I'm a Lutheran. That carries a lot of connotations, too—some good, some bad. But, you know, not every Lutheran in the world has to be great."[3] While the stereotypes of Lutherans elude most of us, those of feminism do not. Nor did they elude many of the women in the Steelworkers. When I spoke with Colette, a Canadian welder of Irish descent, she exclaimed, "Ooh, that word! If you were a feminist at one time it was sort of a dirty word, and nobody wanted to be associated with it because, you know, they didn't wear bras. They were radical."[4]

All three women defined their union activism as an extension of their commitments to social justice and developed a sense of themselves as feminists through their struggles on the job and in the union. Their sense of agency is rooted in the multiple subject positions they inhabit as part of the small generation of working-class women of different races and nationalities who seized the new, nontraditional job opportunities created by the U.S. civil rights movement and by the second wave of the women's movement. The feminism the women in my study grappled to define, and were often forced to defend, was a feminism forged in the day-to-day struggle to keep their jobs in a male-dominated industry during the harshest of economic times for steelworkers, their union, and their communities.

This book is about the remarkable emergence, growth, and development of union feminism in the United Steelworkers of America (USWA)—an international union representing over 700,000 workers in the United States and Canada. It is a story about a tenacious group of working-class women who—like Sandy, Loretta, and Colette—secured space within a male-dominated union from which women could challenge sex discrimination and advocate for women's rights. To do so, women found it necessary to transform the organizations, resources, and networks of both the women's movement and the labor movement. They developed and used "in-between" movement spaces to create a feminism more responsive to their multiple political interests as workers, as women, and as citizens.[5] Union feminism serves as a bridge between the women's movement and the labor movement and has helped to make salient in both movements the reality of multiple, overlapping, and intersecting sites of discrimination, which Collins (1990) labels the matrix of domination. In the process of transforming the steelworkers union to represent their multiple interests as working-class women, these women are themselves transformed into union feminists.

Understanding the opportunities and constraints of women mobilizing at the intersection of two very different social movements—one new and identity-based, and one older, more traditional and class-based—enhances our knowledge of the dynamics of social movement formation. This is particularly useful in the contemporary period when political identities are increasingly fragmented. Union feminism combines the class politics of economic redistribution with the identity politics of difference and represents a unique way to understand the new forms of class politics emerging from the social and economic disruptions of globalization—a politics that requires fusing new (gender) and old (class) forms of solidarity (Fraser 1997). To survive the effects of economic restructuring at the turn of the twenty-first century, the labor movement must develop new approaches to mobilization and new forms of organization, which I believe can be effective only if they are informed by feminism and other social movements.

"Women of Steel" and Union Feminism

As an outcome of women's activism, the Steelworkers have instituted a number of new initiatives to increase the participation and activism of its female members and to increase the number of new women in the organization. In 1998, George Becker, former president of the International, appointed Sharon Stiller to serve as special assistant to the president for women's issues and programs to develop, coordinate, and direct these initiatives. Women's committees have been developed and linked together by a new system of regional councils, and Stiller has put into place an International Women's Committee composed of a coordinator of women's programs from each of the Steelworkers' twelve districts. The committee held its first International Women's Conference from 6 to 9 February 2000, and close to eight hundred participants came together in Pittsburgh to lay the foundation for the future of women's participation and activism in the union. A second women's conference dedicated to building global solidarity and building alliances with grassroots organizations was held in Pittsburgh from 26 to 29 August 2001. The Steelworkers in Canada developed an innovative, educational course on women's leadership that has been adopted and modified for use throughout the United States. The Canadians have held three national women's

Figure 1. George Becker, former president of the United Steelworkers of America, announces the appointment of Sharon Stiller as special assistant to the president for women's issues and programs at the 1998 Constitutional Convention in Las Vegas, Nevada. Courtesy of the United Steelworkers of America.

conferences and have put into place their own national women's committee to advise national director Lawrence McBrearty on women's issues and programs. Finally, through the work of the Steelworkers Humanity Fund, the Canadians are building women's international solidarity, particularly among women unionists in the North American Free Trade Association (NAFTA) bloc (Figures 1 and 2).

These relatively new initiatives are loosely packaged together under the title of *Women of Steel,* and they involve a range of actions from discursive practices such as conference resolutions, to formal structures such as women's committees, to specific campaigns such as the union's domestic violence program in Canada. I also use the term "Women of Steel" to convey their unique collective identity as union feminists. Through consciousness raising, mutual support, and collective action, women are challenging their status as a group disadvantaged by discrimination and using the union to do so. The targets of protest and action are simultaneously the union, the workplace, and the broader society. The activists are concerned with tradi-

Figure 2. Opening session of the Steelworkers' First International Women's Conference, 6 February 2000, Pittsburgh, Pennsylvania. Courtesy of the United Steelworkers of America.

tional feminist policy issues such as sexual and racial harassment, domestic violence, pay equity, balancing work and family, domestic-partner benefits, job training, and reproductive health and rights as well as more conventional collective-bargaining concerns, such as pensions, job security, and wages. Because collective bargaining for gender-specific policies is more effective when there are legislative mandates regarding such issues already in place, union feminists are pursuing collective bargaining and legislative avenues simultaneously.

Union feminism in the Steelworkers is simultaneously discursive practice and goal-oriented collective action undertaken on behalf of women as a group. Activists use discursive tools (conference resolutions, policy statements, educational programs, newsletters, etc.) as well as institutionally sanctioned spaces (conventions, workshops, labor schools, committee structures, etc.) to fashion a network of resources that can be called into action to mobilize their membership and potential supporters at strategically important moments. This network helps to establish and sustain more permanent structures of organizational participation and protest. Their collective identity as "Women of Steel" is forged through the day-to-day activities of building and sustaining these networks.

Union feminism is not a new phenomenon. Historians and sociologists have documented and analyzed the role women played in the history of the labor movement, the way labor history itself is gendered, and how particular unions have served as crucial vehicles for organizing gender protest and advancing women's rights (Baron 1991; Blum 1991; Briskin and McDermott 1993; Cobble 1990, 1991, 1993, 1994, 2003; Cockburn 1997; Cook et al. 1984; Cornfield 1989; Crain 1994; Deslippe 2000; Faue 1991; Ferree and Roth 1998; Gabin 1990; Hartmann 1998; Kessler-Harris 1975; Luxton 1997; Milkman 1987, 1993; Pocock 1997; Sugiman 1994). These struggles have often combined women's demand for economic rights ("bread") with broader social justice issues ("roses") and have traditionally expanded workplace struggles out into the community. As in the past, union feminists often extend women's issues and concerns beyond the economic to encompass dignity on the job, worker education, and improvements to the quality of life and culture in working-class communities (Orleck 1995). They are more likely to fight for work-based policies and practices that recognize and accommodate women's dual commitments to family and work (Cobble 1994; Franzway 2001; Gerstel and Clawson 2001). With the advent of civil rights and human rights legislation, new political strategies and discourses have been added to the repertoire of union feminists. These include affirmative-action initiatives, the creation of separate spaces for women's activism and leadership development, and efforts to use collective bargaining to advance gender-specific concerns such as pay equity, child care, and the prevention of sexual harassment and domestic violence (Cuneo 1993; Curtin 1999; Forrest 2001; Kumar 1993; Munro 2001).

Deindustrialization and Economic Restructuring

My analysis covers the period from 1974 to the present—a period of great change and upheaval for the economy as well as for unions and the workers they represent. The study of gender equity and women's union participation during this time contributes to an understanding of the forces that affect the economic security of women in late capitalism. Rapid technological change, economic restructuring, increased globalization, and the subsequent reconfiguration of state-market relations have created new realities for women workers and new and difficult challenges for social movements. Yet it is in this climate that women's activism has begun to flourish in the Steelworkers.

Globalization and economic restructuring present difficult but not insurmountable challenges to the labor movement and to the feminists within unions. Steelworkers have had to come to terms with these challenges, and their union serves as an illustrative case for understanding the effects of globalization on women's activism. The history of women in the steel industry has always been one of advances and setbacks. Women's labor was needed during World War II but not during the re-conversion to peacetime production, and women were quickly displaced by the men who were returning from the war. In the United States, it would take an affirmative action court order filed on 15 April 1974 before jobs would once again open to women—this time on equal footing with men. At the peak of their employment, women represented 14,500 of the maintenance and production workers in basic steel (Deitch et al. 1991, 42).

But almost as soon as the women were hired, they were displaced again—this time by ravages of deindustrialization. Plant closings and massive downsizing disproportionately affected those more recently hired and left nearly 50 percent of women steelworkers in the United States permanently displaced from some of the best-paying jobs in industrial manufacturing. Between 1974 and 1979, women's share of jobs in basic steel in the United States increased from 1.8 percent to 5.8 percent and, in some select mills in the Chicago-Gary area, the percentage of women had reached as high as 17.5 percent of the production workforce (Deaux and Ullman 1983). However, by 1984, their numbers had dwindled from 14,500 to fewer than 3,000 (Hymowitz 1985). When they accepted new jobs in other industries, steelworkers experienced a 40 percent drop in median weekly earnings (Flain and Sehgal 1985).

This turn of events dramatically reduced the union's membership rolls, and the Steelworkers' path to recovery and revitalization has required a deeper understanding of globalization and economic restructuring. The union restructured its own administration, expanded international networks, and allocated more funds for organizing a broader constituency of workers, including those sectors of the economy that traditionally employ women. Women are more predisposed than men to join unions, and the Steelworkers are very aware of this fact. They know that changing the union's culture is key to organizing women. "We need to examine in what ways we can continue to build an attractive and woman-friendly union. This means attention to internal programs, staff hiring, the way that we communicate—in other words, attention to all of those parts of the union's life which constitute our culture" ("Report of the Organizing Task Force," 1998).

Through union mergers and innovative organizing techniques, the Steelworkers have added new members from the rubber, upholstery, grocery,

Table 1

Membership Diversity in United Steelworkers of America

Industry	Number of members
Basic steel	147,087
Rubber and plastics	80,639
Sheet and structural steel, nuts and bolts, etc.	60,604
Chemicals, petroleum products, nonmetallic minerals	56,139
Aluminum	45,932
Nonferrous metals	40,549
Industrial machinery, fittings and equipment	39,449
Retail, wholesale, and financial services	36,961
Transportation equipment	33,063
Foundries and forgings	25,077
Utilities and construction	22,579
Electrical equipment, cutlery, hand tools	19,472
Health care	15,568
Public sector	10,014
Containers	9,981
Miscellaneous	64,109
Total	707,223

Source: "The Union," n.d. Union brochure, Membership Department, 4–5.

health care, hotels and restaurants, finance, insurance, security, and real estate industries (Murray 1998; Devinatz 1993) (Table 1).

The Steelworkers made further inroads into female-dominated occupations when nearly 4,000 staff and professional workers at the University of Toronto, 70 percent of them women, chose to affiliate with the Steelworkers in 1998. Union membership in the Steelworkers, which has recovered from its earlier decline, is now around 700,000 members, and about 20 percent are female. Women have become the fastest-growing sector of new union membership.

I seek to understand the factors that explain the origin, growth, and changes in women's activism in the Steelworkers over time. What makes it feminist? Why does organizational location matter? What advantages and constraints are afforded by operating in two distinct political fields—Canada and the United States? I also hope to contribute to a theoretical understanding of how gender and social movements mutually inform each other. How does attending to gender and to other categories of difference improve the analysis of social-movement formation? How has globalization changed the nature of the political playing field for women activists in the Steelworkers? It may be surprising to many that union feminism has taken root in a traditionally male-dominated industrial union during a period of history some-times characterized as postindustrial and postfeminist. Steelworker and feminist are two collective identities we do not often associate with each other. Yet women Steelworkers from different backgrounds and occupations are forging a unique working-class feminist collective identity as "Women of Steel."

Gender and Social Movements

My analysis of feminist activism in the Steelworkers is informed by the con-cepts, assumptions, and frameworks developed by scholars of social move-ments and by feminist theorists of the welfare state and gender politics. I view social movements and their organizations as gendered, that is, serving simultaneously as sites of resistance to cultural and social constructions of gender inequality and as sites of conformity to and reproduction of gender norms and structures. By attending to gender we increase our understand-ing of the processes that influence the nature and course of all forms of col-lective action, including social-movement formation, mobilizing frames and collective identities, organization, strategies, and outcomes (Beckwith 2001; Fonow 1998; McAdam 1992; Taylor 1999). Because gender is also consti-tutive of states and organizations, it serves in a very particular way as an or-ganizing principle that structures the political opportunities, mobilization networks, and resources crucial to the recruitment of movement partici-pants and to the ongoing maintenance of activism within social movements (Acker 1995; Lorber 1994).

Similarly, race and ethnicity are constitutive of gender and of labor markets and state relationships and, as social categories, are constantly be-ing transformed and contested by political struggle.[6] Gender cannot be sep-arated from race and/or ethnicity. Women hired into occupations represented by the Steelworkers are hired into jobs that are also structured by race and ethnicity. In the United States, for example, black women hired during World War II were given the job assignments deemed least desirable for white women—jobs that mirrored the existing "Jim Crow" division of labor that placed black men in the most dangerous, least desired jobs handling raw material (Dickerson 1986; Hill 2002; Nelson 2001; Norrell 1986; Stew-art 2001). Women's activism to end discrimination in the steel industry in the United States had to be forged at the intersection of the civil rights movement and the women's movement. It is necessary to trace these link-ages in order to understand how both black and white women developed a sense of themselves as political actors within the union.[7]

Immigration status, ethnicity, and language tend to be more salient in the Canadian context than is race, and much of the politics and discourse there about difference is subsumed under the broader rubric of human rights and multiculturalism. The divergence in racial composition and in racial politics between the two countries poses interesting challenges to union feminists who are trying to build bridges across national borders. Power differences among union women may require different and/or separate forms of mobilization for specific groups of women—women of color, immigrant women, indigenous women. The Canadian Steelworkers developed a special version of the women's leadership course for women of color (primarily Caribbean and South Asian immigrants), which struck some black women in the United States as segregationist.[8]

Class is also at the center of my analysis. I view class formation in much the same way that I view gender and racial formation—as the ongoing, historically specific effects of social-movement activity. Class does not transcend other categories of difference. Class is lived through race, gender, and sexuality (Krupat and McCreery 2001; Kelley 1997; Kurtz 2002). According to Jenkins and Leicht, "class formation is a product of class struggles that come together in a concrete nexus of economic, political, and ideological relationships between specific actors" (1997, 373). By focusing on union women's activism, I seek to explain how a gendered class is produced, at least in part, by a union feminism forged at the intersection of the women's movement, the civil rights movement, and the labor movement.

Model of Collective Identity Formation

The success of social movements seeking to mobilize working-class women depends on the ability of such movements to develop discursive frames of action, collective identities, and mobilizing structures that build solidarity across various lines of difference without suppressing the social and political significance of those differences. Studying a union located in two different political fields allows us to compare the effects of different political opportunity structures on the formation of collective identity and union feminism (Figure 3).

As Figure 3 shows, broad socioeconomic factors such as globalization and economic restructuring help to shape the political opportunity structures and collective action frames that, through the formal and informal mobilizing structures of the union, influence the formation of a collective identity as "Women of Steel." Collective identity formation is necessary for the development of collective action or union feminism. The collective action of union feminists influences the ability of the union to mobilize its

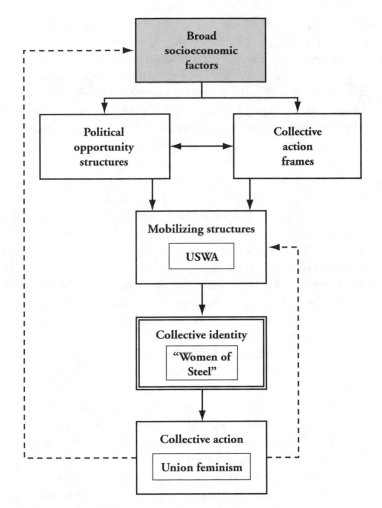

Figure 3. A model of collective identity formation and its outcome.

members and ultimately the broader socioeconomic factors. Gender relations and other dimensions of difference inform each step in the process.

Gendered Political Opportunity Structures in Canada and the United States

The political field structures the political opportunities of a movement—including the repertoires of collective action available to social-movement organizations and to participants—and configures the system of conflicts and alliances that serve as movement resources (McAdam 1997; Ray 1999; Tarrow 1996; Tilly 1984). The state—including the gendered networks of power it generates—plays an important role in constricting and/or expanding the political opportunities that influence the trajectory of social movements and their chances of success. This relationship between the state and social movements is a dynamic one. Social movements actively seek to reconfigure political alignments within the state while, at the same time, the actions of these movements are impacted by the state. In the case of the labor movement, affecting the balance of power among market, state, and family is essential if the movement is to create new political opportunities for women (Kriesi 1996; McAdam et al. 1996; Orloff 1996; Skocpol 1992). Similarly, the women's movement has always focused, in part, on getting the state to ameliorate the effects of the market on women (Brodie 1995). Thus, both labor and feminists are uniquely situated at the boundary of the public and the private—a boundary that serves as a site for political struggles about where that line of demarcation is to be drawn.

The factors that distinguish the political opportunity structures in each country also help to shape the way labor and feminism relate to the state and to each other (Franzway 2000). Despite similar experiences with economic restructuring, particularly a decline in manufacturing, which had been a traditional stronghold of unionism in both countries, Canada has not experienced the dramatic decline in union membership that has characterized the United States labor movement. Canadian labor unions have been more successful in organizing new types of workers in workplaces characteristic of the post-Fordist production regimes.[9] They have also been more effective in protecting and expanding collective-bargaining rights. Stronger labor laws provide unions and the feminists within them more avenues for activism.[10] The parliamentary structure in Canada is more conducive to multiparty formations and has allowed labor a more prominent place in Canadian politics through its affiliation with the New Democratic Party (NDP), a social-democratic party. The Steelworkers are officially affiliated with the NDP, which guarantees them positions in the deliberative bodies of the party. Through its women's committee and appointments of women, the NDP has made feminist issues a more acceptable part of the political landscape of labor in Canada.

The longer history of a feminist presence within the Canadian Labor Congress and the federated labor bodies of the provinces has enhanced "feminist footholds" (Hartmann 1998) in contemporary, mainstream Canadian labor politics more than is the case with similar bodies in the United States, such as the AFL-CIO. These Canadian labor bodies initiated women's committees in 1974, and most developed some form of affirmative action to set aside leadership seats in their decision-making structures for women and minority men, providing a venue for feminist activism within organized labor. In the United States, feminist activism in unions was channeled into the Coalition of Labor Union Women, an association of union women that advocates for women's interests from an autonomous position outside the formal organizational structures of any one union or federated body. This outside location made union feminists in the United States less effective in integrating gender equity within the labor movement than the Canadians (Roth 2003). In fact, the AFL-CIO did not establish its Working Women's Department which has already disbanded until 1996. Some of the functions of the department have been merged with other departments, and its director, Karen Nausbaum, is now a special assistant for women's issues to the president of the AFL-CIO.

The women's movement in Canada has a different relationship to labor and to the state than does the women's movement in the United States. The exchange of ideas, participants, resources, and leaders between the women's movement and the labor movement in Canada has resulted in a more class-oriented feminism, one that has generated greater support for feminist ideas and policies in the labor movement. The coalitional nature of the women's movement in Canada created space and legitimacy for union-based, working-class feminism (Luxton 1997). Unlike the National Organization for Women, which tries to mobilize a large heterogeneous population into one women's rights organization, its counterpart in Canada, the National Action Committee on the Status of Women, coordinates and facilitates the work of more than 600 women's organizations. The coalition has helped to secure a place for union feminists within the broader women's movement. As a result, in Canada, feminist politics are more institutionalized in the labor movement, and union politics are more institutionalized in the women's movement than they are in the United States.

The tension between political and legal discourses of individual rights and collective rights also differs in the two political fields. This is reflected in each movement's notion of equity. Unions in both countries have pursued group rights for workers but diverge in their recognition of differences other than class. The labor movement and the women's movement in Canada operate in political fields where there is less tension between group rights and individual rights. The Canadian Supreme Court has ruled that "accommodation of difference is the essence of true equality." Hence, the path to equality may involve accommodation of difference through special legal and constitutional measures that go beyond the common rights of citizenship (Kymlica 1996, 153). The Canadian Charter of Rights and Freedoms guarantees that laws "be interpreted in a manner consistent with the preservation and enhancement of the multicultural heritage of Canadians" (156). Unlike in the United States, which defeated the Equal Rights Amendment (ERA), women in Canada are guaranteed constitutional equality as women. This legal and political climate strengthens class-based claims of organized labor and gender-based claims of the women's movement while it opens the door for labor and feminists to recognize other group-based interests even within their own ranks. In Canada, attention to individual rights was added to an earlier emphasis on group rights, while the reverse is true in the United States (Lipset 1990).[11]

The State as the Object of Protest

Feminist theories of the welfare state and critiques of politics suggest that while the state has shaped political-opportunity structures in important ways, there are also other institutional locations for these opportunities, including new transnational sites for politics outside of the nation-state. Some feminists have concluded that an exclusive focus on the state as the site of politics may exclude most of women's political activity and the politics of the private sphere (Naples 1998; Randall and Waylen 1998; Shanley and Narayan 1997).[12] Others have found the state to be so thoroughly implicated in the construction and reproduction of gender relations that the extent to which and the manner in which the state can serve as vehicle for change is compromised (Brown 1995).

Sassen (1998) suggests that feminists and other social theorists need new ways to think about the state in the age of globalization. Regulatory functions once managed by the nation-state are increasingly being transferred to supranational, nongovernmental, private economic institutions and regulatory bodies, such as the World Bank, the International Monetary Fund, and the World Trade Organization. This is a process she refers to as the "unbundling of sovereignty." It is important to understand how these new sites for politics can be used by union feminists to build international or transnational forms of feminist solidarity—particularly in the face of globalization. The increasingly transnational political opportunity structures for organized labor and for the women's movement include nontraditional sites for organized politics, such as international law; international labor institutions; nongovernmental organizations (NGOs); the United Nations' tribunals, conferences, and covenants; human rights platforms; and cross-border organizing campaigns (Boswell and Steves 1997; della Porta et al. 1999; Smith 1997b).

The Steelworkers are taking notice of these new opportunities for collective action that transcend the boundaries of a particular nation and are mobilizing their members around free-trade issues. They are also building and maintaining better links with other unions within the NAFTA trading bloc. There have been worker-to-worker exchanges across borders, efforts to pursue legal remedies under the NAFTA sidebar agreements, participation in various International Labour Organization conferences, people's summits, and NGO networks and campaigns positioning workers' rights as human rights. The Steelworkers played a very visible role in the free-trade protests in Seattle in 1999 and in Quebec City in 2001. The participation and activism of union feminists in this area will be crucial. Union feminists can help the labor movement understand the gendered implications of economic restructuring and help unions fashion a political response that takes into account the needs and concerns of working women. Effective mobilization strategies must be informed by the understanding of how race, culture, and language situate women differently within the global economy (Bakker 1996; Gibson-Graham 1996; Sassen 1998).[13]

Gender and Collective-Action Frames

Political opportunities must be discursively framed as such (Gamson and Meyer 1996; Gamson 1997; Snow et al. 1986; Snow and Benford 1992). Discourse transforms issues, problems, and events into grievances about which individuals believe something can and should be done. Frame, according to Snow and Benford (1992), refers to "an interpretive schemata that simplifies and condenses the world out there by selecting, punctuating, and encoding objects, situations, events, experiences and sequences of actions within one's present or past environment" (459). To be successful, such frames must seek congruence and complementarity between the interests, values, and beliefs of the potential movement participants and the activities, goals, and ideologies of social movements. Discursive frames must mobilize new union participants and win allies among existing participants. It is sometimes hard to see how different and at times conflicting frames of the women's movement and of organized labor can be reconciled. Yet union feminists in the Steelworkers are learning to extend traditional trade-union frames to feminist issues. Likewise, they are introducing new, feminist frames to standard trade-union issues.

Innovative frames are being used to socialize an already mobilized group (workers) to a specific set of new actions—for example, ending violence against women. Canadian feminists in the Steelworkers appropriated the symbols and rhetoric of the bargaining table, a frame that already resonated with unionists, to construct a "kitchen-table" campaign on the prevention of violence against women. By coupling the kitchen table with the bargaining table, they were able to position the issue of violence against women as more than a private issue—as something that belonged on the collective-bargaining table in full view of the public. Men in the union were being socialized to look at a new issue in terms they could understand as trade unionists. In turn, this led to the successful organizing of domestic-shelter workers who were then positioned to help the union construct a class-based strategy to address a classic feminist issue—domestic violence.

Gender itself (as well as class and race) can actually be the frame through which the repertoire of collective action is constructed. A gender frame, according to Beckwith (2001), "connotes both generalized and movement-specific understandings of difference embedded in conceptions of "women" and "men," and in "masculinities" and "femininities" (301).[14] The symbols, behaviors, or actions (war metaphors, boycotts, strikes, rallies, etc.) that protest participants learn are legitimate for use in specific situations are already gendered, but this may not become apparent until women's activism in male-dominated settings brings gender into stark relief (Faue 1991).

As an occupation, steelworker was historically gendered as "masculine" so that by entering the occupation women challenged the cultural meanings that organized work, gender, and even protest (Fonow 1998). The presence of women in a previously gender-segregated work environment produced in some men a defensive reaction—a need to differentiate from anything feminine. In many protest situations this need to shore up masculine boundaries has led to expressions of what Hewitt (1991) labels "virile unionism." Exaggerated displays of masculinity on the job and in the union tended to conceal women's activism, to make solidarity more difficult to achieve, and to limit the range of protest activity deemed appropriate—all of which limited the union's effectiveness (Fonow 1998). It is possible to transform collective repertoires through deliberate innovation and strenuous bargaining—often at the margins of established repertoires—a process of collective learning through struggle (Beckwith 2001). Feminists in the Steelworkers have become an integral part of this "strenuous" bargaining process.

Mobilizing Structures and Women's Separate Space

Mobilizing for collective action takes place through mobilizing structures—the network of groups and organizations prepared to mobilize for action (Rucht 1996). These structures—both formal and informal—serve as organizational mechanisms to collect and use the movement's resources. Although often designed for other purposes, these structures can serve as sites for collective identity formation. To choose and develop mobilizing structures effectively, activists must successfully frame them as useful and appropriate to the social-change tasks they will be used to facilitate. Strategic framing and stable political opportunity structures are central in shaping the available range of mobilizing structures (Freeman 1999; McCarthy 1996).

The formation of union feminism depends in part on the existence of separate spaces that serve as staging areas for broader forms of organizational and movement participation. As Katzenstein (1998) makes clear: "For protest to occur inside institutions there must be protected spaces or habitats where activists can meet, share experiences, receive affirmation, and strategize for change" (33). Often the reliance on separate forms of mobilization and organizing for women is a reflection of gender significance and specificity already built into social arrangements at work, in the union, and within the broader society; it is not a form of separatism (Briskin 1993). The rationale for creating separate forms of mobilization is predicated on the minority status of women in a male-dominated union and in their experiences of sexual harassment and sex discrimination on the job.

Women can be organized and mobilized from this location, but only if their participation is solicited and effectively channeled for action, such as in unions or mass movements. This is accomplished when the union provides "structured opportunities" for broader forms of participation. "Structured opportunity represents the pressure from above, the support and efforts by those in leadership to open doors, provide education and experience, as well as vehicles for sharing responsibility and power" (Needleman 1998, 187). Briskin and Eliasson (1999) believe that the success of women's separate organizing in unions depends on achieving the right balance between autonomy from and integration with union structures and practices. Too little integration and women become marginalized. Too much integration and women's organizing loses its radical edge. Relatively successful integration brings legitimacy and access to resources. Relatively successful autonomy gives women a stronger voice about women's concerns and greater connection to community-based groups (17).

Brown (1995) suggests that the development of feminist politics actually requires the cultivation of political spaces for constructing feminist political norms, strategies, and agendas. Although these spaces would be clearly defined and defendable by activists, their boundaries would not be permanent or fixed. Women's organizing in unions provides the political space to construct union feminism, and it is within these spaces that women's class interests get defined. According to Curtin (1999), "separate spaces provide the opportunity for women to alter the discursive frameworks through which women's claims are constituted" (33). They serve as mobilizing structures and are not ends in themselves.

"Women of Steel": Gender and Collective Class Identity

Collective identity—the shared definition of a group derived from common interests, experiences, and solidarity—becomes politically relevant when collectively held grievances produce a "we" feeling along with causal attributions that denote a "they" that is held responsible (Taylor and Whittier 1995). Mobilization depends on the collective belief that action can make a difference—a sense of political efficacy—and that there is something to be gained by becoming a part of a group. Collective identity is created and maintained as part of a movement's internal discourse (Gamson 1997) and is constituted not only in the broader social movement, but also within specific organizations and solidarity groups constructed around particular social locations. These layers of identity may be closely integrated or entirely separate, at some times more salient than at others. But according to Gamson, it is the movement's task to fuse solitary and organizational identification into an integrated movement identity. Union feminists must be able to forge a collective sense of themselves as political actors from the integration of their social identities as members of a specific race, class, and gender; as members of a specific union; and as participants in broader movements (women and labor) for social change.

Union feminists develop a unique sense of themselves as political actors within the union movement and the women's movement when their multiple identities become the salient basis for collective action. It is through struggling for their rights, as a diverse group of women workers within a particular union, that women develop a politicized group identity that can be a resource for mobilizing into broader forms of political participation and collective action. "Collective political actors do not exist de facto by virtue of individuals sharing a common structural location; they are created in the course of social-movement activity" (Taylor and Whittier 1992, 505).

Women in a male-dominated union may not be able to identify with the union's actions and appeals if they do not see themselves reflected in its efforts and goals. In these circumstances, women who demand to be included often have to challenge the very organizations or movements that have been authorized to represent their interests as workers. The ability of working-class women to develop class-consciousness is impeded when they cannot identify with the struggles and campaigns that are essential to class formation.

Women need a union sensitive to other identity categories—race, sexuality, nationality, and gender—in order to identify with their class interests.

In addition, working-class women must negotiate the differences among themselves in terms of race, language, culture, and sector in order to achieve the level of solidarity necessary to be effective advocates for women's collective interests within the union. As Johnston and colleagues explain: "Shared definitions of the situation are the result of a process of negotiation—by this process of interaction, negotiation and conflict over the definition of the situation, and the movement's reference frame, members construct the collective 'we'" (1997, 282). These sensitive negotiations must recognize that the collective "we" cannot be constructed in a way that denies the differences among working-class women or undermines class solidarity with men.

During acts of protest, participants construct a collective identity through interaction and negotiation. However, that collective identity can also be more deliberately constructed and strategically deployed by organizations, movement leaders, and mobilizing structures (Johnson et al. 1997; McAdam 1997; Morris and Mueller 1992). For example, union feminists often appealed to the unique class/gender identity of union women by asking their members to wear their union logos at events designed to show broad-based support for the women's movement. The effort by union feminists and activists to get their union to support the ERA campaign further politicized the women and helped to solidify their collective identity as feminists. When union women play an active role in framing grievances within both movements and in the construction of a collective identity as union feminists, they increase the possibility of expanding both the class base of the women's movement and the gender consciousness of the labor movement.

Collective identity, with its emphasis on the socially constructed nature of identity, is a useful concept. It avoids essentializing notions of identity as something totally a priori to collective action (Rupp and Taylor 1999). One cannot assume the coherence of an already constituted essential category of "woman." Yet, without some way to conceptualize women as a group, it is not possible to conceptualize gender as a basis of inequality. "Feminist politics evaporates without some conception of women as a social collective" (Young 1994, 719). Young attempts to resolve this dilemma by proposing that women constitute a group only in the politicized context of feminist struggle. Gender is relational; it is not an essence. Solidarity and political consciousness are the outcome of discussion and struggle among people of diverse backgrounds. Feminist class consciousness and the formation of a unique collective identity as union feminists must be studied in the context of mobilization and action (Fantasia 1988; Kurtz 2002).

Conclusion and Direction

I have studied the twist and turns of women's activism in the Steelworkers for more than twenty-five years and have found advantages to sticking with one topic over such a long period. For one, it has deepened my understanding of the process of social change and social-movement formation. I have watched, recorded, and analyzed the ongoing struggles of working-class women to forge a social-change agenda that makes sense to them as union women. I have followed their persistent efforts to make the Steelworkers more responsive to their needs and more accountable as the representative of their interests as women and as workers. Such lengthy forays into the field have allowed me to take the long view and to avoid making premature judgments about the success or failure of social-movement efforts. For another, from the standpoint of theory, my understanding of that field has been enhanced and deepened by more recent developments in feminist theory, in social-movement theory, and in the theorizing about the intersections of gender, race, and class.

I have tried to tell the unfolding and ongoing story of women's activism from their perspective, but it is really my analysis and my interpretation of their activism that is at the center of this representation of working-class feminism forged in the Steelworkers. In the next chapter, "Women in the Workshop of Vulcan," I present a brief history of the gender and racial division of labor in steel, emphasizing the implications of these divisions for the social construction of union solidarity. I discuss the experiences of women steelworkers during World War II and their efforts after the war to maintain their status in the industry. Chapter 3, "Bread, Roses, and Rights," provides my analysis of the legal and political climate that led to affirmative-action gains for women in the steel industry in the United States and in Canada. I explore the strengths and weaknesses of legal strategies and arguments for gender equity and examine the divergent meanings of equality embedded in Canadian and U.S. antidiscrimination law. I discuss the implications of Title VII of the U.S. Civil Rights Act, the U.S. Consent Decree in the steel industry, and the Canadian Charter of Rights and Freedoms for women's employment in the steel industry and for their activism in the union.

In chapter 4, "What's a Nice Girl Like You Doing in a Place Like This?" I examine in some detail the experiences of the first group of women hired by Wheeling-Pittsburgh Steel in Steubenville, Ohio, under the 1974 consent decree—an industry-wide affirmative-action order. I describe what it was like for women to integrate a male-dominated industry, and I explore their nascent efforts to organize as feminists. I examine mobilizing networks, union participation, experiences with sex and race discrimination, and attitudes toward the women's movement. I situate their understanding of feminism within the media discourses about working women and feminism in the 1970s. In chapter 5, "Mobilizing Women Steelworkers for Their Rights," I explain why and how women in the Calumet (Chicago-Gary) region established a Women's Caucus while efforts in other parts of the country were unsuccessful. Here I explore the unique political opportunity structure in the region and the way in which activists were able to coopt particular mobilizing networks. Chapter 6, "Making Waves," documents the efforts of women to mobilize around their "collective interests" as women in the union and in the broader women's movement. I focus on the efforts of women Steelworkers in the Chicago-Gary area to establish a multiracial Women's Caucus within the union and their alliances with the Chicago women's liberation movement. Here I make visible the contributions of working-class feminism to second-wave feminism.

The renewed efforts of women to organize as women within the union—this time originating in Canada in the mid eighties and early nineties—are examined in chapter 7, "*Women of Steel* Crossing the Border." I discuss the programs, activities, and campaigns aimed at strengthening women's participation in the union during this period. I highlight mobilizing efforts on the part of feminists who were committed to building and sustaining a broad network of women activists within the union and across borders. Finally, I examine what feminism means to the women involved in these initiatives and their efforts to build solidarity across various lines of difference. Chapter 8, "Building Feminist International Solidarity in the Age of Globalization," examines how economic restructuring and globalization are creating new and challenging realities for the Steelworkers. I explore the impact of globalization on women and the role women are playing in helping the union construct and deploy new forms of transnational solidarity and activism. I examine efforts of union feminists to build solidarity and advocacy networks between women Steelworkers and women in the Authentic Workers Front—a federation of labor, community, and peasant groups in Mexico and other worker-to-worker exchanges. In chapter 9, "Forging Union Feminism and the Fight for Social Justice," I summarize my argument and draw out the implications of my analysis for social-movement theory and for women's activism in the Steelworkers.

2

Women in the Workshop of Vulcan:
Gender and the Making of Steel

There is a glamour about the making of steel. The very size of things—the immensity of the tools, the scale of production—grips the mind with an overwhelming sense of power. Blast furnaces, eighty, ninety, one hundred feet tall, gaunt and insatiable—these are the things that cast a spell over the visitor in these workshops of Vulcan.

—John Fitch, *The Steel Worker*

Steel—the product and the dangerous and arduous process of making it—has always been associated with things masculine. Metaphorically, steel, and the mostly male workforce that once produced it, came to represent America's strength as a nation from the building of railroads and battleships to skyscrapers. Images of machines and muscles adorn the covers of books about the U.S. steel industry with such audacious titles as *A Nation of Steel* (Misa 1995), *Running Steel, Running America* (Stein 1998), and *Big Steel* (Greer 1979). Even the U.S. rap singer Cam'ron posed seductively as a pumped-up steelworker on the cover of his first CD, *Confessions of Fire*—advertising posters for which I found plastered along a side street in Toronto near the national office of the Canadian Steelworkers.

In the latter half of the twentieth century, the steel mill, once the icon of industrialization representing strength, might, prosperity, and class struggle, came to symbolize rust, decay, and broken dreams.[1] Culturally, the mills, their workers, and their communities came to represent the plight of the postindustrial working class. In fact, Wheeling-Pittsburgh Steel, one of the mills in my study, served as the bleak and gritty location for an Oscar-winning Hollywood film, *The Deer Hunter* (1978), an epic about war, masculinity, and male bonding among a group of steelworkers who experienced the Vietnam War together. The same mill was featured in *Heart of Steel* (1983), a made-for-TV movie (nominated for a Golden Globe award) about a group of male steelworkers in the Ohio Valley who take over their abandoned mill for one last shift. Finally, the mill served as background for an independent gay video, *Danny* (1987), a story about a gay man dying of AIDS who returns home to Steubenville to die.[2] In a reversal of the standard trope (gay man returns to the healthy heartland to be nurtured in the bosom of traditional family values), Danny returns to a dying steel town. Danny, not a steelworker like his father but a hairdresser whose former good looks are dissipated from the disease, tells his story on a dark and dreary day while standing in front of the Wheeling-Pittsburgh Steel plant, like a refugee from a concentration camp, a narrative that conflates a dying industry with a dying man.

Because the steel industry was among the most visible casualties of deindustrialization, for journalists, social scientists, and cultural critics it became a metaphor not only for decline and decay but also for the loss of manhood. The misfortune of the industry came to represent the erosion of the "American Dream" for the common working man. For feminist journalist Susan Faludi (1999), the average working man got stiffed, perhaps even betrayed. "Rustbelt" became the term used to describe the steel-producing regions of the country that were hardest hit by deindustrialization. Community studies and newspaper profiles of steel towns chronicling the impact of deindustrialization carried titles like *Rusted Dreams* (Bensman and Lynch 1988), *Recast Dreams* (Livingstone and Mangan 1996), *Beyond Rust* (Smith 1995), and *Homestead: The Glory and Tragedy of an American Steel Town* (Serrin 1993).

Similarly, the struggles of workers to unionize the industry were portrayed in hypermasculine terms. Organizing was every bit as difficult as making steel, and historically the struggle to do so was painted in highly gendered terms—as a struggle between men. A central metaphor for labor struggles in the steel industry was war. According to Brody (1987) "American labor history was a record chiefly of industrial war. Periodically the struggle burst into the open; mostly it remained hidden and silent. But war it was" (9). The metaphor of war worked because it captured something true about the difficult struggle to organize the steel industry. On occasion, these struggles did erupt into state-sanctioned violence involving the police, private detective agencies, and the National Guard.[3] While I do not wish to diminish the magnitude of working-class struggles in the face of real danger, the over-reliance on gendered iconography and metaphors to represent labor struggles obscures the role of women in the history of steel and in the history of union organizing (Faue 1991).

The cultural narrative of the rise and fall of steelmaking has made a more recent comeback in the acclaimed film and Broadway play, *The Full Monty*.[4] Less macho perhaps than other stories, it is, nonetheless, a masculine story and remains so even when the Broadway version moves the action to Buffalo, New York, and sets it during a period in time when women would have been working in the area's steel mills. The movie and the play focus on the gender dilemmas faced by male steelworkers who lose their jobs and must come to terms with what it means to be a working-class man in the postindustrial era. If being a steelworker made you a man, what happened to your masculinity when you lost that job? Do you become more like a "woman" or redefine what is means to be a "man"? The story line obscures other questions: What happened to the woman steelworker who lost her job? Did she lose her honorary status as "man" and return to being "woman" again? Stripper does not carry the same gender-bending connotations for women steelworkers.

The story of women steelworkers and their activism is hard to imagine because women are absent from the cultural scripts about steelmaking except occasionally as the wives, lovers, and mothers of steelworkers—very conventional gender scripts for working-class women. The popular media's representations of the working class is often that of the resentful, white, ethnic, usually Catholic, male—a bona fide member of the "silent majority." Even the image of the hard hat, associated with construction workers and steelworkers, evokes a particular cultural stereotype of a hard-drinking, tough-talking, even rude form of manliness prone to patriotic violence, sexual harassment, and racist confrontations (Freeman 1993). It is very difficult for women steelworkers and men of color to insert themselves in the public and cultural discourse about the economic upheavals of late capitalism. It is even harder for all workers to fashion a collective political response to deindustrialization that does not reinscribe gender and race in ways that are counterproductive to building solidarity and collective action.

There are two periods in history when women entered the workshop of Vulcan in significant numbers—during World War II and again in the mid-seventies when a court-ordered, affirmative-action consent decree set timetables and goals for hiring women at nine of the major U.S. steel companies. In order to understand women's activism as workers with a direct stake in the steel industry and its union, it is necessary first to examine the historical and cultural context of each period in terms of political opportunity structures, mobilizing networks, and prevailing public discourses about gender, work, and class. Under what circumstances did women enter the workshop of Vulcan? Did women's employment in such a quintessential male occupation challenge gender relations? How did other categories of difference, such as race, facilitate or inhibit collective action?

Women in the Steel Industry before World War II

Traditionally, the only jobs open to a woman in the steel industry before the war were those of nurse, matron, attendant, secretary in the administrative office, and inspecting and sorting tinplate within a female-segregated department—all nonproduction jobs that were reserved for white females. In the tinplate department, women called tin floppers were responsible for flipping the tin sheets, inspecting for surface flaws, and grading and judging the thickness and weight of the metal by touch. Management believed women were better suited for this job because of their greater finger dexterity, speed, and sensitivity of touch.[5] I interviewed three women who had worked in the mills before, during, and after the war. Theresa Ogresovich, a woman who grew up in a family of sixteen in a mining camp, told me that as soon as you were old enough to work you went to work, even if it meant you lied about your age. She joined her older sisters in the tinplate department in 1934 at the age of fourteen and worked in the mill on and off in "women's jobs" until 1974 when the consent decree gave her access to the jobs previously held only by men. She recalled her early days as a tin flopper. "It was considered women's work. They only hired women. The foreladies wore pink uniforms. The girls wore blue uniforms with white collars. They had to be stiff starched. You had to look real neat."

Theresa remembered how the women were treated before the plant was unionized. She told me that bribery and favoritism were often the norm, and the women worked in fear of losing their jobs for failing to play along. Inequities were suffered without any recourse for grievance. "At that time, the ladies brought gifts so they could hold their jobs, and the forelady treats them good. I did not go for that. At $2.44 a day I couldn't afford it." She walked two miles to reach the streetcar that would take her to the mill—for a fare of five cents each way. She described the difficult situation she faced as a working mother. "We walked. Cold weather, zero weather, and I nursed my baby at night when I come home. I was scared to eat in the mill all day for fear you'd have milk running down. It was rough, I'll tell you. It was real rough."[6]

World War II: Mobilization of Race and Gender in U.S. Steel Industry

When the United States joined the war effort, the tin floppers were among the first to be offered men's jobs. Many were eager to have the opportunity, but they had to face strong reservations—of the government, of the companies, and of their own families about their ability to do a man's job and about the appropriateness of such employment for women. Peggy Piazza, another former tin flopper, jumped at the chance to bid on a job as a crane operator during the war and told me, "The tin house girls got first choice. It was a man's job, but women could do it. When I told my mother I would be wearing slacks, she said, 'Oh Lord, what kind of job did you get?'"[7]

What was it really like for the women in the mills during the war? In 1943, the Women's Bureau of the U.S. Department of Labor (Erickson 1944) conducted a survey of women's employment in forty-one steel mills throughout the steel-producing regions of the country, including Pittsburgh, Youngstown, Buffalo, Chicago-Gary, and Baltimore. Researchers tallied the number of women employed and their occupational distribution within the industry and described in some detail the types of jobs the women performed and the conditions under which they performed them, including wages, hours of work, and health and safety standards. The purpose of the research was to assess the "suitability" of continuing to use and (expand if need be) the use of women to help meet increasing labor shortages in steel production. What did the experiences of women in the industry suggest about the possible future uses of their employment if the war dragged on? What effect did doing a "man's" job have on women? What were the optimal conditions for employing women—under what specific conditions did they best perform? What was the safest way to use women? Women represented 8.1 percent of the production workers, higher in the more modernized facilities (16.1 percent) and much lower in older facilities, and 35.2 percent of the office and technical workers. While in a few mills women could be found in almost any job, most of the white women were concentrated in rolling mills, in finishing and fabrication, and in shop maintenance, while black women worked in the more dangerous areas of the mill, such as the coke oven and blast furnace (Erickson 1944).

Suitability of Steel Employment for Women

The bureau's report adopted a "protective" tone regarding the war employment of women in the steel industry. Management was described as "cautious" in assigning jobs to women and as "reluctantly" doing so only "as a measure of last resort." During the war, some states relaxed protective-labor standards regarding such issues as night work and hours of work. The bureau sought to safeguard protective-labor legislation for women, and, at the same time, to make sure that such laws were not used unfairly to pay women less than men for doing the same work. When it came to wages, employers used these standards as the rationale for paying women less than men doing the same job. For example, protective-labor laws required that women workers be given a half-hour lunch break, but because companies did not pay for the lunch break in the steel industry where production is continuous, women were paid for seven and a half hours of work while men were paid for eight hours. Women did not actually take a lunch break but instead like the men they ate during "spell" time (Erickson 1944, 5).

During World War II, male clerks on the shop floor were transferred to production jobs, and women from the front office replaced them but at a much lower rate of pay. Male clerks at Carnegie-Illinois Steel, for example, were paid $160 a month for tasks that were not that much different from those required in the administrative offices where women were paid only $90 a month. A woman's wage transferred with her to the shop floor. The company could get away with the pay differential because the women were placed on salary and therefore not covered by the union contract's equal-pay clause. In one particular case, the union filed a complaint with the War Labor Board. Male clerks, who counted on returning to their old clerical jobs when the war ended, were particularly wary of any pay differential between men and women. They certainly did not want to return to these jobs at a "women's" rate of pay.

The protective tone of the report is not surprising, given the origins of the Women's Bureau (1918) as the Women in Industry Service (WIS). This agency was established during World War I to respond to the political pressure on the Labor Department by progressive women's organizations, including the Women's Trade Union League. Women's organizations lobbied the government to monitor the working conditions of women in factories that held government defense contracts. The WIS conducted research to help establish standards for safety, minimum wages, and hours of work for women working in war industries. Its mission was to "develop in the industries of the country policies and methods which will result in the most effective use of women's services in production for the war, while at the same time preventing their employment under injurious conditions" (Skocpol 1992, 419). The WIS was not given the authority to initiate legal sanctions but rather was forced to rely on its powers of investigation and persuasion.

World War I opened the door for advocates of protective-labor laws for women and children, and they were able to establish national standards that reflected the best labor standards of the day. "These standards stressed safe working conditions, eight-hour days and forty-eight hour weeks, and minimum wages that were equal between the sexes and adequate to cover the costs of living for dependents" (419).

In 1920, President Wilson made WIS a permanent agency by establishing the Women's Bureau of the Labor Department. The first director, Mary Anderson, was still heading the bureau when World War II broke out, giving leadership and policy continuity. A member of the International Boot and Shoe Workers Union, she helped institutionalize many of the goals of the Women's Trade Union League into the mission of the Women's Bureau. According to Skocpol (1992), this gave the advocates of "protective" labor standards for working women a niche in the federal bureaucracy from which to campaign for women's economic rights.

The steel industry was late to employ women for wartime production and did so after women's employment had peaked in other industries.[8] The government and the media generally treated the situation of employing women in steel mills as undesirable. The Women's Bureau believed that "the heaviness of the raw materials, the weight of the steel products, the massive equipment, the spatial spread, the heat, fumes and hazards do not offer employment possibilities that would normally be considered desirable or attractive to women" (Erickson 1944, 3).

To make the employment of women in men's jobs more acceptable to the public, the press ran national stories about the heroic efforts of women war workers. However, it would take special effort to justify the employment of white women in the steel industry. Only as a measure of last resort—a measure so extraordinary that *Life* magazine called it "revolutionary"—could U.S. women, characterized by the magazine as far more "feminine" than their European counterparts, be employed as steel workers. "Although the concept of the weaker sex sweating near the blast furnaces, directing giant ladles of molten iron, or pouring red-hot ingots is accepted in England and Russia, it has always been foreign to American tradition. Only the rising need for labor and the diminishing supply of manpower has forced this revolutionary adjustment" (*Life*, 9 August 1943, 75). The media worked especially hard to convince the public that it was patriotic and not "un-American" for women to work in heavy industry and that women steelworkers would not become masculinized in the process—unless they were already masculinized, as was the case with black women.

Public discourse about women and war work, according to Hartmann (1982), contained three conditions that made it socially acceptable for women to replace men at work during the war: if it were considered temporary and only for the duration, if women maintained their femininity while performing masculine duties, and if they were motivated by a desire to bring the men home more quickly. Appeals to patriotism underscored the temporary nature of wartime employment (Rupp 1978). Such propaganda highlighted women's femininity and positioned their wartime contributions in terms of their relationship to men. This allowed the public to accept the participation of women in unusual jobs without challenging its beliefs about women's traditional sphere.

At the same time that femininity was emphasized, safety required that women don clothing and equipment that would hide it. The bureau reported that it was impossible sometimes to tell the women from the men. Hair, a marker of femininity, was a particular safety hazard in most industrial workplaces. More than thirty years later, Peggy recalled a poster—of a woman with long blonde hair in high heels and wearing a nice dress in the mill—which read: "No cap confines your golden hair / you wear a dress with quite a flair / loose sleeves, high heels is cute, my dear, / but a hell of a garb to wear in here."

In the black press, women war workers were similarly portrayed as supporting their men, but they were not represented as housewives who would return to the home after the war. According to Honey (1999), black women were depicted as "trailblazers able to escape low-wage domestic service." It was assumed that they would continue working once the war was over. "Indeed, 40 percent of all Black women already were in the labor force when the war broke out, as opposed to only 25 percent of white women" (12). Despite the reservations of the government, the companies, and the media, the supply of women seeking work in steel exceeded the demand throughout the war (Erickson 1944).

Caste in Steel: Black Women on the Job

Most of the jobs that women obtained in steel during the war were concentrated at the less skilled end of the production process, a pattern true for industries such as auto and electronics as well (Gabin 1990; Milkman 1987). The majority of the women were classified as laborers and were involved in auxiliary services such as cleaning track, sweeping, hauling, handling tools and small equipment, hooking up cranes, and stacking brick (Erickson 1944). In general, white women were assigned jobs at the "cleaner" and "safer" end of the production process, away from raw materials, and they were more likely to be involved in the fabrication of steel products rather than the production of basic steel.

Jobs in the steel industry were harder for black women to obtain, and, when they did get them, they were assigned jobs more like those held by black men.[9] A "Jim Crow" racial division of labor was prevalent in the steel industry and placed black men in the most dangerous, least desirable jobs handling raw materials. These jobs paid less and offered little chance for promotion (Dickerson 1986; Hinshaw 2002; Needleman 2003; Nelson 2001; Norrell 1986; Nyden 1984; Stewart 2001). Not only were black women assigned jobs deemed least desirable or suitable for (white) women, such as cleaning scrap metal and iron from the bottom of shipping freighters, but the bureau's report presumed that black women did not mind such assignments (Figure 4).

> A crew of women—chiefly Negro—with a woman gang leader has been employed for several months, going from boat to boat as needed. When there is no boat ready for cleaning, they are employed around the docks and stockyards as part of the general clean-up labor gang. Only the strong and husky woman who does not mind close association with dirt can be placed on such work. (Erickson 1944, 5)

To maintain the color bar, it was necessary to masculinize black women by attributing to them characteristics such as strong and husky. Black women, however, did mind discriminatory treatment and joined black men to protest racist treatment in the steel industry during the war by staging wildcat strikes, filing union grievances, and registering formal complaints with the Fair Employment Practices Committee (Dickerson 1986). In some plants, white women were given hiring preference over black men and women, and one steel executive in Pennsylvania revealed he did not hire black women in his plant because he thought "white women wouldn't have it." In other plants, white women refused to work with black women or to share dressing facilities with them.[10]

Race, ethnicity, and gender were linked to job classifications in the steel mills, but the bureau's investigators never seriously questioned the racial/ethnic/gender hierarchy of women's wartime employment in the steel industry. Instead, they reinscribed the prevailing discourses about race and skill and, thus, reinforced racial and ethnic stereotypes. The boundaries between work that was sex-typed male and work that was sex-typed female appeared more permeable than the boundaries between jobs that were racially coded.[11] Even the emergency circumstances of war could not fully erase the color

Figure 4. "'Pan Man' at Gary Works is Mrs. Rosalie Ivy, a husky Negro laborer. She is mixing a special mud used to seal the casting hole through which molten iron flows from a blast furnace." Original caption in Life, *9 August 1943, 76. Courtesy of TimePix. Photograph by Margaret Bourke-White.*

line that separated the work of black women and the work of white women within the mills. The "protective" impulse of the Women's Bureau did not extend to black women who risked their health and safety to supply the steel needed for the war. Instead, it was assumed that black women, described in the report in masculine terms as "strong and husky" and "who worked as hard as a man," did not need nor were they entitled to "protection." Black women were treated more similarly to black men than to white women. The report contends that "unhardened" women should not be assigned to work temporary jobs in the blast furnace because the risk of injury was not worth the marginal value that women added to the process. "Unless there is a critical shortage of male labor, the inexperienced, 'unhardened' woman who comes to the steel mills as a war worker for a temporary period with little probability of remaining long enough to be eligible for the better jobs, should not be given strenuous or hazardous work" (Erickson 1944, 9).

To justify the employment of black women in jobs that were not considered suitable for women, they had to be disqualified as women—made more like men, that is, black men. On the other hand, for white women, production jobs were feminized, that is, modified in ways that allowed the women to remain women. Greater gender shifting was required of black women than of white women. White women were allowed to exercise race privilege and to collect the wages of whiteness.[12] The black man's work and wages were suitable for black women but not so for "unhardened" (white women). She required jobs that had been reconfigured to protect her from becoming more like the hardened black woman.

In a department-by-department assessment of women's occupations in the steel mills, the bureau concluded that, in general, the blast-furnace department did not provide "suitable" employment for women. Yet the final report treated the employment of black women around the blast furnace as an "objective" and not objectionable fact. The report described the jobs in the sintering plant, where ore dust and dust from the furnaces are salvaged and recycled into the sintering block that fuel the big blast furnaces, as "dirty and chiefly of a labor grade—work done by 'Negro' women."

> Quite a number of women in sintering plants work on dumping the cars of ore and dust, inspecting along the sides of the conveyor to remove lumps of slag and foreign matter, shoveling up spills along the conveyor lines, screening coal and dust, carrying test to the laboratory, and so forth. All the work is classed as labor. Most of the women are Negro and they are purported as moving as much dirt and materials as men. Everything around a sintering plant is covered with iron dust. Siderosis from exposure to such dust may cause pulmonary difficulties, but the workers seen were not wearing respirators: nor did they wear goggles. (Erickson 1944, 8)

In addition to general labor, a large number of white women—up to one fourth in some mills—worked in the fabricating and finishing departments. In finishing, women operated machines that sanded, polished, and bundled the finished steel products for shipping to customers. In fabrication, women operated machine tools, including drills and boring machines, lathes, milling machines, grinding machines, punch presses, saws, and special-duty machines. In the armor-plate division of one mill, women were fully integrated into the production of combat vehicles, including reading blue-prints, lay-out, cutting sheet metal, and assembly (Erickson 1944,15). The types of jobs the bureau favored for "unhardened" (white) women were away from the blast furnace where the actual steel is made from the raw materials of iron, coke, and ore. These women's advocates thought that handling the controls that open and close the furnace doors (from a distance) was about as close a woman should come to being a steelmaker. The rolling mills, where the hot steel is stretched out and molded to fit the specifications of the customer, were judged to be a more "auspicious" utilization of women than work in the blast furnace (14).

Equal Pay

Many jobs the Women's Bureau considered suitable for women were not open to them. These jobs belonged to white men with seniority rights—workers who, in the past, had had the opportunity, by virtue of their race or ethnicity, to work their way up to the cleaner, safer, and better paying jobs. Many of these jobs involved the chance to earn incentive pay for meeting or exceeding production goals—an important way to augment relatively low wages paid to steelworkers at that time. In fact, the bureau reported that representatives of the union believed that women were being hired in the first place because wages were so low for the most undesirable jobs that men would not take them. "In many instances these hard laboring jobs are not suitable for women, and the primary reason why women have been employed is that the firms became unable to secure men at the rates paid. Had the industry upped the wage rates for the lower jobs, men would have been available and women could have been employed for work for which they are better adapted" (Erickson 1944, 34).

There were no separate male and female seniority lines in steel. But, that did not really matter, because most women did not have the seniority that would have allowed them to move up to the higher paying jobs. According to the report, industry representatives were eager to crow about equal treatment of men and women. When it came to wages, "A highly virtuous feeling seems to imbue managers when they pay the same rates to women as to men on the same, similar, or comparable work" (22). The union insisted on equal treatment and equal pay. "Organized labor has insisted that women shall not compete unfairly with men by taking their jobs at lower prices" (22). Those women who did hold the same jobs as men experienced both an absolute and a relative increase in wages during the war.

The principle of equal pay for jobs different from, but comparable to, men's was harder to institute. Women who entered the mills as tin floppers—a traditional female job before the war—were paid an hourly rate of 63 cents per hour, considerably lower than entry-level jobs that traditionally employed men at 78 cents per hour. According to the bureau, this differential reflected the general attitude toward "women's wages." In other cases, lower rates for women were justified because they were not required to do all aspects of the job in the same way that men were or because the women were being paid a "learner's wage." In one plant, women crane operators were paid 11 cents an hour less than men, because they were not required to oil or repair their machine, a requirement of the official job description. In reality, however, the male crane operators rarely repaired their own machines and relied instead on mechanics from another department. In another instance, the bureau found that women were being paid a "learners' rate" while the men, who also required training, were not—a practice successfully challenged by the union (22).

The Union

The attitude of the union toward women steelworkers is described in the report as "welcoming," and women joined the union at the same high rates as men—as high as 98 percent in one plant. Women served as shop stewards and on grievance committees but did not serve on negotiation committees, which were the preserve of senior officials. The bureau also found that some locals did not encourage women's participation in the union because women "are regarded as having tenure only for the duration of the war and so it seems hardly worth while to encourage their activities or develop leadership among them" (Erickson 1944, 33). At Duquesne Steel, male co-workers were often outright hostile, as when they walked off the job in a wildcat strike to show their solidarity with a foreman who refused to work with women. Management fired the women, and the foreman returned to work (Rose 1995, 41).

A bureau survey[13] of unions conducted in 1944 included Steelworkers Local 65, which represented 9,000 workers (out of 14,000) at Carnegie-Illinois Steel in South Chicago. Of the 2,000 women employed there, only 50 percent were in the union, while 67 percent of the men were. There were no women on the labor-management committee or on the grievance committee in this particular mill. There were 354 male shop stewards and 30 female shop stewards. The contract contained the standard equal-pay clause. The bureau's investigator interviewed local officials and members, including Katherine Martin of the Women's Organizing Committee, Virginia Lasser, a shop steward, and Joanne Kennedy, editor of the local's newspaper about the experiences of women in the union.

The only activities directed by the local specifically to increase women's participation in the union were social in nature. Martin believed that the women did not come to union meetings because they were afraid of management. Lasser felt that "the company was very anti-union and foremen fomented much talk in mills against the union."[14] Albert Towers, the local president, said he did not know of any plans or programs by the union to increase women's participation or to develop women's leadership. No women had been employed on staff of the union for organizational or educational work, and he was not aware of any plans to hire women, although he did express interest in women's outreach programs offered by the United Auto Workers.

The survey recorded how the subjects felt about women's continued employment when the war ended. George Mischeau, the union's staff representative, did not think permanent jobs in the mill were suitable for women or that women would want to remain in the mill after the war. Towers stated, "The girls signed cards when employed indicating they would give up their jobs after the war." No one, according to M. Bagwell, who authored the report, said that the union had tried to prevent this or stop it.[15] Elsa Graves, a slow cool operator, said that while male officials pledged that they would back up the women if they were laid-off and that they would try to prevent any discrimination, she thought there was a good chance "they would change their minds" when the war was over. She believed that "a good many of the women will want to remain in the mills rather than go back to lower paying jobs in service trades." The Women's Bureau sided with the view that the jobs were temporary and probably should be. It was not an advocate for women's postwar employment in steel. "It appears to be generally agreed that women's employment in steel is a temporary war expediency and that men returning from the armed services will have seniority and priority on the jobs in the industry after the war, so it seems hardly fair to ask women to do extremely heavy labor and dangerous jobs and dissipate their strength on employment that is of a temporary nature."[16]

The Problem Every Supervisor Dreads

In 1940, only 5,000 women were employed in basic steel and another 15,000 in steel fabrication (Clark et al. 1987). Even as late as 1942 women were less than 1 percent of the production workforce in basic steel (Rose 1995, 25). Their employment in the steel industry during the war peaked in 1944 when their numbers rose to more than 80,000 or about 8 percent (Erickson 1944, 42). Even during the war there was considerable resistance to employing women. At the Duquesne Steel Works, the introduction of women workers during World War II met with opposition and hostility from management and from workers. According to Rose (1995), both groups held deep-seated prejudices against women working in the steel mill and paternalistic attitudes about women's place in society. Management resisted because it was costly to replace male production workers with females. State protective-labor laws, women's lack of experience, and the demanding nature of the jobs made the hiring of women "the problem every supervisor dreads." Management relied on a "mixture of common sense, stereotypes, and pseudoscientific thought" about women as a group to guide their decisions about women workers. Supervisors had their minds made up before women walked through the mill gate. Women were considered more temperamental than men: "The dislikes of women are much deeper and much more venomous than the dislikes of men." Much stock was placed in physical differences. "Women have different muscular control from men which accounts for the fact that they have trouble throwing a ball but can button the back of a dress with ease" or "The fact that women's thigh bones incline inwardly toward her knees makes her more susceptible to tripping than a man." Again, "Women admire men because they realize nature favors them. They have a desire to act like men and be treated as men" (34). Even at the end of the war, when women were 12 to 13 percent of the production workforce, management clung to cultural stereotypes about women workers. The list of things they thought women could not do as efficiently as men included climbing and using shovels, picks, sledgehammers, jackhammers, wheelbarrows, or hand tools (39).

The Bren Gun Girl: Canadian Women and World War II

The Bren Gun Girl, like her U.S. sister, Rosie the Riveter, became the Canadian icon of the woman war worker. The Steelworkers organized the real-life Bren Girls employed at the John Inglis factory in Toronto. Their experience is illustrative of how work was gendered in Canada during the war. Originally Inglis made large-scale factory machines, such as blast furnaces, engines, and boilers but, under new ownership in the thirties, began to manufacture the lighter weight, Czech, Bren machine gun. The Inglis trademark came to stand for Canadian industrial might. "Inglis machinery, equipment, and expertise beat at the heart of industrial operations in Canada" (Sobel and Meurer 1994). Lynn Williams, past president of the Steelworkers International, got his start at Inglis, and current president, Leo Gerard, once served as the Steelworkers staff representative for Local 2900 at Inglis. Despite a valiant struggle by the workers, including the women who helped to establish the early *Women of Steel* initiatives, to keep the company open, it was sold to a U.S. conglomerate in 1988 and closed the following year. But it was during the war years that women at Inglis rose to fame as the Bren Gun Girls.

Their real story, of course, differs from the way it was told to win the Canadian public to the idea that it was acceptable for women to work in heavy manufacturing. Much like the U.S. campaigns, the Canadian government emphasized the temporary nature of women's war work and reassured the country that such work would not diminish a woman's femininity. "A promotional photo series on the 'the typical Bren girl' showed her in her boarding house 'dolling up' before an employees' party and jitterbugging after she got there" (Pierson 1983, 20). What better way could a woman help to ensure the speedy return of her man than to produce his gun? The motto of company newsletter *Shotgun* was "They Shall Not Die Because We Faltered" (69).

Inglis introduced new ways to manufacture guns that made it possible to hire women. In part, the process of making guns was "re-organized as 'women's work', or at least what suited the image of appropriate work for 'girls'" (42). This required moving from the traditional craft approach to gunmaking to an assembly-line style of production. One company official thought there might even be an advantage to hiring women. "They were much more sensitive with the feel of their fingers. They could do things that a man with clumsy fingers couldn't get at, and in many cases, we were probably better off having the ladies doing the job" (43). Inglis did not use women to fill men's jobs. Much of the plant remained male dominated and firmly in the control of the metal craftsmen. Women worked in segregated departments specifically designed for them. These jobs paid less and offered little by way of training or promotion. Women did not acquire the skills during the war that would give them a chance to keep their jobs after the war or to move into other jobs in manufacturing. Even with modifications in production, the hiring of women at Inglis was controversial. After many debates, the government decided that Inglis could employ a small number of women, at lower rates of pay, but only in specific, female-job classifications. Women could be employed on light-machine operations and as inspectors if they were confined to the government-owned ordnance division and did not displace any men. Employing women "did not represent a shattering of all shop floor traditions. Confining women to the Ordnance Division created distinctions in the minds of both the workers and management. New jobs were created that simplified tasks and, by design, involved repetitious, semi-skilled operations" (53). This deskilling was used to justify paying women lower wages than the men.

During the war, Inglis was the largest employer of women at 10,000 women workers. Overall, women's employment in Canada increased from 638,000 in 1939 to a little over a million in 1944. Unlike the United States, the Canadians instituted a national registry for all women between the ages of twenty and twenty-four, and women from all over Canada were required to register. Opposition to this policy was particularly strong in Quebec, and the government and employers worked hard to allay fears and concerns about the corrupting influence of nontraditional work on young women. Inglis created a "girls' club" to "build up the correct mental attitude of the women" and to "discover personal grievances"—a form of worker surveillance that was gender specific (Sobel and Meurer 1994). The club was a part of a paternalist network of programs and activities aimed at building morale among women living far away from home. These included beauty pageants, employee-of-the-month programs, and sports teams (Pierson 1983).

There had always been unions at Inglis. However, the AFL craft unions did not welcome the women. Craftsmen were against hiring women and, once they were hired, would not train them for skilled jobs. They insisted there were competent, unemployed men who could be hired. When the CIO began its campaign to organize basic industry, the Steelworkers Organizing Committee made inroads at Inglis, which by 1942 employed 14,000 workers. They employed a woman organizer, Eileen Tallman, and made a special effort to organize women. As the production of guns accelerated, the women became increasingly dissatisfied with their pay and with the way production goals were set. Tallman remembered, "As soon as the women's group reached their quota of production, the quota would be raised. That was one of the major grievances amongst the women. That made it easier to organize them" (90). During the CIO organizing drive, the issue of women getting less pay became key. On 19 April 1943, workers voted to become Steelworkers (Figure 5).

Canadian women went to work in the war industries for the same economic reasons U.S. women did, and most—72 percent—wanted to keep their jobs at the end of the war. While many women were forced back into unpaid labor in the home, some remained in the workforce. Most found employment in the growing service and retail sector although some managed to stay on at Inglis as it reconverted to making fishing rods and washing machines. The Canadian labor market, like the market in the United States, remained stubbornly resistant to female integration, an arrangement not significantly challenged by labor unions in either country. In fact, many collective-bargaining agreements after the war reinforced the sexual division of labor (Creese 1996). Once in place these agreements had great staying power and served to limit economic opportunities for working-class women until such practices were challenged by the equity legislation passed in the sixties and seventies in both countries.

The Post–World War II Period

The situation at the end of the war was similar for women in both countries. While many women voluntarily quit their jobs, others who wanted to

Figure 5. Canadian women at the Inglis factory join the union during the CIO organizing campaign, Toronto, Canada, circa 1943. Courtesy of the City of Toronto Archives, Globe and Mail *Collection, 84534.*

stay in the industry and its powerful union were pressured to leave, were laid-off, or were simply fired. Peggy Piazza, employed at Wheeling-Pittsburgh Steel, described to me the situation at the end of the war. "On VE day, we all left the factory and jammed the streets to celebrate. We didn't know whether to go back to work or not. We went back the next day, and we didn't work very much. They said they would get in touch with us. After several months, they reconverted to making car air conditioners. We worked for awhile on that, but it wasn't steady." A few women were allowed to return to their previous jobs as tin floppers, but most were let go. Lola Murrin told me that it was "just an understanding," a "verbal agreement," that you were working for the duration.[17] Most of the women in wartime employment needed to work to make ends meet while their husbands were overseas or to compensate for the losses of the Depression, while others were responding to patriotic calls to help bring the men back home. Peggy, who did not want to relinquish her job after the war, told me:

> Then too, there was this feeling that you were helping your country. They
> made you believe this by the ads on the radio. . . . The boys at war were
> short of this and short of that. It gave you a feeling that you were directly

helping. There were some who wouldn't have been there except that there was a war on. Not me, I had to work. I needed the job. Before the war, I made $17 a week; in the plant I made $5.44 a day. That was a big difference.

After the war, the women at Wheeling-Pittsburgh Steel were laid off and told they would be called back on a seniority basis. Most were never called. Some women were brought back as sorters and inspectors, but the opportunities to transfer to other departments—where the pay was higher and the promotional opportunities greater—were extremely limited. The women at Wheeling-Pittsburgh Steel were pushed from one company division to another and often endured long periods of layoff. By exercising their seniority rights, they were able to find work in a fabricating division that made garbage cans. At one point, they were offered jobs that required giving up ten years of seniority, and those who accepted the deal worked an additional ten years in order to collect full retirement benefits. While the majority of women who had been employed in steel during the war were displaced from the industry after the war, enough remained to allow women to register a net gain in their share of steel jobs. In the United States, more than twice as many women were employed in iron and steel after the war compared to before the war and, by 1947, women were 9.4 percent of all workers employed in steel (Pidgeon 1947).[18] More women in Canada remained in the labor force after the war than in the United States. Although women's labor force participation during the war was higher in the United States than in Canada, it dropped farther after the war. Between 1945 and 1947, women's labor force participation fell by 19 percent in the United States and by less than 9 percent in Canada (Prentice et al. 1988, 311).

Union Feminism after the War

In the postwar period, technology changed the way work was organized, and for the first time it became possible for women to seriously challenge their exclusion from better paying jobs in manufacturing on the grounds of "suitability." Cultural assumptions about the naturalness and inevitability of the sexual division of labor were exposed during the war, and afterward increasing numbers of women, particularly those employed in male-dominated industries, came to question the necessity of protective-labor law. Many of these women did not want to return to the low-pay ghetto of women's work—particularly under the rationale that it was for their own protection—once they had demonstrated they could handle nontraditional "male" jobs in steel, auto, and aerospace. Women holding jobs that placed them in direct

competition with men came to see protective-labor legislation as an imped-
iment and joined together to lobby for its repeal (Cobble 1994).

For many women, wartime employment was their first experience with
organized labor, and women's membership in labor unions rose from 800,000
in 1939 to more than 3 million by the early 1950s (Cobble 1994, 2003).
The postwar expansion of jobs in the traditional domains of female employment such as retail, communications, food service, and clerical added
much of the growth in female union membership. Female-dominated unions
provided working-class women with new opportunities for leadership development and activism, and the women took full advantage by organizing
strikes, boycotts, sit-downs, and organizing campaigns. According to Cobble (1994, 2003), working-class feminism "flowered" in the postwar decade
and not only survived but flourished in the 1950s. The feminist anchors in
this period were in the female-dominated unions and not in steel.

Union women, with the help of the U.S. Women's Bureau, created a
feminist economic agenda for working women in the postwar years. The
labor activism and the organizational networks of working-class women
and their professional allies in the government helped to lay the groundwork for the emergence of the contemporary women's movement. Their
economic program of equal rights in the workplace challenged the sexual
division of labor and the unequal wages and working conditions that resulted.
Union activists were very aware of the need for policies that would help
working women balance the demands of work and family, and they believed
that collective bargaining could help women to achieve this goal. They sought
to institutionalize their vision of economic equality within individual unions
and lobbied for women's departments and greater avenues for leadership
development and for women's full participation in their unions (Cobble 1994,
2003; Deslippe 2000; Gabin 1990; Hartmann 1998; Kessler-Harris 1990,
2001; Laughlin 2000; Milkman 1987; and Sugiman 1994).

The Women's Bureau played an important role in bringing union women
together in the postwar years. It held conferences, conducted studies, and
published government reports and articles for the popular press on women,
unions, and economic policy. According to Laughlin (2000), the bureau
brought union women and their allies together to forge a national action
plan for social change that was rooted in their work during the war years.
"In the postwar years, the Women's Bureau provided one location where a
loose coalition of female government officials, union members, organizational
leaders, politicians, and media professionals forged a 'reconversion blueprint'
anchored by the goal to pass federal and state equal-pay-for-equal-work and
minimum-wage legislation" (13).

According to Stepan-Norris and Zeitlin (2002), the CIO did not put women's concerns high on its organizing agenda. And, while the CIO's stated aim was to organize "working men and women," there were only four women delegates at its founding convention (1935), and no specific resolution on women's rights was adopted (191). The CIO did not focus on women in the postwar years. Few women were hired as organizers or staff representatives, and typically not more than about 5 percent of the delegates at CIO conventions in the late 1940s and early 1950s were female (198). The CIO adopted a very progressive agenda of women's rights in 1944 that included equal pay for equal work, maternity leave without seniority loss, support for daycare centers, and women's leadership development in member unions. However, the level of commitment by individual unions in the CIO to such an ambitious equity program was very uneven. In their survey of CIO member constitutions and local contracts, Stepan-Norris and Zeitlin found that fewer than half (43 percent) of the international constitutions included explicit language regarding the inclusion of women as members, and only 21 percent of local contracts included an equal-pay clause (199). The commitment to women's equality and to women's greater representation within unions varied greatly among the CIO member unions. Those that maintained ties with the Left did better than other unions. Those that severed such ties, like the Steelworkers, did not fair as well. Only 2.4 percent of the Steelworkers' local contracts contained an equal pay clause and no women, as of the year 2000, have held national, international, or district office. There were only 18 women delegates (out of 1,700) at the union's founding convention in Cleveland in 1942. At the second convention, in 1944, their numbers rose to 61 (about 3 percent), still considerably below their 8 percent of the industry employment. Four hundred and forty-six women held local union office—with only 32 serving as local union presidents (Clark et al. 1987, 52). In general, women's involvement in the union was lower than their numbers in the industry.

During the postwar years there were no Steelworkers' convention resolutions dealing directly with women's rights and only one on the need to organize women salaried employees. The Steelworkers' legislative agenda did support, however, policies that would benefit women indirectly, such as the extension of social-security benefits to domestic and agricultural workers and support for raising the federal minimal wage. The union also supported government subsidy for daycare centers for working women (53).

After the war, union feminists in the United States transformed the discourse on equal pay from the need for equal pay to prevent employers from using women's cheaper labor to replace men to a discourse on equal pay as a woman's right—a question of justice and fairness. They questioned why women were paid a lower rate to begin with and fought for the notion that a fair rate of pay should be assigned to the job, regardless of the worker's gender (Cobble 1994).[19] Union feminists also expanded the definition of equal wages to include equal wages for work of comparable value to men's work. "By this we mean not only equal pay for identical work but equal pay for work of equal value no matter where it is done" (61). Even though the Equal Pay Act of 1963 was a watered-down version of what union feminists had proposed originally, the campaign for its passage changed the underlying cultural meaning of equal pay. According to Kessler-Harris (1990), "The struggle for its enactment expanded notions of justice, encouraging perceptions of male/female equality that had been previously invisible" (67).

While there was a good deal of consensus regarding the benefits of equal pay and comparable worth, there was more debate and opposition regarding protective-labor law and the Equal Rights Amendment (ERA). According to Cobble (1994), unionists from the pink-collar sector wanted to upgrade and expand the female work sphere and argued for the inclusion of more workplaces, such as drug stores, restaurants, and department stores in the Fair Labor Standards Act. The struggle to obtain the minimum wage for women and the protective standards regarding hours of work, weight restrictions, rest periods, and overtime were hard-fought battles, and there was great reluctance to let go of such policies in the name of equality. Union feminists had hoped that such labor standards could, in the name of equality, be extended to men. Many union feminists also believed that the ERA could be used to undo these protections, and it was not until the 1970s that union feminists and their unions changed their positions on both issues.

Pay-equity legislation was achieved more than a decade earlier in Canada, in 1952, even before the creation of a Women's Bureau in the Department of Labour in 1954.[20] Pay equity and the campaign to establish a Women's Bureau similar to the one in the United States gained momentum immediately after the war. Women's organizations, particularly the Business and Professional Women's Association and the Young Women's Christian Association, were at the forefront of the effort to improve the economic lives of women in Canada. Pay-equity legislation was first introduced in Canada in 1950 and was framed in part by the 1949 United Nation's "Universal Declaration of Human Rights" that prohibited sex discrimination. The Female Employees Fair Remuneration Act was introduced on International Women's Day, 8 March 1950, and on 1 January 1952, Ontario became the first province to put equal-pay legislation into effect (Prentice et al. 1988, 332).

Conclusion

Women Steelworkers did not develop a collective identity as union feminists during this period of the union's history. Women, "the problem every supervisor dreaded," were hired into steel mills late into the war effort, and in the United States, jobs were refashioned to make them more "suitable" for women—with the important exception of black women. Women took advantage of the union membership during the war and joined the union in record numbers. While some of the women like Peggy, Theresa, and Lola desired to remain on the job after the war, the vast majority of the women were let go or reassigned to female-segregated departments. Lola was one of the lucky few who got to keep her job as a crane operator after the war.

Popular and government discourses in both countries conveyed the idea that making steel and guns were only temporary occupations for women. The U.S. Women's Bureau, the one place where there might have been the opportunity to create a counter discourse about women steelworkers, did not come through for those women who wanted to remain in the mills. Nor was the bureau up to the job of challenging the industry's "Jim Crow" practices. In fact they participated in masculinizing black women as a way to justify their employment in jobs the bureau considered "unsuitable" for (white) women. The Canadian government, bowing to conservative pressure from Quebec, provided a "paternalistic" system of benefits for women who left their homes for work in the munitions factories and steel mills. It was hoped that women could be protected from the corrupting influences of doing a man's job and be sent back home relatively unchanged.

3

Bread, Roses, and Rights: Gender Equity and the Law

Equality is, at the very least, freedom from adverse discrimination. But what constitutes adverse discrimination changes with time, with information, with experience and with insight. What we tolerated as a society one hundred, fifty, or even ten years ago is no longer necessarily tolerable.
— Rosalie Abella, "The Dynamic Nature of Equality"

Equity law and the jurisprudence it generated were perhaps one of the biggest accomplishments of the "new social movements" in both the United States and Canada. Without such legislation women would not have gained access to better paying, nontraditional blue-collar jobs in either country. Yet the payoff for working-class women in the United States was not as great as it was for their sisters in Canada. Almost as soon as the ink was dry on U.S. equity legislation, the courts were flooded with angry litigants, often backed by powerful business interests, charging "reverse discrimination." Canadian equity jurisprudence does not recognize reverse discrimination claims, and litigants in discrimination suits must demonstrate a history of disadvantaged treatment (Colker 1998).

Laws help to shape political opportunity structures in ways that both constrain and facilitate collective action (Katzenstein 1998). The doctrine of equal rights forms the backbone of sex-discrimination litigation and legislation in U.S. law. Women in the United States gained access (no small feat) to educational opportunities, to male-dominated occupations, to unions, to the military, to sports, and so on, by proving that their exclusion constituted differential treatment under the law. They were excluded as individuals because of their membership in a particular social group. Katzenstein (1998) argues that over the past two decades the extension and enforcement of individual rights to disadvantaged groups within the law in the United States has opened up and legitimated protest inside mainstream institutions, creating a climate more receptive to feminist political claims for group-based gender rights. Yet only because these claims rest securely on the foundation of individual rights do they gain a measure of acceptance.

Because unions may legitimately articulate class-based group claims through collective bargaining, strikes, filing of grievances, and arbitration, the addition of equal-rights law as one more tool in their repertoire expands in principle their options for protest.[1] Union feminists took advantage of antidiscrimination law and the equal opportunity norms it created along with the tools of negotiation and political action to gain economic rights for working women. Equity law gave ammunition to those women who were predisposed to claim discrimination and provided greater leverage at the bargaining table to those union leaders who were already sympathetic to gender equity (Hartmann 1998). Union feminists and their allies urged the union to press employers to comply with equal opportunity law because they reasoned that, if it failed to do so, the union could be held liable for the employer's discrimination. Of course, creating the political climate and the will to use the legal tools is a part of the overall struggle to advance gender claims within the working class. A serious limitation of the equal-rights approach is the inability of the law to entertain the simultaneous effects of multiple forms of discrimination. Black women in the United States, for example, must base claims of discrimination on either race or sex but not on the unique "compoundedness" of both forms of discrimination (Crenshaw 1988, 386).[2] Black women must grant legal privilege to one source of discrimination over the other.

Title VII and Its Impact on Steel

Title VII of the Civil Rights Act made a difference in the lives of working-class women by outlawing discrimination in hiring, wages, and conditions of employment on the basis of race, color, religion, national origin, and sex. It was a much broader law, with stronger measures of enforcement, than any previous efforts to outlaw employment discrimination (Hill 1993). For one, it opened the door to more "aggressive," private litigation and, in the early years, provided the Equal Employment Opportunity Commission (EEOC) with an avenue to file amicus curiae briefs on the interpretation and application of Title VII. According to Hill (1993), "This dual feature of the process resulted in a new body of law that transcended anything known under previous fair-employment-practice statutes and administrative orders" (306). Before Title VII, the only other avenue for legal redress for employment discrimination was the National Labor Relations Act (NLRA), which was passed in 1935 and required unions to provide fair representation of its members (Iglesias 1997). Unfortunately, these two laws often came into conflict; the older law pitting class or majority rights against the newer law guaranteeing individual rights based on sex and race. Women of color often paid a particularly high price for this contradiction in law.[3]

Struggles over the passage, interpretation, and enforcement of Title VII of the 1964 Civil Rights Act exposed the gender and racial fault lines in the U.S. labor movement. For different reasons unions and employers vigorously opposed the idea of extending civil rights to the workplace. While businesses were concerned primarily about the financial costs of eliminating discrimination, unions worried that federal legislation like Title VII would undermine the collective-bargaining system put into place under the NLRA. After all, they reasoned, unions were already required by law to represent all members fairly regardless of race, color, creed, or national origin *(but not sex)*. If an individual experienced discrimination, there were existing ways to remedy the situation. Initially unions opposed any government intervention into the collective-bargaining system, and they feared that categorical relief for black workers would undermine seniority. Unions did not favor independent enforcement powers for the EEOC and insisted that the commission be regulated by the Department of Justice (Hill 1993).

Title VII of the 1964 U.S. Civil Rights Act, the introduction of affirmative action and the subsequent erosion of protective-labor law, allowed women to gain a foothold in the steel industry. Not surprisingly, women steelworkers were among the first women to use civil rights initiatives to challenge protective-labor laws. When they had the support of their union they used the grievance procedures to challenge sex discrimination, and when they did not they pursued their equity claims with the help of civil rights organizations and the EEOC. In some instances women used both approaches.

Women Steelworkers, like Alice Peurala, who were hired after the war were often inspired by the women who worked in the mills during the war.[4] U.S. Steel South Works hired Alice, an Armenian American and a socialist, as a metallurgical observer in 1953. This was a job women had held during the war, and a few had remained in that position after the war. Alice, a single mother of a one-year-old daughter, wanted to transfer to another job in the metallurgical lab that would afford her the opportunity to work steady days so she could be at home with her baby at night. Whenever she asked about new openings she was always told by the company, "We have someone else in mind" or "We don't want women in these jobs." Alice had been active in the civil rights movement, so when the Civil Rights Act was passed in 1964, she didn't hesitate to use the new law. In 1967 she asked again for a transfer to an opening as a product tester and was told that she didn't have the educational background for the job and that, because the job required overtime and heavy lifting, as a woman, she was ineligible. The union did not press her case, and so she went to the EEOC. Their investigation revealed that over a two-year period only two hours of overtime were ever required and that nothing heavier than five pounds was ever lifted. In addition, there were no special educational requirements beyond what Alice already had acquired on the job. The EEOC recommended that Alice file a sex-discrimination suit, and she did. The judged ruled in her favor and, after much haggling, she was assigned to the job of product tester. The legal route was long and costly, and by the time Alice was assigned the new position, her daughter was fifteen years old and presumably not in need of daycare.

In the long run, Alice's persistence paid off for other women as well. She was a veteran of many labor struggles and was instrumental throughout the seventies in many of the rank-and-file insurgency campaigns in Local 65 and in District 31 in the Calumet region. She was at the founding convention of the Coalition of Labor Union Women in 1974 and, with Roberta Wood, helped to create one of the district's first women's committees. She served two terms as president of Local 65 but failed in her bid to become the first woman elected to direct a district. Alice saw her plant dwindle from a mill employing 9,000 workers to one employing only 772 and eventually closing altogether. She died of cancer in 1986 but not before opening many doors for other women (O'Farrell and Kornbluh 1996).

Unlike the case of civil rights, there was no grassroots women's movement in 1964 demanding an end to discrimination against women. In fact, the differential treatment of women in many workplaces including steel was often considered "natural" and not an act of discrimination. Separate want ads for men and women simply reflected the taken-for-granted nature of the sexual division of labor. Even after Title VII passed, not many involved thought that women would actually use the legislation. Franklin Roosevelt Jr., the first director of the EEOC, thought extending civil rights protection to women was laughable (Friedan 2000).

Working-class women did not think that the inclusion of women was laughable, and once the law was in place, feminists made it a tool that women workers could use to their advantage.[5] Working-class women were at the forefront of filing EEOC complaints, according to Deslippe (2000). In the first year alone, women filed 2,500 sex discrimination complaints—accounting for 27 percent of all complaints. Their most common complaints involved unequal employment benefits (30 percent), separate seniority lists (24 percent), unfair restrictions due to state protective laws (12 percent), and discrimination in hiring and firing (5.6 percent). When their unions did not respond, women used the EEOC mechanisms to file complaints against them as well, and between 1966 and 1977 women filed twenty-seven complaints against the Steelworkers, a number second only to the International Electrical Workers Union (Deslippe 2000, 124).

Sex Discrimination and Arbitration

In 1964 the Steelworkers added a nondiscrimination clause to the basic agreement to demonstrate its compliance with Title VII of the new civil rights law, thus enabling women to make greater use of the union's grievance mechanisms to challenge sex discrimination. The clause stipulated that "there shall be no discrimination against any employee on account of sex, race, creed, color or national origin in any matter pertaining to wages, hours of employment and other conditions of employment." Sex-discrimination cases that made it to arbitration provide insight into how gender, culture, and law influenced the prevailing discourses about women's rights on the job. In addition, such cases also shed light on the process that transforms a complaint about sex discrimination into an official grievance and finally into a political rights claim.

The *Steelworkers Arbitration Reports,* published monthly, feature select grievance cases that might be of interest to the whole steel industry. The criteria for inclusion in the publication are significance of the contract involved, importance of the points to other contracts, the degree to which the reasoning appears in the decision, and the novelty of the issue at stake. Only a small number of the total cases are ever published in the reports and, therefore, these cases cannot be considered representative of sex discrimination grievances in the steel industry. I view them more as illustrative of the way sex discrimination was defined in the steel industry, and a close reading of sex discrimination cases reveals the strengths and limitations of using the grievance procedure to fight sex discrimination. Fifteen cases of sex discrimination were published in the *Steelworkers Arbitration Reports* between 1964 and 1979 (Table 2).

Twelve of the fifteen sex-discrimination cases specifically invoked the nondiscrimination clause of the contract. Ten of the fifteen cases involved seniority issues, three involved wages, and one each involved working conditions

Table 2

Sex discrimination arbitration cases, 1964–79

Case number and firm	Date	Grievance	Violation	Decision	Rational and remedy
1: Rockwell-Standard Los Angeles	20 April 1964	Wages: women were transferred to all-male department and not paid equal wages.	Discrimination* (wages)	Sustained.	Stop practice. No back pay award on technicality.
2: Wheeling Steel Corp. Yorkville, OH	19 May 1967	Women prevented from exercising transfer rights to avoid layoff; men with less seniority retained.	Discrimination (seniority)	Denied: protective laws limit civil rights when it comes to transfer, but in all other cases seniority clause governs.	Upholds the principle that women must be judged on individual merit—except when covered by protective statutes.
3: ALSCO Gnadenhutten, OH	19 June 1967	Women with greater seniority being laid off while men with less seniority worked.	Discrimination (seniority)	Denied: state protective laws take priority.	Company should request state to reevaluate the jobs given to men to see if they can be done by women.
4: Gibson, Inc. Kalamazoo, MI	17 Nov. 1967	Woman with greater department seniority denied bid; man with no experience and less department seniority was given the job.	Discrimination* (seniority)	Sustained: state law does not stipulate a weight-lifting requirement, only that females not be assigned jobs dispropor-tionate to strength.	Grievant awarded job for a test period of sixty days; her right to the job becomes permanent if she shows she is able to handle it.
5: General Fireproofing Youngstown, OH	27 March 1967	Men with less seniority recalled to work before women with greater seniority.	Discrimination* (seniority)	Denied: state protective laws take priority.	Company can consider physical requirements of the job in recall decisions.

6: Wheeling Steel Corp. Yorkville, OH	2 Feb. 1968	Women not given inter-plant transfer rights over men with less seniority.	Discrimination* (seniority)	Mixed: cannot cling to state law as a way to exclude women if reasonable accommodations are possible.	Company not required to assign women to jobs that violate state protective laws but may alter some minor job requirements.
7: National Can Corp. Los Angeles	21 Oct. 1968	Woman with more seniority refused bid on job vacancy over men with less seniority.	Discrimination* (seniority)	Denied: state protective laws take priority.	Company not required to assign women on the basis of seniority if from "time to time" lifting more than 25 lb is required.
8: Chamberlain Corp. Burlington, NJ	9 June 1969	Woman forklift operator in an all-male department is involuntarily transferred to another department to make it easier for her.	Discrimination* (seniority)	Sustained: company's right to make assignments does not mean it can do so on the basis of sex.	Company must return grievant to former job if she wants it.
9: Sterling Faucet Morgantown, WV	7 Jan. 1970	Modified weightlifting requirements for women and not for men in the same job classification.	Discrimination* (wages)	Sustained: cannot alter requirements for one sex and not the other.	Require all women to participate in all activities of the job; create new job and open for bidding; relieve all workers in this category of lifting assignments.
10: Republic Steel Gadsden, Alabama	22 March 1971	Practice of giving only females parking passes is discontinued, thereby revoking an established benefit before contract is up.	Discrimination (local working conditions)	Denied: cannot treat men and women in same job classification differently.	Nondiscrimination clause takes priority over local working conditions.

Table 2 (continued)

Case number and firm	Date	Grievance	Violation	Decision	Rational and remedy
11: U.S. Steel Fairfield Works	28 March 1972	Woman is involuntarily transferred to less desirable vacancy simply to ensure a same-sex work crew.	Discrimination* (seniority)	Sustained: cannot use speculation about some untoward event occurring in a mixed-sex group to deny a woman seniority rights.	Must not assign grievant to janitor vacancy if her seniority permits her to hold another job.
12: S. G. Taylor Chain Company Hammond, IN	12 April 1972	Women transferred to male department and not paid new rate	Discrimination* (wages)	Denied: rate is determined by job content and not by where the job is performed.	The women were moved to all-male department but not asked to do different work and therefore not entitled to to a different pay rate.
13: National Steel Portage, IN	24 June 1975	Woman disqualified from position because management believed women were unsuitable for the job of feeder-helper and not because of poor evaluation.	Discrimination* (seniority)	Denied: assessment of individual ability to do the job guided management, not sex.	Discrimination did not occur because grievant did not have the physical ability to do the job, which required heavy lifting. Slowing production and impeding incentive cannot be used to disqualify.

Case	Date	Issue	Type	Ruling	Outcome
14: Bethlehem Steel Burns Harbor, IN	18 Feb. 1977	Differential discipline on the basis of race; unfair discharge without due process; right to refuse polygraph test.	Discrimination (discipline)	Sustained: hearsay evidence cannot be used to determine the grievant's guilt or innocence; polygraph not admissible or required; race discrimination denied.	Grievant is reinstated and awarded back pay because of contract.
15: Bethlehem Steel Sparrows Point, MD	12 Dec. 1979	Termination during probationary period because of sex.	Discrimination (seniority)	Sustained: cannot discharge a woman on the basis of similar standard is used for men.	Grievant is reinstated and awarded back pay. Company has the right to discharge probationary employees but must be evenhanded.

*These cases invoked the union contract's nondiscrimination clause.
Source: "Steelworker's Arbitration Awards," USWA Steel Arbitration bulletins 1964–1979, volumes 12, 14, 15, 16, 17, 18, 19, and 21.

and discipline. Arbitrators were almost as likely to sustain a grievance as to deny it. In most of the rejected cases, arbitrators ruled that state protective-labor laws limiting hours of work and the amount of weight that women could lift took precedence over the contract's nondiscrimination law—even after the EEOC issued guidelines to the contrary.

Using the grievance procedure proved more successful in challenging state protective-labor statues when such laws were not well defined. In Michigan (case 4), the law did not stipulate an actual amount of weight but instead said that a woman could not be assigned work that required her to lift a "disproportionate" amount of weight. The arbitrator sustained the grievance and ordered the company to give women the opportunity to prove whether they could do the job or not. In Ohio (see cases 2, 3, and 5), the law stipulated that women could not be required to lift more than 25 pounds. This left little room for discretion, and arbitrators were more likely to rule that state law held sway over the nondiscrimination clause of the contract. As the influence of protective-labor law began to wane throughout the United States, arbitrators in Ohio (case 6) began to rule that companies could not deliberately cling to state law and that, if reasonable accommodations were possible, then some modifications that would allow women to perform the job could be made.

Women involved in cases 2 and 6 argued that even under the protective-labor restrictions there were many more jobs for which women were eligible for but from which they were excluded. Protecting their seniority rights eventually became more important than the protective-labor laws—particularly when women felt the law was deliberately being used against them. Women with greater seniority than men were being denied transfer and recall rights because the new openings might require, even if only on rare occasions, lifting something heavier than 25 pounds. Exercising transfer and recall rights was the only way workers could protect their job status in an industry racked by cyclical downturns and eventually more permanent cutbacks. Peggy, one of the women involved in both cases and a mother of six, told me that she did not feel the need to be "protected right out of a job."

Union staff, arbitrators, and company officials were not immune to cultural stereotyping about gender to justify or explain their arguments. In a case (15) involving a female employee who was fired during the probationary period for reasons of "physical stature," the union was successful in establishing that sex discrimination had occurred. The grievant believed she was fired not because she was overweight but because the foreman thought women in general did not have the physical stature to do most of the jobs in the mill. The company offered no specific examples to show that the grievant was not able to do her job, and the union could find no instance where a man was discharged on the basis of "physical stature." The foreman was acting on the assumption that there might be, at *some time in the future,* jobs that she would not be able to do because of her size. Company officials mistakenly clung to the idea that the company had the unilateral right to fire probationary employees. During the hearing, a company representative said, "If we want, we can discharge a probationary employee because they have green hair." The arbitrator ruled in favor of the union and ordered the worker to be reinstated with back pay. "It is quite true that the Company can discharge a probationary employee for having green hair, but it cannot discharge a female employee for having green hair unless it would also discharge a male employee for that reason. The same is true of 'physical structure,' which, upon this record, is the only reason for the discharge." The employer's right to fire probationary employees had to be exercised in a nondiscriminatory or evenhanded fashion. In this case, the union's nondiscrimination clause took precedence and established the fact that civil rights had to be protected during probation.

In three other cases (8, 10, and 11), arguments about chivalry obscured the question of who was responsible for sexual harassment. In two of the cases, women are asked to pay a price for their own protection from harassment or potential harassment, and, in the third case, it was women themselves who laid claim to a "privilege" as a way to protect themselves from sexual harassment. One woman (11) was demoted to a janitor's position—a demotion she did not request—because the company did not want to assign that job to a man. For a "safety reason," the company did not want a mixed-sex work crew cleaning offices on the second shift when not many other workers were around. The arbitrator ruled the grievant, a woman with twenty-seven years of seniority, did not have to accept the assignment if her seniority permitted her to hold another job just to protect other women from sexual harassment. The company's fear that "something" would happen in a mixed-sex group was unfounded and could not be used as the grounds for assigning work using gender as the criteria. Another woman (8), a forklift operator, was involuntarily transferred to another department in order to avoid a situation where she would be the only woman in an otherwise all-male department. She alleged that her supervisor told her the transfer was done in order to make it "easier" for her. In her own defense she wrote in her grievance, "Since I have worked at this company I have never in any way asked anyone to make work easy for me, nor have I ever complained about any amount of hard physical work assigned me." The arbitrator ruled she was allowed to return to her former job if she so desired.

In another case (10), it had been the past practice of the company to give women office employees, but not men, parking passes that would allow them to park closer to the work site. The union advised the company that, if it did not stop the practice, men would complain about reverse discrimination. The company stopped the practice and the women filed a grievance claiming that, since this practice had such long standing, it had became a part of their conditions of work and was thereby protected by the contract. On this basis the union went to bat for the women. Noted in their complaint were a number of hardships that walking to the office inside the mill would pose to women. In addition to damage to "ladies'" shoes and walking in the rain, women would be subject to the "embarrassing whistles and catcalls." The arbitrator ruled against the women on the grounds that it was discrimination to give passes to women and not to men—a clear violation of the union's nondiscrimination clause. In the ensuing discussion the plant superintendent felt compelled to apologize for depriving the women of the passes. He described himself as a "southern gentleman who hated to be in a position of picking on ladies." The arbitrator responded with similar claims to chivalry when he expressed regret that he had to rule against the women. "The standards of gentlemanliness do change with the times." Neither man addressed the question of the harassment the women experienced as a result of the change in policy nor who was responsible for it.

The Consent Decree and Women's Access: The Case of the United States

Women in the United States gained access to nontraditional job opportunities in the steel industry in 1974, when women were included in an industry-wide consent decree fashioned by the courts to remedy systemic patterns of discrimination that stemmed from an internal labor market. The structure of this internal market featured an elaborate job classification system, horizontal ladders of progression, and differential wage incentives based on job classification and exaggerated the long-term effects of initial job placement.[6] Race, ethnicity, and gender were an integral part of the internal labor market that advanced the opportunities for some workers at the expense of others. Black and Latino men typically were assigned initially to the least skilled, least desirable, and most hazardous jobs and then locked into a seniority system that favored the length of department service over plant service. When jobs with better pay, higher production incentives, and greater opportunities for promotion were open they were quickly filled by white men who held less plant seniority but more department seniority.[7]

White women, on the other hand, were segregated within a very small number of specific job classifications that were less skilled and desirable, and there were no opportunities for promotion other than those specially designated for women. Undoing the discriminatory effects of such a complicated job structure required an outsized commitment to equality and to the equity tools of affirmative action during a time when there was considerable backlash against such measures—particularly in the United States.

The consent decree, the outcome of decades of civil rights litigation and activism, put into place one of the most extensive affirmative-action plans in basic industry. The decree set hiring goals for women and minority men: 20 percent of all new hires in production and maintenance had to be female, and 15 percent of all new hires into clerical and technical jobs had to be black and Latino. Twenty-five percent of the employees selected for management training and for supervisory positions had to be minorities and/or female. In addition, the consent decree established measures to increase women and minority representation in the crafts and skilled trades and restructured the entire seniority system to facilitate the transfer of workers out of previously segregated departments. The change from department seniority to plant-wide seniority required by the decree was applicable to all workers, including white men (Tannenbaum 1979).[8] Legal counsel for the union believed that the "even-handedness" of the approach to changes in the seniority system would help to mitigate white resistance to affirmative action.[9]

The scope and magnitude of the decree was large. It involved nine of the largest steel companies, which at the time accounted for 73 percent of all steel production in the United States and covered workers at 250 plants. These nine companies employed 347,679 workers, of whom 52,545 were black, 7,646 were Spanish surnamed, and 10,175 were women. A consent decree is a legally binding agreement between government agencies, industry representatives, and unions and usually results from threatened litigation. Like the one in steel, they are negotiated in lieu of an imposed court decision. This method of settling discrimination suits was first used with AT&T in 1973 when the company agreed to give back pay to whole categories of women workers and to institute a company-wide promotion package for women and minorities (Deaux and Ullman 1983). The steel-industry decree followed on the heels of the AT&T agreement and was described by *Business Week* (12 May 1975) as "the most far reaching legal remedy for past discrimination ever applied in U.S. industry" (36). Unlike the AT&T agreement, the steel decree was the first to make the remedy available to all workers whether they were members of the aggrieved class or not. At the time both settlements were considered to be the wave of the future.

The effect of the decree on women in the steel industry was immediate, and their numbers in production increased by 38 percent in the months

Table 3

Distribution of women by race and company, 1977

Company	Number of Employees	White women Percent	n	Black women Percent	n	Women with Hispanic surname Percent	n	Total women Percent	n
Armco	13,133	1.5	191	0.7	86	0.0	8	2.2	285
Allegheny Ludlum	5,346	2.2	115	0.2	13	0.0	1	2.4	129
Bethlehem	44,784	1.9	859	1.2	525	0.0	7	3.1	1,391
J&L	20,663	3.4	708	1.3	273	0.0	3	4.7	984
National	10,352	2.7	279	3.3	339	0.2	18	6.2	636
Republic	22,715	1.4	321	1.8	410	0.1	22	3.3	753
U.S. Steel	73,567	1.6	1,255	1.8	1,396	0.1	94	3.5	2,745
Youngstown	16,723	1.1	180	1.1	186	0.1	17	2.3	383
Wheeling-Pitt	9,098	1.1	97	0.1	12	0.0	0	1.2	109
Total	219,181	1.8	4,005	1.5	3,240	0.1	168	3.4	7,413
Percent of study		54		44		2		100	

Source: Audit and Review, b32, HCLA, Penn State University, University Park, Pennsylvania.

following the signing of the decree—mostly in the Northern and Midwestern states. African American women were nearly half of all the women who went into the mill, and they were counted as female rather than as minority for the purpose of affirmative action (Table 3). Some women moved into the jobs vacated by minority male workers who used the decree to transfer out of undesirable jobs in the coke plant. However, the new flexibility in the seniority system would mean that these women were not trapped there.

As it turned out, the wave of the future did not last long. By 1977 the U.S. Supreme Court ruled that seniority systems that resulted in advantages for white workers over black workers were not necessarily illegal. Expressing the majority opinion in the 7–2 decision (T.I.M.E.-DC and Teamsters)[10] was Justice Potter Stewart, who wrote, "Bona fide seniority systems with no overt racial underpinnings are not unlawful, even though such systems may in practice have the impact of discriminating against certain workers" (*Time*, 13 June 1977, 60). The court also ruled that no worker could be given retroactive seniority prior to the passage of the Civil Rights Act in 1964. Potter held, "It was not the intent of Congress to destroy or water down the vested seniority rights of employees simply because their employer had engaged in discrimination prior to the passage of the act" (60). In that case, which involved a trucking firm, the courts ruled that dual systems of seniority for different types of jobs were not illegal as long as all workers in each department were treated equally.

Support for and Opposition to the Decree

The steel decree withstood opposition and legal challenges. It was initially opposed by lawyers and civil rights organizations representing the aggrieved class for not going far enough and by opponents to affirmative action for going too far. Under Title VII, lawyers for the National Association for the Advancement of Colored People's (NAACP) Legal Defense Fund had won class-action suits on the behalf of black steelworkers and did not believe that the industry-wide, negotiated settlement provided sufficient relief to the victims of discrimination. In addition, they were critical of the fact that the decree required the victims of discrimination to sign away their rights to sue for pre-decree discrimination in order to collect a relatively small amount of money. Once the decree went into effect, the government would be obligated to intervene on the side of the companies charged with discrimination in order to "protect the integrity of the consent decree." The NAACP's Herbert Hill charged that steel corporations and the Steelworkers union were attempting to buy immunity from litigation under Title VII (*New York Times,* 14 April 1974, sec. 3, 1). The average amount of back pay awarded was between $250 and $500. Women hired after 1967 received $3.25 for every month they were employed before the decree.

The NAACP solicited the support of the National Organization for Women's (NOW) Legal Defense Fund, and together they filed a motion to have the courts vacate the decision. Both organizations were worried that the powers of the EEOC were being eroded and that the right of individuals to file lawsuits for discrimination was jeopardized. NOW entered the case on behalf of all women who had been excluded from the industry, including those women who were forced out after the war. NOW argued that some of the provisions were unfair to women. For example, if utilization studies showed that women and minority men were underrepresented in the skilled crafts in proportion to their employment in production and maintenance, then the companies were required to promote women and minority men into craft jobs on a one-to-one basis with white men. Since so few women were already employed in the mill it would take some time before women would advance to the apprenticeships. In the end, the appeals court for the Fifth Circuit upheld the decree.

There was also organized opposition from white steelworkers. Some who opposed argued that the affirmative-action measures of the decree constituted "reverse discrimination." Brian Weber successfully challenged affirmative-action measures at his Louisiana plant of Kaiser that were similar to those required in the decree. He was denied access to an apprenticeship because the quota for whites was filled, while black workers with less seniority were allowed to enter the program. However, his case was overturned by the U.S. Supreme Court in 1979.[11]

A coalition of nine Pennsylvania State legislators introduced a bill in the Pennsylvania State House to overturn the decree; they too were unsuccessful. A small group of workers in Youngstown, Ohio, organized an opposition group they called the Committee of Concern for the Rights of Steelworkers and put together a media and legal campaign to overturn the decree. A year later, they claimed a membership in the hundreds and a potential base of sympathizers in the thousands. The group filed an unsuccessful reverse discrimination suit in the federal court in Cincinnati, picketed the International Steelworkers headquarters in Pittsburgh, lobbied their congressional representatives in Washington, and appeared on local television and radio to plead their case against changes in the seniority system. The group, critical of the change to plant seniority as a remedy for ending discrimination in the industry, claimed there was no proof that discrimination had occurred in any of the mills in Youngstown. They believed they were being penalized for acts of discrimination that had occurred elsewhere—mainly in Alabama.

To get the attention of the International, the group threatened decertification—a drastic move to divorce themselves from the Steelworkers. "What will hurt the union more than anything else is to leave it." A cartoon in their newsletter entitled "Sobering Up Time" depicted a drunk (representing the International) lying down in the street in front of a fire hydrant with the word "steelworkers" painted on it, clutching a bottle of liquor labeled "consent decree." The backlash group raised money for their antidecree cause by selling raffle tickets and bumper stickers, holding a Big Band dance that "the wife won't want to miss," having card parties, and hosting the ubiquitous stag with free beer and sandwiches. Their flyer announced, "Anyone who likes to play cards and shoot craps will enjoy themselves."[12]

Opposition to the decree was anticipated by legal counsel for the Steelworkers who thought they had found a way to harmonize the interests of white workers with the interests of minority workers and women. Bernard Kleiman (1975), an attorney with the union, argued that the resulting "turbulence" from Title VII and other efforts to end discrimination was an "inconvenience"—the price to be paid for the elimination of discrimination. New ways of organizing work would be needed. "We cannot expect minority employees and women to be responsive to our collective bargaining systems until they have been shown that the system will work for them as well as they do for white male workers. Hence, if we want to improve the labor relations climate and maximize the fruits of collective bargaining, we must get at the task of assuring equal employment opportunity for all workers, and soon" (1).

Not all white workers opposed the consent decree. Some white workers would benefit, and they welcomed the broadening of seniority rights. Mary Kearney, the government's representative to the implementation committee with jurisdiction over Wheeling-Pittsburgh Steel, told me that an older worker, an Italian immigrant, dropped by her office in Wheeling unexpectedly to tell her she was doing a good job and that he knew for a fact that race discrimination existed.[13] He told her there were black men who had worked with him as helpers and who were more than capable of doing other jobs, yet were denied bids on better jobs.[14] Mary also received a handwritten letter from an anonymous steelworker who thought that opposition to the consent decree was not a majority opinion and that such opposition was unjustified. The author of the letter wrote on behalf of an unknown group of workers "to commend the federal govt. and all who initiated legislation to remedy a situation long discriminatory in the working-class field." He thought that opposition to the decree was being expressed by workers who in the past benefited from an unfair advantage. "The issue of departmental seniority only without being able to use Plant seniority was only originated for favoritism, nepotism & payola-& as you know some people cannot exist without these practices, so as long as these few got their way the majority legits pay." He believed that the decree was in the best interest of all workers including the majority of white workers. He went on, "The Consent Decree—has been the most significant and just thing to happen to the American working people in 40 years." He also recognized that the decree had unanticipated benefits for white workers: "The irony first all is that within just a few more years when a very majority of elderly people retire the dissidents will be the eventual winners of the whole thing. Common sense & lack of selfishness & greed will tell you that." He claimed there were many like himself who supported the government's efforts and wanted Mary to show his letter to her boss. "I hope you will hold onto this letter to show to your superiors. The names are not important—we can put a thousand names on here."[15]

Thus, women entered the industry under an unpopular court order at a time when court orders regarding affirmative action and desegregation were generating considerable hostility and backlash in white, working-class communities across the United States. According to Robert Moore, the lawyer from the Justice Department who had responsibility for its implementation, sex was added to the consent decree at the eleventh hour so that the decree would conform to the intent of Title VII regarding the inclusion of women as a protected class. Moore did not remember any cases where women had filed class-action suits regarding sex discrimination in the steel industry prior to the consent decree.[16]

Yet women did use a variety of means to stake their claim in the industry before the consent decree, sometimes using the grievance procedure and sometimes using the mechanism established by the EEOC under Title VII. But these were women, already employed in the industry, who wanted to transfer to better jobs or who wanted equal pay for jobs that were similar to those done by men. Others were women who, when threatened with job loss, like Gloria Reehill, a seventeen-year employee at the Fairless Works of U.S. Steel, demanded to be transferred to jobs not previously held by women.[17] In 1973, the union used Title VII to file a class action suit on behalf of female members and former female members at the Loraine, Ohio, works of U.S. Steel to challenge protective-labor laws as unequal treatment.[18] Even though the EEOC issued guidelines in 1969 that said conflict between protective-labor law and Title VII had to be resolved in favor of Title VII, the courts ruled against the union because no such cases had been resolved in Ohio courts to guide the employer. I could not find one legal case involving the use of Title VII by women outside the industry to gain entry into the mills on the same basis as men.

Small numbers of women were hired into the mills in the late sixties well before the 1974 consent decree because of labor shortages caused by the Vietnam war. These new openings for women were not widely advertised. For example, Republic Steel in Buffalo, which hired 100 women, asked the New York State Employment Service to send them female applicants. Once the media began to cover the novelty of women in the mill, though, Republic received more applications than it could handle. The *New York Times* (28 December 1969, sec. 3, 1) carried a story about women steelworkers in Buffalo, emphasizing that unlike Rosie the Riveter, this new generation of women steelworkers was expected (with a few exceptions) to perform most of the same jobs as men did. They were described as working hard, "shoulder to shoulder" with the men, and those women that made the grade were described as "somewhat more agile and robust than the average woman." To ensure that their femininity was not diminished, the reader was reminded that, though the women wear traditional protective boots, safety goggles, and hard hats, some were "painted bright pink and further adorned with the sort of flower decals that hippies plaster on their Volks-wagens." The women are further "normalized" as feminine by reference to heterosexuality. One woman's worries about whether she will be free for the "big date" on New Year's Eve and another woman is characterized as baking a cake for the "boys in the Bar mill."

The *New York Times* story claimed that there was some initial resent-ment of the women and cited the response of a male worker who was asked by a woman co-worker where the water fountain was and replied, "You make as much money as I do, girlie. Why don't you find it?" Yet the reporter, Robert Walker, insisted that such signs of hostility were "unusual" and "have since evaporated." The superintendent of industrial relations at Republic was quoted as saying that "women without a husband, especially one sup-porting children, would be unlikely to arouse resentment by taking a job among the male steelworkers, who still outnumber the women in the plant by about 32 to one."

With one important exception, the women reported that their work in the mill was only "a little harder than anything they have done in the past." The exception is forty-four-year-old Maria Markiewicz, who was born in Poland and survived a Nazi labor camp where "she worked 18 hours a day at jobs much harder than her current activities in the steel plant." The bar-riers to women's nontraditional employment were being eroded, however slowly, before the advent of the decree. Yet, it was the courts that finally opened the plant gates to women and provided opportunities for advance-ment into skilled crafts and apprenticeships. The courts also made it possi-ble for those women who had remained in the industry after the war to transfer to new departments and retain their plant-wide seniority.

Audit and Review

The consent decree contained an elaborate system of implementation, re-view, and oversight that operated on a local, regional, and national level. I examined the records of the union's national Audit and Review Committee, the committee charged with responsibility for the implementation of the order, to determine whether and how the committee responded to sex-discrimination complaints filed by women steelworkers. The committee had responsibility for the interpretation and resolution of disputes not re-solved at the local level of the implementation process, for clarification of the terms and specificity of the court order, and for the coordination of com-munication between all of the parties involved.

The technical details guiding administration of the decree did not lend themselves to quick or easy resolution of disputes, and much of the sex discrimination experienced by women did not actually fall under the authority or purview of the oversight committee. All grievances regarding sex and/or race discrimination were first submitted to the local implementation committees. The decree stipulated that women and minority workers were to have representation on the local committees and that, if the local committee decided a worker's charge of discrimination was related to the consent decree, it would have the jurisdiction to try to resolve the complaint. All other non-consent-decree-related grievances regarding sex or race discrimination were to be sent to the EEOC. However, correspondence between the EEOC and the national Audit and Review Committee suggests that this procedure was not always followed.

In my review of the docket of cases that reached the national Audit and Review Committee, I found twenty cases filed between 1976 and 1985 that involved sex discrimination (Table 4). These twenty complaints involved forty-eight women and were filed against five of the nine steel companies involved in the consent decree. In nine of the cases, the committee ruled that it did not have jurisdiction in the matter and referred the cases back to the locals or to the EEOC. In cases where it did have jurisdiction, it ruled against women in all but one case. Only one woman was able to use the oversight committee to win a case of sex discrimination (docket 77-4). In this case, which involved filling temporary vacancies, the committee ruled that "where a company has no contractual obligation to assign a specific employee and a choice between equally satisfactory options are possible" then the spirit of the decree should be upheld.

Battle in Seattle: The Bethlehem 10

From the beginning there was confusion on the part of workers concerning how to use the decree to process a grievance or complaint about discrimination, and, in some cases, workers did not even know of the decree's existence. One case (docket 65-16)[19] involved charges brought by ten women in 1977 against the Bethlehem Steel Works in Seattle, Washington, and is illustrative of the type of discrimination the women faced. Neither the company nor the union explained to them what rights and remedies they had under the consent decree. In addition to the claim that they had been improperly laid off while shorter service male employees at the plant had been retained, they also charged that the company engaged in a general pattern of sex-discrimination by "allowing men but not women to refuse potentially dangerous work assignments; bumping women off certain jobs before they were able to accrue seniority in those positions; and consistently giving the less favorable work assignments to women." Rebuffed by their union local, the women went to the Seattle Office of Women's Rights and, with the help of that office, secured the assistance of a law firm. Some of the women also filed separate complaints with the EEOC and with the Washington State Human Rights Commission.

Most of what the women charged did not constitute a violation of the decree, and after reviewing the data regarding the women's date of hire and those of the men recalled before them, the Audit and Review committee concluded that no violation of seniority rights under the decree had taken place. Furthermore, six of the women had exhausted their recall rights, were no longer employees of Bethlehem Steel, and therefore were no longer covered by the decree. (If a worker had less than two years' seniority and was laid off for longer than two years, he or she was automatically removed from the company's list of employees.) The committee was upset that the women had not been informed about their rights under the consent decree and ordered the company to prepare materials to distribute to all new employees regarding these rights—a requirement that the company claimed was too costly.

The Audit and Review Committee held a hearing in Seattle about the women's situation but warned their attorneys that it was extremely unproductive to try to verify "mill rumor" that arises in a reduction-in-force situation. Equally unproductive were attempts to deal with general allegations that unnamed supervisors or turn foremen had harassed particular employees. The women would need to provide detail, such as names of male workers with less seniority who received more favorable treatment, or the charges could not be verified. The committee would not accept that the women did not know the names of fellow employees and supervisors in their departments. Personnel records were made available for all parties to view, and the committee also sent a female attorney to interview the ten women. But in the end there was very little the committee could do for the women, and they ruled that most of the charges were not adequately substantiated or that they were for issues that did not fall under the jurisdiction of the committee.

Using the apparatus of the consent decree to register concerns about the violation of rights was difficult, cumbersome, and hard for workers to understand. This caused much frustration on the part of workers.[20] Much of the gender and racial harassment workers encountered on the job were not formal civil rights violations or even violations of the basic contract. Some union locals helped workers to find the appropriate avenues for complaint and others did not. Even overt acts of sexual harassment encountered by women on a day-to-day basis on the shop floor were not yet named as such or illegal. When women tried to complain about sexual harassment

Table 4

Audit and review sex discrimination cases, 1976–85

Company (city)	Year	Participants	Nature of complaint	Outcome	Docket number
J&L (Pittsburgh)	1976	3	Union's refusal to process grievance	No jurisdiction; insufficient detail	47-7
Bethlehem (Seattle)	1977	10	Seniority violation on layoff and recall, failure of union to represent	Not valid	65-16
Bethlehem (Burns Harbor)	1977	1	Excluded from training program, nonsexual harassment	Not valid	S76-58
Republic (Warren)	1978	2	Filling job vacancies; seniority	Valid; all things being equal uphold spirit of decree	77-4
Bethlehem (Sparrows Point)	1979	2	Recall rights of probationary employees	No jurisdiction	91-8
USS (Irvin)	1980	2	Transfers and reduction of force	Withdrawn	96-6
USS (Irvin)	1980	1	Failure of union to arbitrate	No jurisdiction	97-7
USS (Duquesne)	1980	1	Filling job vacancies; seniority	No violation	99-3
Republic (Youngstown)	1980	1	Transfer from production and maintenance to office and technical	No violation	100-3
USS (Gary)	1981	4	Exclusion from apprenticeship	Not valid	107-8
USS (Gary)	1981	1	Filling job vacancies; seniority	Lost record	107-10
USS (Homestead)	1982	2	Job elimination	No jurisdiction	112-3
Allegheny (Brackenridge)	1983	1	Performance evaluation	No jurisdiction	121-13

Bethlehem (Burns Harbor)	1983	1	Bona fide occupational qualification	No jurisdiction; refer to EEOC	122-7
USS (Gary)	1983	2	Job reclassification	Not valid	125-1
Bethlehem (Sparrows Point)	1984	5	Layoff and recall	Not valid	125-13
USS (Birmingham)	1983	2	Layoff and recall, job assignment	Not valid	126-4
J&L (Pittsburgh)	1984	1	Job reclassification	No jurisdiction	128-2
Republic (Canton)	1984	5	Job assignment, sexual harassment	No jurisdiction; refer harassment charge to EEOC	124-5
USS (Imperial)	1985	1	Layoff	No jurisdiction	133-10

Source: Audit and Review, b3, 6, 7, 16–19, HCLA, Penn State University, University Park, Pennsylvania.

under the consent decree, they were referred to the EEOC. In one case, a woman was told by the Audit and Review Committee that if she had only stayed long enough on a particular job, she would have discovered that, over time, the harassment "goes away."[21]

Canadian Equity Law and Women Steelworkers

Canadian women became Steelworkers by a different legal route. The consent decree was strictly a solution fashioned under U.S. law, so there was no sweeping, industry-wide affirmative-action order in Canada that opened up the entire steel industry to women at once. Canadian women relied on human rights legislation, primarily in the provinces, to gain access to jobs with particular companies. There were two important gender equity campaigns involving the Steelworkers in Canada. One involving the Steel Company of Canada (Stelco), one of the country's largest steel mills located in Hamilton, Ontario, and the other involving Inco, the world's largest supplier of nickel, located in Sudbury in Northeastern Ontario. Both campaigns were well organized, had secured union backing, and had captured media attention. They were part of a broader strategy by feminists to get women hired in nontraditional blue-collar occupations. They were launched in larger cities and targeted major companies in key industries, such as mining and steel (Luxton and Corman 1991). In 1979, an ad hoc "Women Back into Stelco Committee," with the support of the Steelworkers Local 1005, urged five women to file a sex-discrimination complaint with the Ontario Human Rights Commission of Canada.[22] The committee's name was chosen to reflect the notion that women had once, during World War II, worked at Stelco. After the war they were fired, and between 1946 and 1961 only a few had been hired to work in the tin mill and then only in female-designated jobs. Between 1961 and 1977, no women were hired at all—even though estimates were that about 30,000 women applied for jobs during those nineteen years. The union arrived at this figure by estimating that 10 percent of all applicants each year were women, and the government used this figure in setting new hiring goals for Stelco. By 1978, there were only twenty-eight women working in the mill—all in tin inspection—and there were about 13,000 men working in production (154).

Union support for the employment of women in production came by a circuitous route. The company had hired a female doctor, Dr. Lilly Chung, and, despite the opposition of some of the membership, the local president, Cec Taylor, complimented the company on its enlightened thinking and urged them to do the same for women in production. Taylor told reporters that he would support women who wanted to apply for jobs at

Stelco, but that none had ever approached the union about wanting to work there. When his words appeared the next day in the *Hamilton Spectator,* eight women contacted him immediately to take advantage of his offer. A sex-discrimination complaint was filed by the union on behalf of the women under two sections of the Human Rights Code. The code stipulates that "every person has a right to equal treatment with respect to employment without discrimination because of . . . sex" and also authorizes "the implementation of a special programme designed to relieve hardship or economic disadvantage or to assist disadvantaged persons or groups to achieve or attempt to achieve equal opportunity." The women won their case, and Stelco was required to hire women on the same basis as men. Stelco hired 200 women before major downsizing reduced their numbers drastically. These women encountered the same problems on the shop floor that I report elsewhere in the book—sexual harassment, lack of washroom facilities, inadequate training, etc.

In 1974, Inco became the first mining company to hire women for hourly rate jobs, and between 1974 and 1976 the company hired 100 women to work in surface operations. They usually started as laborers doing routine maintenance. It was not until 1992 that the first woman went underground. During World War II, more than 1,400 women had worked at Inco when Canadian laws preventing the employment of women were temporarily suspended. Women's employment in production ended after the war, and the only jobs open to women were in technical, clerical, or domestic job classifications. According to Keck and Powell (1996), the mining laws were amended to include "such other capacity that requires the exercise of normal feminine skill or dexterity but does not involve strenuous physical effort." The Ontario Mining Act was changed in 1970 to allow for the employment of women in production and again in 1978 to allow for their employment underground—changes that were recommended in the 1970 report by the federal Royal Commission on the Status of Women. The women did not fare well under economic restructuring, and by 1994, after drastic reduction in the Inco labor force, only 46 (1 percent) women remained on the job.

Conclusion

The struggle to end race and sex discrimination in the U.S. steel industry was shaped, in the main, by civil rights law and by the political discourse of equal opportunity, which constructed the substance and implementation of the decree.

Women entered these jobs in 1974 under the auspices of equal-employment opportunity legislation, but they did so well before any of the legislative and legal refinements regarding sexual harassment, pregnancy discrimination, or family leave were in place. Furthermore, women gained the opportunity to be employed in nontraditional jobs in the steel industry at a time when the future of such jobs was already in jeopardy. Women steelworkers, like minority men, were positioned between governmental policies that were, according to Stein (1998), often at cross-purposes—one regarding equity and the other regarding free markets. The courts at the time were responding to broad universal principles of equal opportunity that treated all sectors of the economy the same and not to the realities of an industry like steel, which was contracting not expanding. At the national level, she argues, the emphasis in government policy was on job training and not on job creation, which was left up to market forces. Since no new jobs were being created, equity became a zero-sum game—a situation that exacerbated hostility and divisiveness between those workers who already had good jobs and those who had bad jobs or no jobs at all. Equity policies created job demand by minority and women workers, but industrial policies produced fewer and fewer good jobs to meet this demand. "There were no new jobs just new rules about who would get them. . . . Policies attending to demand and ignoring supply set off quite a noisy conflict within the working-class" (315).

Transforming seniority was a monumental task, and the decree probably did more in the long run to save the jobs of all long-term employees, black and white, than it did to create new opportunities for women. The large influx of women into the steel industry would not have happened without the consent decree, and it did improve the opportunities for women who had managed to remain in the industry after World War II. However, the consent decree could not save jobs that were eliminated or restructured by deindustrialization, jobs the women fought desperately to retain. Yet, women did register increases in their share of jobs in the steel industry (Table 5). The largest increase was in sales (20.5 percent) followed by office and clerical (18.2 percent). Women made sizeable gains in professional jobs (14.5 percent) and technical (9.3 percent) but only miniscule gains in craft jobs (2.6 percent) and in management (5.5 percent). Moderate gains were made in laborers (9.5 percent) and operatives (6.4 percent). In the end, it might be argued that women in mid-level white-collar jobs benefited more from the decree than did women in the blue-collar categories.

Gender equity initiatives including affirmative action did not meet the same level of hostility in Canada that they did in the United States, even in the face of similar downsizing of the steel industry. The Canadian law has limited the types of persons who make claims of legal discrimination. "Plain-

Table 5
Percentage of women by occupation in the steel industry

Occupation	1975	1980	1985	1990	1995	1998	Percent of change, 1975–98
Officials and managers	1.2	2.2	3.3	5.2	5.9	6.7	5.5
Professionals	6.0	10.4	14.4	17.7	18.4	20.5	14.5
Technicians	7.7	12.1	15.4	16.1	17.2	17.0	9.3
Sales	11.5	15.7	28.2	45.4	17.0	32.0	20.5
Office and clerical	46.8	54.6	58.5	63.1	63.4	65.0	18.2
Craft	0.2	1.0	1.2	1.8	2.5	2.8	2.6
Operatives	2.2	5.1	5.7	7.7	9.5	8.6	6.4
Laborers	4.7	12.8	12.3	11.5	14.1	14.2	9.5
Service	13.2	15.7	11.4	18.4	20.6	23.3	10.1

Source: U.S. Equal Opportunity Commission. Data compiled from *EEO-1 Reports for Basic Steel Industry, 1975–98.*

tiffs ... must demonstrate that their claim of discrimination is based on an enumerated or analogous ground to a disadvantaged group" (Colker 1998, 55). Enumerated grounds include race, national or ethnic origin, color, religion, sex, age, and mental or physical disability. Analogous grounds include marital status, sexual orientation, citizenship, and adoption. "Thus not all persons can bring claims of discrimination, they must be able to demonstrate a history of disadvantaged treatment (56)." Protection against "reverse discrimination" charges are built into section 15 of the charter where it explicitly states that remedies to eliminate the effects of past discrimination are allowable. In the Canadian context, affirmative action is a type of "reasonable accommodation" and a way to remove barriers to equality (56).

Without the changes in employment equity law in the United States and Canada, women would not have gained access to nontraditional better paying jobs in the steel industry. Male-dominated unions such as the Steelworkers would not have changed discriminatory practices without the pressure of the law and the social movements that helped to create the new laws. Once inside the industry, women did not hesitate to use the law in conjunction with the union's grievance mechanism to advance their economic interests. Title VII and the Canadian Human Rights Charter were important tools for shaping a response to race and sex discrimination that was "caste in steel."

4

What's a Nice Girl Like You Doing in a Place Like This? Life on the Shop Floor

I was shocked that women would even want to work in the mill. I know this might sound like prejudice, but my idea of a woman is a step above a steelworker.

—Foreman at Wheeling-Pittsburgh Steel Company

In this chapter I explore women's motivation for becoming steelworkers, their experiences on the shop floor and in the union, and how these experiences informed their activism. I assess the potential for collective identity formation as women, as feminists, and as Steelworkers, including the role of media discourse. Was the union a vehicle for addressing sexism and gender-specific problems on the shop floor? If not, how did the women handle issues such as sexual harassment, pregnancy discrimination, and sexist bias? Did they form women's committees or unique women-centered spaces to construct gender-specific politics? What networks might be available for mobilizing women and were they open to the ideas of feminism? Was gender solidarity even a possibility? How could it be achieved, and what were the obstacles? I focus my attention on women employed at Wheeling-Pittsburgh Steel Company (Local 1190) whom I interviewed in 1976 in Steubenville, Ohio, to better understand working-class women in a small, industrial community and how they developed a sense of themselves as political actors during a period of rapid social and cultural change (Figure 6).[1]

At the national level, the political climate of the 1970s was marked by

Figure 6. Wheeling-Pittsburgh Steel stretches between Steubenville and Mingo Junction, Ohio. From Follansbee, West Virginia. Mingo Junction is on the west side of the Ohio River. Photograph by Andrew Borowiec, copyright 1994.

a rapid succession of legal gains for women, rank-and-file insurgency among steelworkers, and backlash against affirmative action and other equity initiatives for women and minorities. Women were taking advantage of new economic opportunities made possible by the civil rights and women's rights movements, and I was interested in whether they saw themselves as agents of social change or even as the beneficiaries of social-movement activism.

While many of the pioneers at Wheeling-Pittsburgh Steel were sympathetic to the goals and accomplishments of the women's movement, most did not see themselves as feminists as they understood "feminist." Some white women did not think that affirmative action was necessary because discrimination was already against the law. The mere fact that they had gotten jobs in the mill was offered as proof that there was no longer discrimination or a need for affirmative action. The women did not feel entitled to jobs in the steel industry nor did they want to take any responsibility for the changes. "The mill was being forced to hire women so it might as well be me," was one woman's attitude. The women saw little connection between acts of protest and social-movement successes—like the new jobs in steel. It was as if these women thought of themselves as innocent bystanders forced to take advantage of affirmative action before someone else did.

Discursive Fields

Postmodern feminists have made us aware of the role of discursive fields in constructing multiple and contradictory subject positions for women to inhabit. The women in Local 1190 could not develop a collective identity as union feminists—a sense of themselves as political actors collectively organized around gender-specific issues—because the emerging discourses at the time about feminism and working-class women did not open enough political space for them to claim such an identity. In fact, these identities were often constructed as opposites, as suggested by this Chicago *Tribune* (26 May 1974) headline, "Feminists vs. Working-Class Women." Discourses of femininity, gender, and sexuality complemented and competed with discourses of feminism. To become political subjects, particularly at the local level, women steelworkers had to challenge prevailing discourses about what it meant to be a working women of a specific class and race as well as what it meant to be a feminist.

By the mid-seventies the national press routinely covered stories about women who were "the first" to hurdle the barriers that had blocked their access to previously all-male bastions of employment. The more "masculinized" the occupation, the more newsworthy the event. Stories and photos of women police officers, firefighters, coal miners, construction workers, and truck drivers seemed to be everywhere. The juxtaposition of lipstick and safety goggles was too much for the popular press to resist. The title of an *Ebony* (June 1977, 103) cover story on black women holding down nontraditional blue-collar jobs was "What's a Nice Girl Like You Doing in a Place Like This?" The title captured the media's fascination with the novelty of a woman doing a man's job. This feature about black women working in oil refineries, auto plants, and subway stations was careful not to undermine the "femininity" of women holding down "masculine" jobs.[2] The story began, "In lockers of some coal miners, factory workers and pipefitters today might be found tubes of lipstick and mascara alongside the hard hats and safety goggles."

General stories about women's increased labor-force participation, such as a *Newsweek* (6 December 1976, 68–81) feature "Women at Work," disproportionately focused on women in a variety of nontraditional occupations. The cover photo showed a determined, hard-hatted, tool-toting white woman perched on a telephone pole. Yet most of the women profiled inside were actually white professionals in male-dominated fields—executives, investors, and scientists. The only blue-collar woman prominently featured in a box insert of the *Newsweek* story was black steelworker Marilyn Butsey, a worker in the forge plant at the Ford Motor Company in Dearborn, Michigan. There is a dramatic photo of Butsey lifting a red-hot steel rod off the "hot press." Titled "Woman of Steel," the text of the insert opened with, "Once it was considered man's work—and a hellish job, at that" (70). Marilyn's job, usually performed by men of color, though not marked as such by *Newsweek,* was described as demanding and dirty but well paid. "The temperature on the plant floor is sweltering, the hissing and pounding never stop. But the money is good—a base wage of $6.88 an hour, up to $10 an hour with incentive and overtime pay—and for Butsey the pay makes the effort worthwhile" (70). Her success on the job was framed in the standard liberal discourse of "rags to riches"—one the press often uses for the working class. She was described as a high-school dropout, married at sixteen, and divorced by age twenty with a history of low-wage services jobs that paid $2.50 an hour or less.

Her experiences were not framed within the context of the political struggles or victories of the women's movement, the civil rights movement, or for that matter the labor movement, but instead relied on a narrative of rugged individualism, of making it against the odds.[3] It might be hard to work in a man's world, but it is well worth it if it allows an individual woman to pursue the American Dream. Butsey did not discuss racism or sexism directly, but there were clues in her own remarks that she understood the dynamics of discrimination and the significance of gender solidarity. For example, she reported that although her "acceptance" by the men was not easy—and in fact she did not socialize with co-workers—she was proud of her accomplishments as a woman paving the way for three women who were hired after her. She tells women "not to let the job get them down" (70). The article concludes on a characteristic note of optimism about how Marilyn is saving her hard-earned dollars ($400 a month) for a house and a car of her own. The fact that she is in no hurry to remarry and raise a family is not taken as a rethinking of heteronormativity but rather as a demonstration of her willingness to defer gratification—a sign that she is serious about bettering her life. Butsey's desire to trade in her blue collar for a white one was praised as a working-class version of upward class mobility. "Right now her ambition is to finish high school and perhaps move into an office job with Ford" (70).

The same woman of steel was featured six months later in the *Ebony* story quoted above. A photo of her, hard at work at the hot press, not only dominates the page but also is used to introduce the entire feature on black women in men's jobs. The photo, very similar to the one in *Newsweek,* shows Marilyn dressed in coveralls and wearing a hard hat and goggles, stacking hot steel rods. The reader is reassured that Marilyn and other women like her are taking nontraditional jobs for the money and not to make a point about sexual, racial, or class politics. In the text she compares the gendered reaction of friends when they hear about the work she does. She reassures women who might be afraid to tackle such masculine work that men will not be turned off. "My women friends don't understand how I can work here. They say they wouldn't want to get that dirty, and they're afraid they might get burned. But my men friends say they like a woman who's not afraid to go out and do hard work" (108). Both *Newsweek* and *Ebony* represented the female steelworker as something new—as though there were no historical precedent of black women doing the hard and dirty work of men—particularly that reserved for black men.

Throughout the seventies, traditional women's magazines (*Ladies Home Journal, Redbook, McCall's,* etc.) routinely featured stories about changing gender norms and roles, including ones written by feminists like Gloria Steinem and Betty Friedan. Readers were invited through polls, letters to the editor, and personal accounts to share their thoughts about the changes in women's lives. For example, *McCall's* initiated a regular column it entitled "Women on the Job: A Reader's Story" and published first-person accounts of women's experiences on the job. Readers were prompted to write about the special problems, conflicts, and opportunities they confronted while trying to balance work and family, but they were encouraged to be upbeat by focusing on the rewards of successfully resolving the pressures of such a balancing act. Readers were further prompted to think of the following as special problems: resistance from family, worry about childcare, strain on marriages, relationships with employers and co-workers, job discrimination, money, and education and training. A prize of $1,000 was offered for those stories chosen for publication. One of the winning essays I found particularly interesting was "Why I Decided to Go Underground," by West Virginia coal miner Barbara Burns (*McCall's,* September 1977, 69, 73, and 82).

Barbara described herself as white, twenty-six, married ten years, and the mother of sons, aged eight and six. Her motives for taking a nontraditional job underground were similar to steelworker Marilyn Butsey. She had held low-wage, female-dominated jobs as a waitress, a cashier, and a foundry worker in fabrication. The work underground was no harder, and the pay was considerably more. Self-described as "no stranger to hard work," the most she had ever made before becoming a miner—starting pay $6.14 an hour—was $2.10 an hour (69). In addition, she now had union protection and a substantial package of fringe benefits. "All things considered, I did not understand why women were not flocking in droves to file applications at the mines" (69). These benefits outweighed the costs of "the constant opposition I knew I would get from every corner of my private world" (69). In time she won over the skepticism and opposition of her mother, husband, and father (both men were miners) as well as the resistance of managers, foremen, and co-workers. She was constantly tested and had to earn the respect of the men. "They feared me at first, stared at me constantly and refused to talk to me. I had to work at earning their respect" (73). Like Marilyn, Barbara knew that her response to various forms of harassment would affect the chances of other women who wanted nontraditional jobs. Given an unusually demanding task for the first three months underground (an unusually long time on the same assignment) she persevered as a way to show the men she could hold her own and thus earn their respect. "I did not complain about this assignment. I knew that my actions would directly affect the employment of other women in the industry" (73). Both women took pride in being able to do physically demanding work and made it clear that they wanted no "special" treatment because they were women. Barbara wrote, "I am strong physically and have been able to perform every job assigned to me. I have asked no quarter because of my sex and have received none" (73).

Barbara made a point of dramatizing her femininity. She demurred, "I never thought of myself as pretty," when she let us know that the bosses thought her good looks were a liability. "You are too attractive. We expect trouble," they told her, not just from co-workers but from the wives of male miners. "The first night I worked the wives threatened to set up a picket line at the mine." The men tried to run interference by telling their wives she was unattractive. "My fellow workers had told their wives that I was ugly, but this did nothing to quell the women's anger or distrust of me" (73).

As with much of the press coverage of the time, Barbara's personal narrative and the two features about Marilyn fit within the confines of what Jones (1992) calls the field of allowable images. These are images that contain a core of traditional images and those newly incorporated or on their way to incorporation. Marilyn only delayed remarriage and motherhood until she could get back on her feet financially, while Barbara, who worried about her husband's safety more than her own ("women tend to be more careful"), contended that her relationship with her husband had improved. "My going to work in the mines has made my marriage much better. Before Sam took me for granted, but now we appreciate each other more" (73). Conveniently, they both worked the night shift and found a baby-sitter who would sleep over while the children were asleep. The kids barely knew she was gone. Barbara reassured readers that she was still a woman who valued her "femininity." She noted a shop in Charleston, West Virginia, that sold mining belts in "feminine" colors, that her hair was long enough to be pulled up in a bun under her hard hat, and that she was careful to apply cold cream to her face to protect her skin underground. She concluded her account with an anecdote about a compliment she received from her son. He exclaimed that she did not look like a tomboy. "In his eyes I could tell I looked feminine and pretty as a mother should, and I know he respects me and is proud of me" (73).

There were also contradictory and competing representations of feminism in the coverage of working women. The *Ebony* article pitted unions against feminism. In seeking to understand why women were making greater progress in male-dominated professional fields than in their blue-collar counterparts, a senior economist at the Women's Bureau of the U.S. Department of Labor told *Ebony*, "This could be because, in professional fields, there is less of a union barrier. Unions have been traditionally anti-feminist" (106). Women were breaking through employment barriers in nontraditional blue-collar occupations, *Ebony* concluded, because attitudes about women and work were changing, families were smaller, an increasing number of households were headed by women, and sex discrimination in employment was illegal. No mention was made about the role of the women's movement or feminism in effecting any of these legal or attitudinal changes.

Symbolically, the nontraditional, blue-collar female workers like Marilyn and Barbara came to represent all women in nontraditional jobs in the seventies. Their experiences took on the status of a trend story; told so often, they gained credibility through repetition. According to Faludi (1991), the trend story "professes to offer 'news' of changing mores, yet prescribes more than it observes" (79). Yet the reality of the seventies was very different. While the implementation of Title VII enabled some women to earn better wages in male-dominated occupations like steel, the reality was that most women workers were employed in standard, female-dominated fields. According to Reskin and Roos (1990), "Occupational sex-typing remained robust, even in a decade in which women reportedly posted revolutionary gains" (20). Their extensive analysis of the sex composition of all occupations revealed that the only occupations in which women made significant inroads were security guards, bakers, typesetters and compositors, and bus drivers. Very little headway was made in blue-collar, craft occupations such as mechanics, carpenters, and electricians. Though serving perhaps as an inspiration for some women to challenge sex discrimination, these accounts of the pioneers tended to exaggerate greatly the ease and speed of social change.

The Pioneers in Local 1190

Despite national media attention, it would take time for the local communities in the steel-producing regions of the country to adjust to the reality of women steelworkers. One plant foreman at Wheeling-Pittsburgh Steel told me informally that the company never dreamed women would actually apply for the new openings in the mill. "I was shocked that women would even want to work in the mill. I know this might sound like prejudice, but my idea of a woman is a step above a steelworker."

How did the women learn about the new affirmative-action policy creating job openings for women at Wheeling-Pittsburgh Steel, and what motivated them to apply? Many of the women first heard about the openings in the mill through word of mouth in the community. A friend or family member in management or in the union who was in a position to know about the consent decree told them about the new opportunities for women and encouraged them to apply. Or it was "common knowledge in the community," they heard "talk around my high school," and one "heard about it on my old job."

Sometimes information about openings for women was not communicated so benignly. In a climate of suspicion and hostility about affirmative action, it was not surprising that some women heard negative comments about the new hiring policies. Some of the pioneers filtered out the negative characterizations and applied for the jobs anyway. One woman learned about women working as telephone line repairers in a magazine article about affirmative action efforts at AT&T. Even though no jobs were being advertised at the time, she decided to put her application on file at the local phone company "just in case." The company representative who accepted her application told her, "You know, the mill is being forced to do this, too. Why not try there?" Another woman heard about the new hiring policy through a friend who was a secretary in the main office of Wheeling-Pittsburgh Steel. "When my friend told me about it, we laughed. We thought it was ridiculous. Later, I had second thoughts and put my application on file." A waitress at a coffee shop near the mill overheard foremen talking about the court order. "This one was saying, 'We are going to hire broads down there. The government is forcing us.'" The next day she went down to the mill's personnel office, applied, and eventually was hired.

Some women felt the company used the interview process to make them think twice about accepting the job if it were offered. Interviewers emphasized the negative aspects of the job, including the potential hostility of the men with whom they would work and the physically demanding aspect of the work. One woman was told she would have to lift 100-pound bags. Another was asked, "Do you think can handle a job like this? You are going to be working around some very vicious people." Another woman said, "They kept saying how it was going to be hard work. 'You are going to have to put up with a lot, especially working with men.'... They kept emphasizing the harassment from men." A fourth woman reported, "They kept stressing that the men didn't want the women in there, and they would be rough on me. One man went into all the details. When I left, I was a little scared about beginning a job in the mill."

The majority of women hired were assigned to standard, entry-level positions in the general labor pool. These jobs, done by a crew known as the "labor gang," involved mostly maintenance work—sweeping, shoveling, painting, washing walls, cleaning track—as well as semi-skilled work—breaking up cement and laying concrete. Women in these jobs were frequently transferred to other departments to fill in for absent workers. This made it difficult for them to become integrated into the work culture, but it allowed them the opportunity to experience a variety of jobs and departments before bidding on a more permanent assignment. Some women did not bid on jobs because they wanted more predictable and stable work relations, and they talked about how difficult it was to constantly switch work crews. One woman said, "They put me in so many different departments and that makes it hard. It gets a little hairy. The first couple of days you spend feeling out new people and learning the job. Just when you get used to the set up, you get transferred." On the other hand, some women deliberately requested jobs that isolated them from or minimized their contact with men who might be hostile. "I like it best when I work by myself or just one other person. It cuts down on all the hassles."

Job History

Jobs in the mill, even the more physically demanding ones, were preferable to the jobs many of the women held before landing the mill job. In terms of salary, the mill jobs were elite, blue-collar jobs. Women who had been employed in sales and retail preferred the autonomy, union protection, and the pay and benefits of the steel job. They rarely missed the patronizing treatment and status inequities typical of service-sector jobs. One retail worker reported, "The money was a lot less and basically what... you had to put up with... from the public and from the people over you... was a lot harder than the mill. In the mill you have your job and you do it. The supervision can be rough, but they are not always looking down your neck. Then, too, in the mill you have the union behind you, so you do have job protection." Another woman told me, "It was tougher being a sales girl.... There is all this pressure to get a quota of sales. The customers don't understand this. Some would boss you around.... 'Get me this, get me that.' They feel as if you are their servant. I am the same as the person that comes in, and I don't want to be treated like I am below them." Yet another reported, "It sounds funny, but sales was more difficult. I was hassled constantly, if not by my employer, then by the customers. We had to attack them when they came in, and this makes some people belligerent. They treated you like you weren't there. For a $1.80 or $2.00 an hour, I don't feel it was worth it."

The pay differential between old jobs and the new jobs in steel was substantial, and the women were quick to point that out. "In clothing I made $60 to $65 a week. Now I make $280 a week." Or, "In the hospital I never made more than $100 a week. One day last week I made $87—just one day in the mill." Some service-sector jobs involved high levels of stress at low levels of pay. A former practical nurse said, "There was more tension involved with nursing. You were always afraid, even when you got home. You wondered did you do all you were supposed to do or did you leave something undone? People's lives are at stake. Now I can go home at the end of the day without bringing my work home with me."

Assembly-line production workers who had previously worked in non-union shops were also aware of the differences in working conditions between their old jobs and their new jobs, particularly in the areas of health and safety. One woman who ran a drill press at a small factory commented, "On my old job, I had to stand on one foot all day. We worked a constant, eight-hour day.... In the mill you can work at your own speed. At the factory they pushed you and pushed you. They didn't care if you lost your fingers in the press; they just wanted their production." The women tended to compare their new jobs in the mill to their old jobs outside the mill, and even those assigned to the worst jobs in the mill compared them favorably. One woman who worked in the coke plant told me, "I have to work forty hours a week regardless, so I might as well go somewhere and put up with a little bit of dirt, a little bit of noise and make the money and be able to do what I want and have what I want, than go somewhere else outside the mill where it's nice and not make any money."

Women who take as their reference group other workers similarly discriminated against may not develop a sense of relative deprivation nor develop the political consciousness to challenge the status quo through union participation or activism. This holds true, as well, for women who compare their status to previous states of deprivation rather than to the current situation. The women at Wheeling-Pittsburgh Steel were grateful for the opportunity to earn considerably more money and to have union protection, and they were all too aware of the alternatives.

Shop-Floor Culture

How hostile was the work climate in the early years? Some women reported a no-win situation. "If the guys talk to me, I talk to them. But I never go out of my way to talk to the men. If you don't talk to the guys, they say you are stuck up, conceited, a bitch. If you do talk to them, they say you are a whore. So you can't win." Some women wanted to participate in routine conversations with the men but found the topics less than engaging. "The men talk a lot about sports, and I'm just not interested. They go into great detail about some hunting trip or fishing trip. They talk a lot about cars.... I don't even like to wash mine." For black women the ability to establish social relationships with other workers involved complicated negotiations across both racial and gender lines. One black woman talked about how hard it was to relate to whites—both men and women.

> I prefer to work with another black person, because it is hard to talk to a white person all day. You are afraid to say what you are doing...like fixing up your house or buying a new car. If it looks like you are getting on your feet, the white resents it. They think you are getting too far ahead of yourself. Black and white workers get along fine as long as a black person lets a white person feel as though they are still on top. There are times you would like to say something but you don't.

When a person is in a statistically rare group, it may take them more time to untangle mistaken identities and to establish competence-based working relationships, particularly with the numerically dominant category (Kanter 1977, 57). This may account for why some women did not bid out of lower paying, physically difficult jobs in the coke plant or blast furnace. Once they had built up a work relationship based on competence, they were reluctant to change jobs and have to reestablish new relationships. Others used isolation and invisibility as strategies to avoid conflict while some women sought to minimize gender-based assumptions in order to blend into the predominantly male culture. One woman who attended union meetings regularly became annoyed when the men went to exaggerated measures to avoid swearing in her presence. "This made me nervous. Finally, I stood up and shouted every cuss word I ever heard. I don't have to do this now. I only swear when the occasion calls for it."

Union Satisfaction

Few of the women had any previous experience with unions or with the type of protection a union could afford workers. Once hired in the mill it became even clearer what had been missing from prior, nonunion jobs. The women continued the pattern of comparing their new jobs in steel with past jobs in the pink-collar service ghetto or with the jobs of other women they left behind. One single mother of four children told me, "About three years ago, my son got real sick and needed a lot of hospital care. I was working as a sales clerk, and we didn't have a union. No benefits at all. I panicked. I had to quit my job and go on welfare to get the assistance to pay the hospital bills. I swore I would never let that happen to me again." A former hospital worker, who had been part of an unsuccessful organizing drive there, felt the criticism that a union would pit caregivers against patients was unfair. She said, "If you are tired from overwork, you will make mistakes and that hurts the patient. I felt if we had a union, we could get more help to take care of the patients." Other women compared their new opportunity to that of female friends and relatives. "I've seen too many instances where people work for virtually nothing, and they worked harder than I do in the mill. My mother worked as a waitress, making 70 cents an hour and took a lot of abuse. She didn't have a union."

In principle, the women valued the protection, support, and advocacy of the union: "If you are ever in trouble, the union is there." "You can go to the union if you feel you are being treated unfairly." "With a union you have someone to fight for your rights." "If you don't have a union, the company would walk all over you." For some the experience was more specific. Positive experiences resolving job-related grievances strengthened their commitment to the Steelworkers. One woman, in the early stages of a difficult pregnancy, was fired when she failed to follow the right procedures for calling in sick. The union was able to get her job back. Another woman, who refused to work before she received the proper safety equipment, was backed up by her steward and did not have to start the job until they brought it.

The most dramatic recollection of the difference the union made came from Theresa Ogresovich, the oldest woman in my study. She had worked in the mill in the 1930s as tin inspector—an all-female occupation—before the plant was unionized. During World War II she had worked as a crane operator, but after the war she lost her job. She and several other women were reassigned new jobs under the consent decree, and some were able to collect part of their previous service time as seniority. Now in their early sixties, they worked side by side with the younger women.[4]

> Before the union came they worked you harder, and they treated you like you weren't human. They never called you by name. They just hissed at you like you were a cat. When the union came in, I said, "I got it made." Before, if they didn't want you, they gave you the dirtiest jobs. I couldn't stand it. One day the boss told me, "You are going to find yourself outside the mill." ... I said, "When you are ready to throw me out of the mill, you are doing me a favor." After that they never bothered me again. If they could find someone to pick on, someone to buffalo, they would do it. I was scared. I cried. I had nightmares that you would make a mistake and lose my job. You don't know how happy I was when the union came. They couldn't push you around like they did. I'd say that was one of the best things, having a union.

Some of the rank-and-file women made judgments about the responsiveness of the union based on its performance in resolving grievances. Here their support for the union was more ambivalent. One woman, who felt that not all of the union officials were doing everything they could, told me, "In the union there are a few that will go all the way, if you are right. And then there are a few that let it ride and won't back you up but to a certain extent. ... And then there are a few in there who will stick with you till you get what you want and make sure you got what you started out to get." Some women complained about the backlog of unresolved grievances (up to two years) and are turned off by the politics involved. "Some ... will tell a worker they have a good case when I know damn well they don't. ... The union official is only interested in getting reelected, not with the merits of the case." One woman who attended a few union meetings told me, "I went to a couple of meetings, but they all seemed the same. The same people said the same things over and over. It seemed too clique-ish. They fight too much." Another woman was upset by "squabbles." "There was so much fighting when [the new local president] took office. The old group wouldn't give him a chance. They kept heckling. They were poor losers. I stood up and told them my six-year-old knows how to behave better than that." What some of the women pioneers viewed as unhealthy some more seasoned men saw as the dynamics of a democracy in action. "Cliques" comprise a healthy, informal, two-party system. One male union leader told me, "There are two sides to every issue. Most workers who don't come around the union hall see our differences as infighting among cliques. I call it understanding the two sides. This makes the process more democratic."

Male Reaction

According to union officials with whom I talked in 1976 and 1977, the men in the plant had mixed feelings about the presence of women workers in the mill, and they told me that the men's behavior ran the gamut from overly solicitous to outright rejection. "Wow, at first there was a lot of resentment. 'Why don't they go home where they belong?' 'They can't do a man's work.' 'They are taking a man's job.' 'They can't lift.'...A long list of can't." Some union officials described the men as accommodating, even solicitous: "The men were glad to see it.... They break their necks to help" and "The men don't swear as much.... They treat the women as ladies, and I think they should." One official said there was a double standard based on physical appearance that determined the men's behavior. "If they were pretty nice-looking, I noticed she doesn't have to work. Four or five of the guys will be doing her work, which is not good. Some ladies that don't look so good are holding their own." Though one official agreed that the atmosphere had changed as the men and women actually experienced working together, he still felt there was a long way to go. "Regardless of what they say amongst themselves, when it comes down to working with a woman, it's a different story. There are still some that think it's a man's mill."

Conway Owens, who chaired the Civil Rights Committee in Local 1190, compared the women's experience with that of racial minority groups:[5]

> Some of those who are hollering the most about the women are the same ones who don't appreciate the blacks and other minorities achieving goals greater than theirs. This is not everybody. You see, almost everybody in here comes from one class, one working class. We are more or less on the same level.

The union officials expressed their own opinions in more guarded ways. One said, "I have mixed emotions about it. Given the employment picture in [the United States], I feel jobs should go first to heads of the family rather than to movements. The society is based on the family. Of course, the union doesn't have any say about who gets hired. This is just my personal feeling." Another said, "You hear, even among union officials in the mill, that women are taking jobs that should possibly go to one of the younger men getting out of school who need to raise a family. They miss completely the fact that many women have to take care of families too... that some men have walked away and left. I believe the women should have the right to make that buck, too." One official who upheld the rights of women in the plant privately believed the mill was not the place for women. He told me:

> The mill really isn't a place for women. It really isn't. She is exposed to slang, and then there are some jobs women can't perform. Instead of placing women in all the plush jobs and causing the men to come up in arms about it, they should put the women in the coke plant... up on the battery. If they were put in the hard work areas, the men would see it and say that's not fair, and men themselves would bring her down.

Women from the coke plants never reported to me that they were brought down from the coke battery lids by chivalrous men.

I asked the union officials to gauge the interest of the women in union activities. According to one union official, women's interests were no greater than that of men. "Women don't participate any more than the men do. People are lazy, complacent. When they come to a meeting, instead of trying to understand the procedure that has to be followed... if they can't get their point across the minute the gavel hits they get resentful, mad, and walk out. Nobody wants to take the time. They let others do it for them. Everywhere you go, it's the same." Another said, "Not that many women seem interested in union activities. The few that are interested are very interested. Of course not that many men are. Out of 5,000 men, about 80 come to meetings. Sometimes we have half a dozen of women who come. Proportionately women do participate." I asked union local officials whether they thought a special women's committee or caucus was needed in order to encourage more women to participate in the local and to address the specific concerns women might have as women in a male-dominated occupation. Most did not see a need for a women's committee and thought the issues should be addressed through the union's standing civil-rights committee. Historically, there has been tension in the trade-union movement between balancing the need for worker unity and class solidarity with the need to respond sufficiently to the specific concerns and unique needs of different groups of workers. Fear that the acknowledgment of difference will jeopardize solidarity makes it difficult for unions to respond to charges of discrimination by their members either against the union itself or against the industry with which they bargain. The Steelworkers were no exception. Union officials tended to mute the concerns and interests of those workers who had been marginalized within the steel industry in favor of "greater good." While there was little effort to deny that minority men and women were treated unfairly within the industry, there was a greater degree of disagreement about what to do about it. As one union official said, "We don't need outsiders to tell us what to do. We can handle it. We don't need a women's lib group." Another union official said, "The company does its damnedest to keep us at each other's throats. They turn our racism against us."

Sex Discrimination

I wanted to better understand whether and how women's experiences of sex discrimination contributed to collective-identity formation as feminists or as gendered political subjects and how this identity is related to union participation. Respondents were able to identify unfair treatment on the job because they were women, but some were reluctant to label such treatment as discrimination. Ambivalence about the word "discrimination" reflected an unwillingness to recognize or believe the political legitimacy of such a claim in a liberal democracy. For some women it was as if discrimination were so un-American that if it happened it must be the fault of the individual. Several subjects pressed me to define discrimination almost as though I had brought up an unmentionable subject. One woman who viewed claims of discrimination as illegitimate complaints by some workers to get out of doing work said, "Discrimination, discrimination, but they are leaving out qualifications. Some people say, 'I am black. I am woman. I am foreign born. Give me a job.' They get in and ride this wave instead of knuckling down." Just as some white women identified their situation as being similar to that of black men, other white women were quick to distance themselves from black workers. One white woman told me, "Discrimination. That's what all the blacks around here say. If they are asked to do one thing, they cry discrimination." Some women thought discrimination was a thing of the past, eliminated by the consent decree. One woman thought that women had already achieved parity with men despite the fact that there were only 60 women out of about 5,000 workers. The term "discrimination" proved to be politically loaded.

When I rephrased the question, eliminating the word "discrimination" and asking instead whether they had ever been treated unfairly because they were women or whether women were treated differently from the men, the responses were strikingly different. Job training, job assignments, and job advancements were often cited as examples of unfair treatment. One woman was denied entry into an apprenticeship program because she failed the mechanical portion of the aptitude test—a prerequisite for the program. She successfully argued that the test itself was gender biased and convinced the company that her failure on the aptitude test did not mean she was not qualified for the program. "I explained that women are not given the opportunity to become familiar with mechanical principles. I threatened that I felt I was being discriminated against. They let me into the program. My work on the job was termed 'above average', and my average in my schoolwork was 89 (a passing grade was 70 percent)." Other women in the local reported that the foremen were not telling them when jobs came open on which they were eligible to bid. Two women said they had to "bump" or challenge men with less seniority for jobs they were entitled to have. Other women thought they had been deliberately assigned to work with men who were openly hostile about women working in the plant.

The women in the local also identified pregnancy as an example of the unfair treatment of women. These pioneers in steel were charting new territory in the policy arena before the Pregnancy Discrimination Act was passed in 1978. Two women who became pregnant during one particularly long layoff period were discouraged from returning to their jobs. The company told one woman—four months pregnant when she was called back—that she could not come back because of the pregnancy. Management called her doctor and told him she would be lifting big cans and pushing wheelbarrows, tasks she had not done before she was pregnant. Her supervisor told her that his boss called him personally and said to make it hard on her. She was also discouraged from collecting insurance benefits, though she eventually received them. "They didn't know I knew my rights. A lot of girls don't know their rights.... Then you take a lot of things you don't have to take."

The absence of adequate childcare options, particularly those that accommodated shift work, also constrained women's opportunities for advancement in the mill. Single mothers deliberately stayed in lower paying, entry-level jobs to ensure a steady shift with weekends off. A sick child could also create difficulties for the women workers. One mother reported off work for three consecutive days because her young child was hospitalized. She was given a discipline notice for calling off though it was her first and only time to do so. She thought men often reported off for weekend fishing trips and football games without facing disciplinary action.

The emotional strain and psychological tension of being the first women to integrate an all-male occupation was apparent in the way the women talked about day-to-day life on the shop floor. They had to prove over and over again that they belonged there. Most men could afford to take this for granted. I heard over and over again from the women. "I have to work double." "I put in two parts to their one." "You are always being watched." The challenges and petty hassles took their toll but also forced the women to think on their feet. Women often heard, "The mill is no place for a woman." "You are taking a job away from a man who needs the money to raise a family." "Women don't do their share of the work." Some women responded to the remarks and others did not. One woman who was told she and another women were taking jobs away from men responded to the charge, "I said, 'No we aren't. The mill has to hire women. It's the law. If they didn't hire us, they would have to hire some other women, so we aren't taking jobs away from a man. We are taking the jobs that would go to some other woman.'" Two other responded with, "You had the opportunities long before we did" and "You have my job.... You got in when we couldn't." One woman who never responded to comments about her right to be there told me, "There are people in the mill who think the mill is no place for women. That's fine, they are entitled to their opinion, but it doesn't stop me from working."

In addition to the daily pressures of sexist attitudes and practices, the women also faced the problem of sexual harassment. Sexual-harassment litigation and advocacy was in its infancy, and the popular press was just beginning to pick up on the issue. A *Ms. Magazine* cover story and a *Redbook* reader survey both appeared in 1977. The experience had barely been named as a workplace issue, and serious research was nonexistent when the first group of women went into the mill.

Frequent cases of sexual harassment involved harassment by a foreman. The forms of sexual harassment ranged from frequent requests for sex or dates, innuendo, gossip, verbal remarks, unwanted touching, leering, and graffiti. Once on the job, one woman's foreman told her that the men were following her around "like dogs in heat." She told me, "That made me sick. It's not a crime for workers to talk to each other. He made me feel it was my fault. I told him, 'Don't blame me, because I am a woman in the mill, dirty and greasy, doing a job.... You want me to quit.'" Another woman who had refused her boss's repeated requests for dates felt that he was retaliating by giving her some of the dirtiest jobs available. "He put me in the oil pits. They had to lower me in this narrow hole.... I was new to the mill, and I was petrified. I had to remove the oil with buckets. It must have been 110 degrees down there. I came up crying." She was scheduled off the next two days, and when she returned he assigned her the same task. Normally the job would have been competed by the crew on the next shift. "You see? He saved it for me to finish after my days off." Some women were totally caught off guard. "Once a foreman grabbed my boob, under eight layers of thermal underwear. It scared the shit out of me.... What do you do?... When it happens, it's a strange thing. At first you think, 'He doesn't know he is doing it' or 'He didn't mean it.'...But he knew." For another woman it was tone of voice and innuendo. "One foreman used to say, 'Come work for my crew. You can sit in the office all day.' Sure, I thought, but what would I have to give in return?"

Sexual harassment was not limited solely to supervisory personnel, though at the time less attention was given to peer harassment. Some women cited married men who asked them out. "If they say something really smart, I say, 'Would you say that in front of your wife?' And they say, 'No, I would-n't let my wife work here.'" Another woman reported, "I get a little disgusted. I am called 'Hey' or 'Hey you', or they whistle or they make weird noises." Other women chose to ignore the comments altogether. "Usually I ignore them. I've been tempted to [speak] quite a few times or to say something but if I do, I am just adding to it. I just ignore them. I feel much better that way."

Feminism and Gender Solidarity

A number of factors inhibited solidarity among the women, including physical isolation from each other, competition over seniority, racism, and age differences. Networks to bring women together at Wheeling-Pittsburgh Steel were rudimentary and not particularly open to the ideas of feminism. It was nearly impossible to form a separate space for women's feminist consciousness building.

Divisions along age lines were common. The older women I interviewed preferred to work with men their own age rather than younger women. They felt younger women did not work as hard as they had in the "old days." One woman, who worked in the plant during World War II, told me, "Some of the spoiled pampered girls today who go in the mill will say, 'I can't do this.' We were never allowed to say I can't do a job. We had to say I'll try." Generational divisions were also apparent around lifestyle issues. One older woman reported, "Back then a decent women didn't go into the factory unless she had to. But the bad woman in the factory then was an angel compared to the ordinary factory girl today."

Seniority generated some of the conflicts between women. Older women had been transferred from plant to plant after World War II. While they had worked for a much longer period of time for the company, they now had less seniority than some of the more recent women hires because the only possible start date the company recognized was 1974, the date of the consent decree. The lost seniority put them at a disadvantage in job assignments, and, despite their longer years of service, they still had some of the worst jobs in the mill. They focused, however, more on the few younger women with better jobs than on the much larger number of men with better jobs and less seniority than themselves.

That most of the new women were hired at the same time created competition between them for openings within the plant. One woman told me that the company wants you to "fight with a woman. They want the women to argue. They want them to bump another woman. . . . You go to a new department, and they'll say, 'She's got this job, and you don't have it.' The first thing off the bat they cause a big jealousy thing because you go home and you say, 'That's right she does have that job and I don't.'" Some women did not like to work with other women for pragmatic reasons, for example, they were more closely supervised with two or more women on a crew.

Identification with the goals and objectives of the women's movement was higher than identification with women as an aggrieved group or with feminism. I asked the women whether they supported the general goals of the women's movement: passage of the Equal Rights Amendment (ERA), greater political representation for women, equal pay and equal job opportunities, daycare, maternity leave and benefits, and shared parenting. A woman might strongly support a feminist goal such as equal political representation but reject feminism and even the women's movement itself. One woman was quick to add the disclaimer that she was not a women libber to a rather radical assertion. "If half the population is women, then we should get half of what there is to get." While there was majority support for the ERA, some women were weary of theoretical equality that left them without any meaningful rights. Angry when the Supreme Court ruled that women did not have the right to maternity benefits because men could not take advantage of such benefits, one activist told me, "We need laws that guarantee equality, but we also need laws that make it possible to exercise that equality. What good is it if I can't be denied a job because of my sex, if I have to quit that same job if I become pregnant?"

Support for daycare and maternity benefits was high. The few daycare centers available did not accommodate shift work, and many women felt forced to remain in lower paying job classifications to ensure their working hours matched their childcare arrangements. Women were coordinating their work schedules with husbands, mothers, and other family members. Most female kin of the working mothers in my sample were in the paid workforce and were not available for baby-sitting. One woman I interviewed had to alternate among her mother, a baby-sitter, and a half-day childcare center. After-school care also posed a problem. The day shift did not coincide with school hours. That left a gap in childcare that created anxiety for many women. Transportation to and from daycare for children of different ages added stress and time to the workday—for one woman, up to two hours.

This was not a new situation, however. Peggy, a mother of six who had worked in the mill on and off since World War II, provided one of the more telling stories of the difficulties of balancing work and family.

> I worked a lot of night shifts. When I had my son, you were given a half-hour lunch break, and you were allowed to go home. My husband would drive to the mill parking lot with the baby. I would nurse my baby and eat my lunch in the mill parking lot. Then he would take the baby home, and I would go back to work. He would bring the car at the end of the shift and go in to work, and I'd drive home. I worked nights, and he worked days and, believe me, it was rough. I was up all day and, with three and four babies in a house, you don't dare take a nap. I'd get the wash done, take care of the children and have supper on the table when he came home. Then I could lay down.[6]

I asked her whether she thought daycare centers were a good idea. "With the last three, I came to see it as important. They would have to be good, and I'd check it out thoroughly. I knew lots of women who had to quit because they couldn't find baby-sitters. There are lots of women in the mill who need them now." Most of the women reported that the men they were married to were doing a lot more childcare than their fathers had done.

Some women were wary of equality if it meant women had to act like men. One woman held the women's movement responsible. She equated her desire to be treated with dignity and respect with the desire to be treated like a lady. "I am not for women's lib at all. A woman's right to vote, yes. To work, yes. I can work better than some men, but I am not a man. I am a lady, and I like that feeling of being treated like a lady even though I am a factory worker, strong as an ox." Another woman told me, "I want to be equal but I still want to be treated as a woman. When I travel...I expect that man to help me with my bags. He better pay for the meal if we go out to dinner. I am still a woman and expect to be treated as one." This response may have been a reaction to working in an environment where many of the conventional reinforcements of gender differences were absent. Sexist attitudes about women in nontraditional occupations often manifest themselves as attacks on femininity and sexuality. Women were entering occupations that had been formally and informally constructed to conform to the model of the male worker. If women wanted in they had to conform to the terms already set up by those in power. Some women responded to assimilation pressures by reasserting difference. Not surprisingly, no one identified as lesbian.

Finally, men who did not like the idea of women working in the plant tended to hold the women's movement responsible. Peggy told me:

> The men are always throwing up women's lib in my face. I say, "Did I tell you I am for women's lib? Did that woman over there tell you, she's for women's lib? How do you know? She might be a victim of circumstances. So am I. When I came in there was no women's lib, so I couldn't have come in for that. But, a lot of you guys are hiding behind the skirts of women's lib. Because you aren't gentleman, you are using it as a crutch." He feels shoddy about pushing the women onto the dirtiest jobs while he is doing easy work so he blames women's lib. Be honest, if you want the job, take it because of seniority. You want the job because it's easy. Don't bring up women's lib, be a man about it.

Whether it was true or not, women were construed as "women libbers" simply because they accepted the jobs.

Conclusion

Affirmative action created new economic opportunities for young women in the 1970s and helped to save the jobs of older women whose employment in the mill dated back to World War II. Few of the women in Local 1190, however, saw themselves as part of the larger women's movement or thought of themselves as feminists. Nevertheless, these women took advantage of the new opportunities for better paying jobs opened to them by civil rights legislation despite little social or political support for doing so.

The consent decree guaranteed women legal access to the jobs on the same basis as men, but there was little in the decree that could be used to challenge sexist practices on the shop floor. Also, there were no laws or policies against pregnancy discrimination or sexual harassment to protect them while they took up the challenge of integrating an occupation long the preserve of men. For women to be successful as steelworkers, they had to leave their gender at the mill gate, which placed many in a double bind.

Wheeling-Pittsburgh Steel (along with many of the major steel companies) did not really want to hire women and did not actually believe women would apply for the jobs. Many women felt that the company not only actively discouraged them from accepting job offers during the interview process but continued that effort throughout the probationary period. Government support for affirmative action—never that popular with the public—had already been eroded by the Nixon administration. According to Mary Kearney, the EEOC representative to the implementation committee of the decree, Watergate made it easier for the opponents of the consent decree to point the finger at big government. She was fond of reminding the parties involved that, while it was technically true that the government had played an important role in fashioning the decree, it did so only after decades of litigation had proved that there was a pervasive pattern of race discrimination in the industry.

Local networks cooptable to the ideas of feminism were very rudimentary and just beginning to emerge at the time of my interviews. These networks began to develop, not on the job, but rather in the union hall, particularly in the civil rights committee. In the sex-skewed work environment of the mill, the women rarely worked in the same department or on the same shift. They did not have enough sustained contact with each other on the job to develop a communications network that could address gender-specific issues. The only opportunities for interaction were in the locker room during shift changes and in the union hall.

Nearly all of the women saw the value of the union and reported that they could get the union to respond to their concerns. A few women began to see the usefulness of the union as a vehicle for organizing around their interests as women. Sissy Humienny ran for and was elected to a minor union office. She then served as a leader and a bridge to the outside and helped to mobilize women within the local to participate in union affairs. Though more women began to come around the union hall, Sissy's efforts to establish a woman's committee in Local 1190 were unsuccessful. Participation in the union was not high for either men or women. The older women, less receptive to feminism, were more likely to go to union meetings than the younger women. This was also true for several middle-aged black women who became active in the local through the civil rights committee.

Neither similar structural location as women pioneers in a male-dominated field nor their experiences of discrimination were enough to create a collective identity as union feminists. The women liked their new jobs in the mills. By comparison to their old, low-paying, nonunion, often-demeaning service-sector jobs, there was little to complain about. At the time of my interviews, the standard female jobs were still fresh in their minds. As one woman told me, the worst job in the mill was better than any job she ever held before. The women were grateful for the new opportunity and felt that they were luckier than their female friends and family members. Under these circumstances it proved difficult to transform their grievances as women workers into collective action.

5

Mobilizing Women Steelworkers for Their Rights

Our caucus brings new strength to the entire union by imbuing the time-honored steelworker tradition of rank-and-file militancy and the legacy of the Civil Rights movement with the fresh enthusiasm of the women's movement.

—Roberta Wood, *Gary Post-Tribune*

The most successful effort to mobilize women on behalf of their collective interests as women occurred in District 31, located in the Calumet region stretching along Lake Michigan from South Chicago to the northwest corner of Indiana.[1] Unlike anywhere else in the United States (including the women in Local 1190 discussed in chapter 4), women Steelworkers in this region were able to create and maintain a visible level of feminist activism. They created a district-wide Women's Caucus in 1977, published a newsletter from 1977 to 1982, and participated in the major women's rights campaigns of the day, including reproductive rights, affirmative action, and passage of the Equal Rights Amendment (ERA). While a few activists were already self-styled feminists when they went into the steel industry, most were not. It was in the process of struggling for their basic rights on the job and for greater representation within the union that many of the women came to identify with the goals and objectives of the women's movement and to develop a collective identity as feminists.

Unlike the rest of the country, the political opportunity structures in District 31 were particularly favorable to the emergence and growth of union feminism in the Steelworkers in the seventies. This region was the center of organizational strength for the Steelworkers and a magnet for social movements and progressive causes. It had the highest concentration of women and minority male Steelworkers in the country, and the political culture and institutions of the region made it possible to mobilize women Steelworkers around a class-specific feminist agenda.[2]

The rich social movement environment of the Chicago/Gary area was an important factor in mobilizing women. The rank-and-file insurgency movement, a vigorous and highly visible ERA campaign in Illinois, a highly mobilized civil rights infrastructure that had elected Richard Hatcher as the first black mayor of Gary in 1968, and the presence of both the old and new Left produced a robust climate for political action. This climate of activism provided women activists in the Steelworkers with mobilizing networks, resources, and collective action frameworks for generating political action. The strength and success of these various movements and the configuration of relationships and alliances between them helped to create and sustain a political environment open to the growth and development of union feminism in this region of the country.

Rank-and-File Insurgency and the Left

By the seventies, the Calumet region had become the center of the grassroots rank-and-file insurgency within the Steelworkers. The construction of a new mill in Burns Harbor, Indiana, by Bethlehem Steel brought a younger cohort of workers, influenced by the antiwar and civil rights movements, into the district and into the Steelworkers. They were exposed to older, more seasoned union members who had a history of rank-and-file activism—particularly in Local 1010 at Inland Steel, the largest steel mill in the country. District 31 was the home of Ed Sadlowski and Jim Balanoff, prominent leaders in the rank-and-file reform movement who supported the Women's Caucus. Both served terms as district director, and Sadlowski made a credible run for International president in 1977. Many of the women activists in District 31 met one another while working within the rank-and-file movement and in the election campaigns of Sadlowski and Balanoff.

These preexisting networks were important for mobilizing women within the district and for building alliances across the lines of race and gender. Many of the key activists in the Women's Caucus were active in the rank-and-file movement, and some were elected to (mostly minor) local union offices on the rank-and-file slates. The caucus was perceived by the International—and accurately so—to be closely aligned with the rank-and-file insurgency in District 31. Once the insurgency movement lost momentum and new leadership took over the district, the Women's Caucus was handed a new set of political realities. Mobilizing women became more of a challenge, particularly when the mill began to drastically reduce its workforce and, in some cases, to shut down production.

There was a strong Left presence in the region that helped fuel the rank-and-file insurgency movement and the activism of the Women's Caucus and the black caucus. The old Left had played an important historical role in organizing the Steelworkers in the 1930s, and many had remained in the region, providing leadership for the emerging rank-and-file movement. Various new-Left groups moved to the region specifically "to move" the working class and their unions to the left—a practice known in some circles as "colonizing." Women from the Left were active participants in the upsurge of new social movement activity in the late sixties and early seventies. Activists from the old Left provided the Women's Caucus with historical links to earlier struggles in the steel industry, some continuity of leadership, and a good deal of practical knowledge about united-front political work.[3] Young radical women, mostly white and college educated, who found it relatively easy to secure jobs in steel under the consent decree, moved to the region with their brothers on the Left to participate in the colonizing efforts in the region (Lane 1996).[4]

Women's Movement

The women's movement was also a part of the rich social-movement environment of the region. The unique character of the Chicago women's liberation movement provided union activists with opportunities to become involved in the women's movement. Both the radical and liberal wings of the women's movement had roots in the region, and both converged on the issue of making the women's movement relevant and accessible to working-class women. The Coalition of Labor Union Women (CLUW), the women's movement of organized labor, was founded in Chicago, and the National Organization for Women (NOW) was particularly visible in Chicago. According to Rosen (2000) over one-third of the charter members of NOW were Midwesterners, which she believes reflected the indigenous character of female activism in the region.

At its founding, NOW placed a strong emphasis on economic issues, and its first president, Betty Friedan, had an impressive history of labor activism.[5] She was uniquely positioned to activate a network of union feminists and women's rights activists within the progressive wing of the labor movement. Union women played an important role in the early days of NOW, and, in the critical first year of the organization, they were able to leverage material resources from organized labor—particularly from the United Automobile Workers. With their years of experience in fighting for workers' rights, union women helped to make class issues a more salient feature of the NOW agenda. It was the activism of union feminists that persuaded the AFL-CIO to change its position on the ERA and to vote to endorse it in 1973. The Chicago chapter of NOW created a task force on labor, and there was even a short-lived NOW chapter of women Steelworkers in Gary, Indiana.[6] Because Illinois was the only industrialized state that had not ratified the ERA, NOW put much of its organizational savvy and financial resources into the state. The women's movement was highly mobilized and very visible in the region at the founding of the District 31 Women's Caucus.[7]

Women from organized labor helped to mobilize thousands of working-class women, including women Steelworkers, to rally on behalf of the ratification of the ERA and mobilized their unions to contribute money and personnel to the ratification efforts in Illinois. The Steelworkers assigned Sharon Stiller, a staff representative at the time, to help organize one of the largest regional ERA rallies in the country. More than 50,000 supporters marched to Grant Park in Chicago on 10 May 1980 (Figure 7). Some of the Steelworkers also participated later that month in a day of lobbying the Illinois State Legislature, and the presence of the men in their ranks brought media attention. *Time* magazine reported, "The feminists and their supporters, including six busloads of burly male Steelworkers, roamed the halls of the statehouse in Springfield" (26 May 1980, 23). The emphasis on the "novelty" of macho Steelworkers supporting women's rights was supposed to make the reader laugh. Lost was the fact that some of the steelworkers were women and that some men were taking women's rights seriously.

AFL-CIO President Lane Kirkland appeared with Ellie Smeal, then the president of NOW, at a pre-rally conference. He told the audience that labor's opposition in the past to the ERA was wrong. "We were wrong. The fact that the labor movement was able to correct its mistake, and now wholeheartedly supports ERA, should be helpful in convincing legislators and others here in Illinois who have opposed ERA in the past to now support ratification" (*Chicago Tribune*, 8 May 1980, 1). Turning its previous position on its head, the AFL-CIO framed its support for the ERA in a way that resonated with the membership's concerns about the effect of the ERA on protective-labor law. "The anti-ERA forces pretend to be the protector of women workers while they are obviously the protective front for corporate abuses and discrimination"(1). The alliance between organized labor

Figure 7. District 31 Women's Caucus at ERA rally, Grant Park, Chicago, 10 May 1980. Photograph by Bill Carey. Reprinted courtesy of Bill Carey and Dorreen Carey.

and the women's movement could not carry the day, however, and the ERA went down to defeat in Illinois.

The records of the District 31 Women's Caucus indicate that the caucus was connected to various women's movement organizations and coalitions. It joined the Coalition on Job Discrimination, which included, among others, Church Women United, CLUW, Mujeres Latinas en Acción, the National Alliance of Black Feminists, the National Council of Negro Women, and Women for Racial and Economic Equality. On 13 May 1978, the coalition held a Mother's Day hearing on motherhood and work at the Chicago Public Library (press release, 12 April 1978). Working mothers were invited to speak out about discrimination in the workplace; sexual harassment, maternity and childcare issues, and job training. Government officials and the media were invited to listen and to observe the women's "testimony."

The caucus newsletter urged its readers to participate in Take Back the Night marches, abortion rights rallies, and walkathons for the ERA and urged them to do so as Steelworkers. They wore T-shirts, hard hats, and work boots, and they carried banners that proclaimed them proud members of their union. They attended NOW conventions and pushed the organization to pass resolutions in opposition to right-to-work laws and section 14-B of the Taft-Hartley Act and in support of unionization drives, such as the drive at J. P. Stevens. Indiana NOW invited the District 31 Women's Caucus to present a workshop on their self-organizing efforts in the union at its 30 January 1979 conference.

The exodus of progressive women from the ranks of Students for a Democratic Society—and, to a lesser extent, from other New Left organizations—provided the Chicago women's-liberation movement with a radical edge and a socialist focus.[8] These women from the Left were deeply committed to creating a community-based women's movement that was relevant and open to working-class women and their organizations. Union feminists, who were taking the labor movement to task for its sexism, found ports of entry into and opportunities to build alliances—however tenuous—with the emerging organizations of the women's movement in Chicago. The Chicago Liberation Union, for example, created Direct Action for Rights of Employment (DARE) to address issues of women's workplace organizing. The members of DARE participated in strikes, union-organizing drives, and job actions and joined NOW to sue the city of Chicago for sex discrimination (Strobel 1995,148).

Civil Rights and the Black Caucus

Much of the success in organizing the Women's Caucus was due to the sustained emphasis placed on building interracial solidarity. This was challenging because the civil rights movement in the Chicago/Gary area had met with considerable white backlash. For example, according to a *Chicago Sun Times* poll in September 1968, 44 percent of Chicago's white steelworkers planned to vote for George Wallace for president (Carter 1995, 352). The election of Hatcher in Gary had to be secured with the intervention of the Justice Department to prevent a voter-fraud scheme. Even Sadlowski's election to be director of District 31 in 1974 required intervention by the U.S. Labor Department to prevent fraud.

Most of the rank-and-file women who joined the white radicals in organizing the Women's Caucus were African American women from the local communities. Dorreen Carey, one of the white radicals, told me the synergy between the two groups was an important factor. "There was just a good fit between [black and white] women who wanted the job, needed the job, and wanted to make every effort to be involved in whatever they needed to do to keep that." From the beginning, interracial solidarity was encouraged and valued by caucus organizers. Dorreen recalled that the primary social base of the caucus movement was located in the African American community. "They set the tone for what made us really successful because, as opposed to being dry politics, which might have been the way some of us would have approached it, we had parties, we met at clubs, went to dances. That's what gave us our base, and our ability to be real was that we were in the community."[9]

Ola Kennedy, one of the key organizers of the District 31 Women's Caucus, served with Roberta Wood as the first co-chairperson of the caucus. Their collaboration fit the model described by Dorreen. Roberta was a young, white radical whose activism was shaped by her commitment to socialism. Ola Kennedy was an African American woman from the community who became a Steelworker when she went to work at Hammond Valve in 1959. She was very active in the Ad Hoc Committee of Concerned Black Steelworkers, a Black Power caucus within the Steelworkers that served as an organizational model for the Women's Caucus. She thought the Ad Hoc was a model the women could emulate. Her resolve to work on the issue of women's rights was strengthened when her daughter, who went to work at Bethlehem Steel under the consent decree, was fired during the probationary period. She helped her daughter, who eventually became an electrician, to fight back and to regain her job.[10] With her ties to the Hammond community and her role in both the Ad Hoc and the Women's Caucus, Kennedy served as a bridge leader—someone who could articulate the interests of different constituency groups.[11]

With the passage of the 1964 Civil Rights Act, black workers who were active in and influenced by the civil rights movement became increasingly vocal within the Steelworkers and stepped up their demand for greater representation at all levels of union decision making. When the union's internal grievance procedures proved too cumbersome or inadequate to challenge racist practices in the industry, workers turned to the legal mechanisms of the government, such as the EEOC, or to the resources of civil rights organizations, such as the NAACP. Because of the external pressure of the civil rights movement in District 31, black workers became more effective in their efforts to secure an organized presence within the union (Nyden 1983; Stewart 2001). Civil rights legislation created the legal infrastructure that provided black workers and, eventually women, with an alternative to the union's grievance mechanism. And, it offered a tool with which to threaten recalcitrant employers.[12] By going outside the "house of labor," they expanded the repertoire of protest action beyond the traditional ones favored by organized labor to include those favored by the more militant Black Power movement.

The goal of the Ad Hoc was to increase the visibility and representation of black Steelworkers in the union as a way to make the union respond to

the racism workers faced on a day-to-day basis in the industry. Their demands included the appointment of a black representative on the International executive board, the racial integration of all International departments, and the reorganization of the Civil Rights Department to give black
members a stronger voice (Nyden 1984; Stewart 2001; Needleman 2003).
Once black votes came to be seen as important swing votes in contested
elections for the International offices, two of these demands were met. The
Ad Hoc endorsement of I. W. Abel in his successful bid for the union presidency in 1964 resulted in the appointment of the first black man, Alex
Fuller, to head the Steelworkers' Civil Rights Department. It was not until
1976, when there was another contested race for the International presidency, that the demand for a seat for an African American on the executive
board was met with the appointment of Leon Lynch as Vice President for
Human Affairs. The Ad Hoc Committee adopted the discourse of the more
militant Black Power movement, a discourse of affirmative action, autonomy, and empowerment, which began to usurp the traditional civil rights
discourse of equal opportunity and integration.

Women in the Steubenville area (Local 1190) were not able to match
the level of women's activism of women in the Calumet region. Greater geographic dispersion of the workforce and a much lower concentration of
black workers constrained the ability of local activists, like Sissy, to mobilize
women or to build the type of alliances between women and minority men
that occurred in the Calumet region. The high concentration of black and
Latino steelworkers in the Calumet region and the stronger civil rights infrastructure provided women there (half of whom were African American)
with greater political leverage, leadership, and mobilizing networks. While the
Civil Rights Committee in the Steubenville local was supportive of women's
activism it did not serve as a link to the broader civil rights movement.

Political Opportunities

There was little opportunity for women in District 23, which encompassed
Steubenville–Mingo Junction and other small towns along the Ohio River,
to participate in the social-movement organizations of the women's movement, such as NOW or CLUW. Lacking such opportunities, these women
Steelworkers relied primarily on unflattering media representations of the
women's movement and feminists. News accounts of the pioneers in nontraditional occupations generally did not credit social movements for expanding the occupational opportunities for women. While many of the
women Steelworkers in Steubenville supported the policy goals of the
women's movement, they did not see feminism as particularly relevant. Tak-

ing advantage of the nontraditional job opportunities was daring enough without taking on the additional burden of labeling themselves as "feminist." Women in small steel communities remained relatively isolated from the women's movement.

Pittsburgh, only thirty-five miles east of Steubenville, could not provide women Steelworkers in the region with the political opportunity structures or mobilizing networks necessary to build a feminist presence within the union. Steffi Domike, a Pittsburgh filmmaker and instructor at Chatham College, who worked for five years at the Clariton works of U.S. Steel, was active in regional efforts to organize a Women's Caucus in the Pittsburgh area. She believed there were a number of key differences between the Pittsburgh region and the Calumet region. First, the rank-and-file insurgents had not been as successful in electing candidates in the Pittsburgh area, so there was little support for women's committees or for the formation of district-wide women's caucuses. The districts located in and around Pittsburgh were under the watchful eye of the International located in downtown Pittsburgh, and their leadership was careful not to rock the boat. Second, within Pittsburgh's municipal government, there were fewer public resources available for civil rights or women's rights projects and for organized labor. Women Steelworkers and activists did forge some ties with the local organizations of the women's movement in Pittsburgh, but Pennsylvania had already ratified the ERA, so the women's movement was not as mobilized as it was in Illinois. White activists, calling themselves "industrialized" radicals, moved to the region to build a more progressive labor movement. However, they did not encounter the same conditions as their counterparts in the Calumet region where women activists were successful because of the strength, diversity, and configuration of alliances among social movements and the mobilization of several social-movement organizations.[13]

Mobilizing Networks

Another important factor that contributed to the success of feminist organizing in District 31 was the way in which activists were able to coopt existing and emerging networks to mobilize women Steelworkers in the campaign for women's rights. Conventions and conferences, often neglected in the literature on social movements,[14] were used by activists as sites for protest and for mobilization and collective identity formation. Two conventions in 1976—the CLUW Constitutional Convention and the Steelworkers Constitutional Convention—were particularly important in launching the District 31 Women's Caucus. Both became vehicles for bringing women together to meet each other, to share experiences, to talk about their issues, and to develop organizing and discursive strategies to effect change—an opportunity not often afforded working-class women. Women activists who were often overlooked for conferences and/or who did not meet the eligibility requirements often pooled resources and attended at their own expense.

Coalition of Labor Union Women

The District 31 Women's Caucus drew inspiration, resources, and legitimacy from the CLUW. Women Steelworkers, such as Ola Kennedy, and women civil rights activists from other unions, such as Addie Wyatt from the Meatcutters, were instrumental in the formation of CLUW in Chicago in 1974. More than 3,000 women representing fifty-eight unions came together to map out the contours of a women's rights organization that could serve as a bridge between labor and feminists. The impetus for establishing the organization came primarily from women who were already in leadership positions in their respective unions. However, the enthusiastic response of the rank and file to their call for action indicated that they had struck a responsive chord among working-class women. CLUW tapped a vein of working-class women's activism that helped to put a class face on the second wave of the women's movement.

The goals of CLUW included increasing the visibility and participation of women in unions, promoting affirmative action in the workplace, organizing the large number of unorganized women workers, and encouraging union women to play an active role in the political life of their unions and of the nation. To meet these goals, CLUW strongly endorsed the formation of women's committees and women's caucuses within labor unions and encouraged unions to develop educational and training schools to prepare women for leadership and policy-making roles within organized labor. It adopted a political agenda that combined the traditional concerns of organized labor with the newer concerns of the women's liberation movement. CLUW advocated for full employment, a shorter workweek, and improved health and safety standards, along with passage of the ERA, policies against sexual harassment in the workplace, and the adoption of childcare legislation. CLUW came to be seen by the women's movement as the voice of union feminists and, within the labor movement, as the voice of women's liberation. CLUW sent delegates to the First National Women's Conference held in Houston in 1977 and was influential in getting the National Plan of Action to include language in support of labor-law reform that would make it easier for unions to organize.

I attended the second CLUW convention in Detroit in 1976 where I observed convention proceedings, talked to delegates, and attended caucus meetings and social events. I met women activists from the Steelworkers District 31, including women who helped to organize the District 31 Women's Caucus. They came to the convention primarily to network and to gain ideas about organizing a caucus from women in other unions.

Delegates had the opportunity to meet in small groups or caucuses by union affiliation, and I joined the women Steelworkers in their breakout sessions. The women used this time to voice concerns about problems of sex-discrimination and sexual harassment on the shop floor and about the failure of the union to respond adequately. They decided to draw up a list of their demands to present to Alex Fuller, the national director of the union's civil rights department, who was scheduled to be at the closing event of the convention. These nine items were to become the staples of women's demands throughout the next twenty-five years and included (1) establishing a women's department at the International, (2) holding a regular International Conference on Women, (3) publishing a regular column on women's issues in the union newspaper, (4) appointing women to staff positions, (5) changing the eligibility rules to run for union office, (6) developing a maternity clause in the contract, (7) giving grievance powers to civil rights committees, (8) recognizing CLUW, and (9) promoting greater democracy in the union. The women Steelworkers agreed to stay in touch with each other and to build collective pressure around their list of demands.

The early success of CLUW depended on the ability of the organization to translate the heightened consciousness about women's changing roles into action. Like many new organizations, CLUW experienced its share of problems.[15] Wertheimer (1977), however, contends that the impact of CLUW in its early years was larger than its numbers would suggest. She cites their successes in gaining support for the ERA from many Internationals, winning the appointment of a woman as associate director of the Civil Rights Department of the AFL-CIO, helping to develop leadership skills among women, and sensitizing women to the organizational politics of their unions. CLUW also helped unions develop model contract clauses that incorporated affirmative action and increased the visibility of women's issues and activism in the union process. Many of the Steelworkers in the District 31 Women's Caucus were also active in creating CLUW chapters and were able to use the legitimacy of feminist issues in the broader labor movement to their advantage in District 31.

The 1976 Steelworkers Constitutional Convention

In August 1976 I rejoined some of the women Steelworkers I had met at the CLUW convention at the Steelworkers Constitutional Convention in

Las Vegas. In addition to the official business, there is a usually a good deal of internal political organizing that takes place at the convention. Constituency groups lobby, introduce resolutions, hold speak-outs and receptions, and caucus in an effort to get a hearing for their particular issues. Many of the women from basic steel, such as Sissy Humienny (District 23) and Roberta Wood (District 31), were there for the first time and learning the ropes, while a few, such as Alice Peurala (District 31), were veterans. Their efforts to organize a constituent group of women steelworkers were just beginning, and the payoff would be felt in District 31 long before it would be elsewhere.

The 1976 convention was no ordinary convention. Even before the gavel hit the podium, there were heated credential fights about who could be seated on the convention floor. The credentials of delegates who supported Sadlowski, the insurgent candidate for the presidency, were challenged, and some delegates were even harassed. Ironically, for the women who were staking their claim to be included for the first time, much of the first day of the convention was spent in conflict over who had the right to be there.

The number of women seated as delegates was exceedingly small at this convention of 5,000 delegates, and they tended to represent small locals from outside of basic steel. Some of the women who attended the convention came specifically to mobilize support for the women's rights resolutions and to organize women as a political constituency within the union and paid their own way. Women who came as delegates from District 31 came as part of the rank-and-file insurgency group and were among the Sadlowski supporters who were unseated in the credential battles. Forced from the convention floor, they sat in the observer section set aside for guests. This made it more difficult for them to mobilize support for the emerging Women's Caucus and to circulate the demands the women activists had constructed at the CLUW conference earlier in the year.

Discourse of Rights and Resolutions

The language of most convention resolutions reflects a strenuous process of negotiation that takes place weeks before the convention between the group offering the resolution and the International. The women's rights resolution submitted by Local 1010 in District 31 was no exception. The version read from the convention floor pledged union support for the ERA as one of a number of tools to fight sex discrimination, for collective bargaining to force employers to cease all practices of sex discrimination, and for lobbying Congress to pass comprehensive childcare legislation. The resolution also pledged union support for the newly formed Coalition for Labor Union Women. The rationale for the women's rights proposal was embedded in the body of the resolution. "Because women are over forty percent of the labor force yet earn forty percent less than males; and because women are systematically exploited as a group; and because women single heads of households are without affordable childcare there is a need for stronger anti-discrimination measures" (*Proceedings* 1976, 456). The resolution passed, but portions of the original proposal did not reach the convention floor. The International tabled a proposal that called for the appointment of a director of women's rights and for the International to hire more women and minorities.

Women's rights were also incorporated into a separate civil rights resolution that was endorsed by seventeen locals. This resolution was carefully couched in the discourse of "equal rights." It recognized that while "great strides have been made by the women's movement," sex-discrimination would remain a "blot" until the ERA had been passed. The consent decree, the International's only official plan for dealing with discrimination, was extolled as "historic" and was characterized as having "virtually wiped out the roadblocks to equal opportunity" while doing so in a way "which advanced the interests of all employees without regard to race and sex" (456). The resolution commended staff and local union representatives for their efforts in the ongoing, day-to-day implementation of the consent decree and promised to continue to "root out all forms of discriminatory practices in the workplace" (455).

However, the resolution also strongly favored collective bargaining and the union's grievance process over the courts and the government as the best tool for eliminating discrimination. "Collective bargaining has proved to be a surer, more effective and more equitable tool to end discrimination than the understaffed and under-funded government agencies, such as the Equal Employment Opportunity Commission, clogged with a backlog of 120,000 cases, or lawsuits which drag on for years, sap everyone's resources and profit no one but the lawyers" (455). The resolution expressed the Steelworkers' ambivalence about affirmative action by defending seniority and condemning "hare-brained" equity schemes that would undermine seniority while at the same time supporting the consent decree.

Politically, it was difficult for the union to acknowledge the costs associated with ending discrimination or to go on record recognizing that some white workers had benefited from past sex and race discrimination. "We have vigorously opposed hare-brained schemes which would discard seniority in layoff situations in favor of retaining junior minority employees on the job, even though they personally had never been discriminated against by the employer, and even though senior employees, innocent of wrongdoing, would, under these schemes, be cast into the streets"(455). In the end, both resolutions endorsed what the International supported, equal rights for individuals, but rejected group remedies such as affirmative action, which is based on one's membership in a social group that had historically suffered discrimination.

Rights Talk off the Convention Floor

Over the course of the convention I interviewed women delegates and observed their efforts to organize women delegates into a gender-conscious constituency. The women I talked to were employed in basic steel, in chemical and small fabrication plants, and in hospitals. Unlike the women at Wheeling-Pittsburgh cited in chapter 4, these women were willing to acknowledge the pervasive sexism and discrimination at work and in the union. One African American woman from a southern local summed this up when she told me that sex discrimination was a serious problem. Raising her eyebrows she said in a hushed tone, "Oh, boy, if you only knew." She also told me she had difficulty getting her local to do anything about it. "It's different in the South. We have to stick together because the anti-union feeling is so strong. Unity is more important than special interest. You don't want to be accused of castrating the men."[16]

A woman who worked in a factory that assembled venetian blinds responded, "God, yes. You better believe it," when I asked about sex discrimination. She said that when they were producing blinds, the majority of the workforce was female, but when the plant retooled to heavier equipment, more and more men where hired until they became the majority. Women with more seniority were denied access to some of the better paying jobs. The women in her plant were challenging the discrimination and were very aware that the law was on their side. She told me, "The Civil Rights Act changed things. They eventually had to open bids to women. Now it's the law."[17]

I also talked with a small group of women from basic steel[18] who met informally to discuss the best way to mobilize women within the union. Roberta Wood, whom I had met at the CLUW convention, organized the meeting in her hotel room. Most of their meeting was spent discussing problems they and other women experienced on the job and what to do about them. They were eager to talk about the subtle and not-so-subtle ways in which sex discrimination operated.

Diane Gumulauski reported that as soon as women were discovered or rumored to be pregnant, they were forced to take a pregnancy test, and, if it was positive, they were forced to take voluntary sick leave. Once a woman took leave, she was ineligible for unemployment benefits or medical insurance. She knew of two cases at Bethlehem Steel where women had abortions in order to keep their jobs. Sissy reported a different situation at her plant (Wheeling-Pittsburgh Steel). "We used a newspaper article about a legal case involving the stewardesses. We met with a company representative and showed him the ruling. Now you get six weeks."

There was not a uniform policy in the steel industry governing pregnancy leave, nor was there federal legislation to protect women from arbitrary firings because of pregnancy. The women in the room believed the companies were using pregnancy as an excuse to get rid of the women they had felt forced to hire in the first place. The women thought that pregnancy was the type of issue that could galvanize support for women's rights. Pregnancy discrimination was an issue on the boundary of the public and the private and was the type of issue that appealed to both feminists and labor.

The women also discussed the lack of promotional opportunities. Alice Peurala felt that her company deliberately picked certain women for difficult jobs, women who, they believed in advance, would fail. "Placement is not done according to ability or aptitude. In order to fill the quotas for apprenticeships, they pick women off the street rather than women already in the mill that [have] a little experience. They build in failure." Another tactic employed by the company involved "playing by the rules." After the women were hired, management often insisted on strict enforcement of work rules, some of which had become relaxed over the years. This caused some of the men to lose the little informal autonomy they had over how to do the job and produced resentment and hostility.[19] Roberta related the following:

> There was an informal agreement between the men working the blast furnace that they could exchange assignments if they didn't want to work a specific job on a particular day. They traded jobs and took turns on the worst assignments. In the rush to prove that women can't do the job, the company came down hard and stupid. They showed us the rules from the book. This caused a lot of resentment toward the women. I think the company knew it would.

The pressure the women felt to prove that all women could do the job sometimes resulted in physical injury. In the beginning, many thought they had to do whatever they were asked to do by the foreman. Diane told me:

While I was working on the lids [coke ovens], I was told to move these 100-pound lead boxes. I wanted to prove that I could do it. That all women could do it. After the third lift, I ripped open my intestines and had to be rushed to the hospital. It took surgery and a three-month recovery period. What I didn't know at the time was that no man would have lifted that much weight. They would have asked for a helper or simply refused.

This account led to an angry outburst by Alice who was appalled that the younger women thought that they had to prove themselves on the same terms as men. She was angry that the women would even attempt colossal feats to prove themselves and did not think it fair to measure women's rights in terms of male standards. "We can't allow men to decide what women's rights are. They aren't the ones who'll get hurt, we are. If those bastards try that trick again, tell them where to shove it. The men never put up with this shit."

Most of the women at the group meeting were from locals where the insurgent rank and file had already challenged the status quo—sometimes successfully and sometimes not. Even though these women reported that sexism was alive and well in the insurgency camp, the women felt they had more room to maneuver in a "maverick" local than in locals aligned with the International. Some were a little more convinced that they had seen improvement in the treatment of women by the insurgents, while others were more ambivalent. Sissy and Roberta, for example, felt they had gained only marginal acceptance in return for their support of rank-and-file issues. For routine tasks they were trusted, but for bigger tasks, such as being selected to run for office on the rank-and-file slate, they were ignored. Both had to run for convention delegate as independents unaligned with either side. Sissy lost the election but with a respectable showing for a first try and, though she was unseated, Roberta won with the "backhanded support" of Sadlowski. Diane admitted that in order to advance the interests of women in her local, she had to be very low key in her approach. "If there [are] more than one or two articles about 'minorities' in the rank-and-file newsletter, charges are raised that 'they' are getting all of the attention. White male workers feel left out."

The meeting concluded with a suggestion from Roberta that the group issue a call for the union to hold a national women's conference—something that would not happen until nearly twenty-five years later. There was agreement among those present, but they did not follow up on the idea. Time at the conference was running out, and the best the women could hope for was to submit a note to the podium the next day announcing that women who would like to meet other women should meet in the guest area. They would gather the names and addresses of the women who came to the guest area and mobilize later.

Conclusion

Women Steelworkers at both the CLUW and the Steelworkers conventions were convinced of the need to organize if their issues were to be heard. This would be a formidable task in a union that was, at best, ambivalent about the presence of women and, at worst, openly hostile to the equity legislation that opened its ranks more widely to women. Most of the women I talked to supported the surge of rank-and-file activism in their locals, but they felt that gender-specific issues took a back seat to other concerns. Women left these conventions with a rudimentary network—not quite a committee or a caucus. Their organizing efforts would pay off later when Roberta and Alice returned home to District 31 with a renewed commitment to the idea of creating a Women's Caucus, which is explored in chapter 6.

Sissy would not be as successful in organizing a Women's Caucus in District 23 or even a women's committee in her local because she did not encounter the same political opportunity structure as did her sisters in District 31. Sissy was elected to another office in her local, and the women in her local continued to participate in union meetings and programs. While they did not construct a collective identity as union feminists or pursue gender-based politics, they were active in various campaigns to save their jobs and communities when deindustrialization hit their region with a vengeance in the 1980s.

6

Making Waves: The Calumet District 31 Women's Caucus

We all know the story "The Emperor's New Clothes," where everyone was tricked into believing the Emperor was wearing a new suit of clothes when he was actually naked. We have the opposite problem with discrimination—everybody can see it as plain as day, but the company just keeps insisting that it isn't there. Moreover, they seem to be able to convince others—namely the government and some of our union officials—that they can't see it either.

—Dorreen Carey (*Bulletin* no. 6)

The Calumet District 31 Women's Caucus came into being in 1977, in part, because the political opportunity structures and mobilizing networks were in place and because the existing union structures were not adequate for solving immediate problems or for integrating women into a traditional male workplace. The union did not anticipate the degree of harassment or the harsh circumstances the new women would face in the mills. Women were concerned about the absence of committees or forums within the union to deal with their special concerns and problems, and activists were appalled at the almost total absence of female representation on the staff of the union and in its elected leadership at all levels. How, they had often wondered aloud to me, could the union know what to do without the input of women?

Women felt isolated in their locals and activists became convinced that they could accomplish more by pulling together their collective resources into a district-wide caucus. In principle, a caucus within an organization can serve as a mobilizing structure for action. It does not depend solely on the parent organization for resources, so it can carve out an autonomous sphere of influence. Participants are free to form alliances with other caucuses within the organization and with groups outside the organization who share their specific political interests. Because their members are also members of the organization they seek to reform, a caucus maintains legitimacy as the voice of protest within the organization. They cannot be labeled as "outside agitators" (Katzenstein 1998).

Goals and Objectives

The District 31 Women's Caucus wanted equality on the job and in the union, and they saw the two as linked. At first, the major concern of the caucus was simply to help women stay in the industry, and the caucus strategically selected issues that they thought had the most direct impact on job security and job advancement for women in the industry. These issues included affirmative action, pregnancy discrimination, harassment and firings of probationary employees, and job training. Strengthening women's participation in the union was important to eliminating discrimination and to achieving equity goals both on the job and in society. With sufficient representation, union feminists and activists believed they could help the union to reframe collective-bargaining issues and to refocus their legislative and political action agenda in ways that would benefit women.

Activists and feminists could not afford to, and in fact did not even try to, distance themselves from affirmative action. On the contrary, they advocated tougher standards and better enforcement of affirmative action and claimed the right to participate in the definition and implementation of affirmative action measures. They viewed affirmative action programs as ineffectual, especially when women were not involved in developing them. The caucus believed that employers were taking advantage of lengthy probationary periods to fire the female employees that they had been required to hire and promote by the Justice Department. They also believed that black women were bearing the brunt of an overt campaign of hostile resistance by the companies. They argued over and over again that by creating a "revolving door" for new affirmative action hires, the companies were undermining and subverting the intent of affirmative action as it was spelled out in the consent decree.

Pregnancy discrimination was another way the caucus member's thought the companies tried to rid themselves of women. Neither Title VII nor the consent decree covered the protection of pregnant women from discrimination as a civil rights entitlement. The caucus charged that pregnant workers were routinely fired, denied full disability and medical coverage while on leave, and forced to return too soon after giving birth. In addition, little or no forethought or planning had gone into assessing the potential reproductive health hazards that women might encounter. Sexual and racial harassment were often blatant and prevented women from taking advantage of training and promotional opportunities. Locker rooms and bathrooms were makeshift, inadequate, and, in some cases, nonexistent (Figure 8).

The caucus proposed to address these issues through a range of activities, structures, and programs. Key to solving the problems women faced in the industry was increasing their level of representation within the union. Toward this end, their original demands were geared toward securing a place for women in the decision-making apparatus of the union. Activists pursued a dual strategy of demanding the integration of women into the existing decision-making structures of the union and of demanding separate spaces within the union for women's self-empowerment. These women hoped that the creation of women's committees, conferences, and educational workshops would give women a niche where they could develop a sense of themselves as political actors. With this enhanced sense of political efficacy, rank-and-file women would then place greater pressure on the union to respond to feminist concerns. The caucus demanded the establishment of women's committees at the district and local levels, the convening of an International women's conference on a regular basis, and the development of a woman's leadership program. Their concerns about greater representation were also evident in the caucus's demands for an International women's department, for a seat reserved for a woman on the International executive board, and for more women appointed to staff positions. For the activists, the success of affirmative action in the workplace was linked to affirmative action in the union.

The officers' report issued at the end of the first year spelled out, with a sense of urgency, the rationale for the formation of the caucus.[1] "Such an organization is of vital concern to the whole union but especially to us [women] not for silly or minor issues but life and death such as; will we have our jobs or will we be pushed out like WWII through harassment and firings? Will we get into skilled trades and survive the apprenticeship programs?" The report viewed women's gains—not only in the steel industry, but also in society as a whole—as precarious and in need of constant attention. Aware of the growing anti–affirmative action backlash, the activists declared a state of emergency. "As women workers we are facing an emergency situation in the nation as a whole today. There is a massive onslaught

Figure 8. Alice Peurala holds a sign protesting washroom conditions at U.S. Steel, South Works, November 17, 1979. Photograph by Dorreen Carey. Reprinted courtesy of Dorreen Carey and Bill Carey.

against us not only on the job by companies but aided by Congress, the Supreme Court, and the President who are trying to wipe out gains we've made" (Wood Papers).[2]

The report took the U.S. Supreme Court to task for the *Gilbert* decision, in which the high court ruled that pregnancy was not a disability, and thereby made it harder, if not impossible, for women workers to secure sick leave and insurance coverage for pregnancy.[3] The report is also critical of Congress for placing limits on abortion rights and for voting against money for school lunches and for daycare services. Caucus leaders were clear about the fact that affirmative action and its promise of better wages was the number one reason women were employed in the industry to begin with: "To close the pay gap we took non traditional jobs mostly through affirmative action." The caucus gave credit to the Civil Rights Act and not to the good will of the steel companies or the union. "Women were hired in great numbers only with the consent decree and quotas." The leadership of the caucus viewed the backlash against affirmative action as a threat to women's progress and argued for the importance of opposing "reverse" discrimination court cases such as *Weber* and *Bakke*.

The report also emphasized the importance of women's self-organizing. Rank-and-file women were in the best position to force the union to respond to their needs. "In this situation it's a disgrace—it's a disaster that no forms within the union exist to deal with emergency problems." The Women's Caucus took credit that first year for getting a maternity clause in the union contract despite the fact that there were no women on the International executive board and only a handful of women on staff, none of whom were on the negotiating committees. The report complained that there were very few women in leadership positions of any type (Wood Papers).

The goals and activities of District 31 Women's Caucus changed over time, in response to changes in the political opportunities structure, to the crisis in the steel industry, and to their own record of success and failure. At first, there was great energy and optimism on the part of activists that the struggle to obtain women's equality and to end sex and race discrimination could be won. In the beginning the caucus focused on the efforts of women to secure the foothold they had gained in the industry through the consent decree. Initially, their concern was how to make the promise of women's equality a reality—how to move from formal equality to substantive equality. Access to better paying jobs in the skilled crafts could not be realized if the qualifying exams were biased and if training programs were designed with the male worker in mind. Women would go nowhere in the industry if they could be fired for simply being pregnant. Without union protection during the probationary period, women and men of color were subject to arbitrary firings.

The accounts of these struggles in the caucus newsletter revealed that the women did not rely solely on the union's grievance procedures to fight discrimination. Caucus activists encouraged women to use the courts and the momentum of the women's movement to stake their equity claims in the industry. They helped women file class-action suits and EEOC complaints and gave testimony at civil rights and human rights forums in the region. The caucus raised enough money to hire a feminist lawyer, Edna Epstein, a member of the Chicago Lawyers Committee for Civil Rights under Law, Inc., to file an amicus curiae brief in the *Weber* challenge to the consent decree. In one of the most important cases in the history of affirmative action law, the Supreme Court overturned a lower court decision that the affirmative action plan negotiated by the Steelworkers had violated Weber's civil rights. The Supreme Court ruled that voluntary plans, negotiated between a private company and a union, could consider race and sex decisions regarding new hiring and promotion.

The amicus brief argued that voluntary affirmative action plans were justified to ensure that past discrimination would not continue into the future. Choosing an expansive[4] definition of discrimination, the brief argues that the intent of the Civil Rights Act was to accord justice to groups and not just to individuals. "The Act seeks not only to accord restorative justice to individuals actually harmed by an employer's past discriminatory wrongs. It seeks also to assure that discrimination against entire groups of individuals will not continue into the future." The brief goes on to argue that no plan devised to remedy past discrimination could be totally neutral in terms of its impact—some white men would be unavoidably and adversely impacted. "Such neutrality of impact is in all events not possible in a situation where discrimination already exists—whether that discrimination has been caused by historic societal attitudes or the particular conduct of a given employer" (Wood Papers; Greenwald 1978; Vogel 1993).

The Women's Caucus also mobilized union members to participate in mass action to overturn *Weber*. Steelworkers participated in a march and rally against *Weber* in Chicago on 2 June 1978. Individual women's committees, such as the one at the Gary Works, participated in the mobilization. They passed out a leaflet endorsing the march and inviting women to come to the next women's committee meeting. The activists saw *Weber* as an effort to strip women and minorities of the few gains that had been won through affirmative action. Because the union leadership and the caucus were on the same side, the caucus did not have to take a stand against the union. They worried that if the Supreme Court did not overturn *Weber*, the union would lose the ability to negotiate antidiscrimination plans with the companies. To the women's committee at the Gary Works of U.S. Steel, the *Weber* ruling by the lower courts, and not the consent decree, was the divisive element. "The *Weber* case is an effort to divide minorities from whites, men from women, and to have us fighting each other for job and benefits" (Wood Papers).

Women's Committees

The caucus encouraged women's self-organizing through the formation of women's committees in the locals. There were no provisions in the union's constitution for such committees, so women formed them on an informal, ad-hoc basis and then lobbied for their recognition.

The campaign to get official recognition for the Gary Works Women's Committee in Local 1014 is informative. The issue of formal recognition of a woman's committee came to a vote at the 27 August 1979 local union meeting. The proposal, put forth by Gayle Douglas, argued that there were already a dozen or so such committees, such as health and safety, veterans, sick, and recreation and that certainly women deserved a committee of their own. Joan Hac spoke in defense of the resolution. "Women have special problems with things like maternity leave and sexual harassment by foremen. No one else in the mill must face these kinds of problems. A committee of women for women would help the union deal with these issues." Although the proposal for formal recognition was defeated, the women were successful in getting sex added to the description of the committee on human relations. The description was changed to read, "The committee on Human Relations shall work to carry out the principles of the USWA in upholding the rights of its members, in and out of the plant, regardless of race, creed, color, nationality or sex" (*Gary Works*, October/November 1979, 2). The women did not consider this a small victory.

The defeat of the proposal sparked a renewed effort to get the district leadership and the International to require that locals set up women's committees that would be organized and run by women. During the debate, the women never vacillated in their commitment to the union. They challenged their union to fight for their "rights as women" and framed their demand for formal recognition of the women's committee as one of the union's responsibilities to be accountable to its members.

> We face discrimination in many forms. The government has ruled that women must be hired—but who protects us when we are the first fired? Federal laws prohibit discrimination based on sex, but who fights for us when we are pushed out of the apprenticeship, when we are denied promotions or when we are physically attacked on the job or in the parking lot? Who takes our side when a foreman feels that his personal property includes all the females under his jurisdiction? We need the union. (*Gary Works*, 2)

While some locals continued to resist the idea of women's committees, the District 31 director, Jim Balanoff, did not. In a meeting with the "unofficial" women's committee at the Gary Works, he told the women he fully supported the proposal that the union officially support the women's committees and the demand for a department of women's affairs at the International. He also announced the appointment of the first woman, Sharon Stiller, now an assistant to the president for women's programs, to a staff position in District 31. Balanoff praised the women activists in the district for "helping to build the union and bringing much needed attention to the special problems that women faced in the industry" (*Gary Works,* 3). He went on to say, "Women are in the workforce to stay and the union must relate to this fact" (3). While expressing their appreciation for his support, the women continued to press Balanoff on their demand for an "official" women's committee in Local 1014.

The Newsletter

The caucus published a bimonthly newsletter, the *District 31 Women's Caucus Bulletin,* which had a circulation of 2,000.[5] The newsletter was distributed by mail to paid subscribers and passed out at no cost at union meetings and at plant gates. Between 1977 and 1982, the caucus published twenty-five issues of the newsletter. While the focus of the *Bulletin* was on district-wide activities, it also reported on the activities of the local women's committees. The Women's Caucus made a strategic decision not to allow the issues of the rank-and-file insurgency movement to overwhelm the focus of their fledgling organization. Although there were disagreements and contentious debates about this policy, the caucus leaders believed they were able to contain the spillover. Ola Kennedy, who was personally involved in the antiwar movement, believed strongly that the newsletter should stay focused on women. "Some wanted to enter things that I thought we ought not to be embracing. It's good to have all these other concerns, but we had so much that we had to do that we couldn't turn the paper into one that wasn't reaching out to what we were organized for." She was worried that the organization would get sidetracked and that disagreements over politics could derail the movement. "Some people said, 'Oh, those wild-eyed radicals. They're not going to last long. They're going to be into this and into that.' But we stayed the course and fought for the issues that we were organized for and really made an impact."[6]

The *Bulletin* announced the formation of each new women's committee in the locals and reported on the regular activities of these committees. Some issues carried news from as many as ten different local women's committees. Individual women's committees, such as the one at the Gary Works, published their own newsletters as well. These may have been more widely read than the caucus newsletter.[7] In addition to serving as a record of the activities of the Women's Caucus and the women's committees within the union and of their participation in the broader women's movement, the newsletter provides insight into how the activists discursively framed their specific grievances as women Steelworkers.

According to Dorreen Carey, who served as editor of the *Bulletin,* the purpose of the newsletter was to keep women informed of their rights on the job and to remind them that they were not alone in their struggle.[8] In addition to connecting the women within the union to each other, the newsletter also provided women with a vital link to the broader networks and activities of the women's movement. For example, the events, activities, and meetings of the National Organization of Women, the Coalition of Labor Union Women (CLUW), and the Committee to Stop Sexual Harassment were listed. The *Bulletin* was used to mobilize support for the women's movement, and it articulated a vision of union feminism. It inspired action through regular features about women's victories against discrimination, and it organized participation in various women's rights campaigns in the Chicago/ Gary area, including the Illinois ERA ratification campaign. The newsletters encouraged participation of women Steelworkers in many of the major women's rights actions, demonstrations, and rallies in the region and in the nation and reported on their activism.

Pregnancy discrimination dominated the pages of the early issues of the *Bulletin.* No legal protections regarding pregnancy discrimination were in place, so women Steelworkers faced the task of forcing the companies to respond to their needs while lobbying the state for protection against discrimination by the industry. They needed the help of their union, yet there were no uniform collective-bargaining provisions regarding pregnancy leave and maternity benefits. Title VII of the 1964 Civil Rights Act said nothing about employers using pregnancy as the grounds for denying women employment. The Supreme Court had already ruled, both in *Geduldig* and in *Gilbert,* that the category of pregnant worker did not meet the equal-protection requirements of the constitution. Therefore, pregnancy discrimination was not viewed as a form of sex discrimination under Title VII. It would take an additional act of Congress to define it as such, and the Women's Caucus was there every step of the way. Members of the caucus went to Congress to testify at congressional hearings on HB 6075 and Senate Bill 995, legislation that would amend Title VII to make pregnancy discrimination illegal, and to lobby legislators for their passage. They secured an endorsement from the International and funding from the district to send a busload of women Steelworkers to Washington. Leon Lynch, an International Vice President, also spoke at the hearings. In addition, women employed at Bethlehem Steel (Burns Harbor) filed EEOC complaints regarding pregnancy discrimination and eventually filed a class-action, sex-discrimination suit on behalf of all women who lost their jobs because of a pregnancy or an alleged pregnancy. Bethlehem Steel not only dragged its feet on resolving the issues, but actively involved company doctors in an effort to intimidate pregnant workers. Eventually, they offered some of the women individual settlements.

Black Women and Discrimination

The caucus was fully aware that black women were on the front lines of discrimination and harassment, particularly when it came to probationary firings. Twelve issues of the *Bulletin* featured stories about probationary firings. The majority of these stories were about the experiences of black women. When the consent decree went into effect, the probationary period for new hires was extended to 520 hours—an unusually long period. Federal antidiscrimination law covered the probationary period, but because probationary workers were not covered by the collective-bargaining agreement, it meant that new workers had little protection against arbitrary and capricious treatment. When it fired six black female probationary workers hired under the consent decree in 1976, Republic Steel argued that they were merely exercising their "exclusive right to fire probationary employees without recourse to union procedure or defense" (*Bulletin* no. 4, n.d.). The company argued that the women were fired because they could not do the job. Local 1033, which represented the women, argued that the disproportionate firing of black women was, in fact, an act of race and sex discrimination and that such acts were illegal under the collective-bargaining agreement. By that time, all basic-steel contracts contained a standard antidiscrimination clause. However, representing probationary employees was new territory for the union, and eventually the International advised Local 1033 to drop the case because of the difficulty of winning probationary cases.

The women who were fired at Republic turned to the District 31 Women's Caucus for help. They were not about to give up. The caucus called for an end to discriminatory firings during probation and, in fact, for a reduction or elimination of the probationary period entirely. The affected workers and their advocates had to pursue the cause without the union. "Women and minorities suffer most from probationary firings and we will be the ones who will lead the fight to end this injustice" (*Bulletin* no. 4, n.d.).

In another case, Gloria Hawthorne, a black woman hired at U.S. Steel's Gary Works under the consent decree, was fired after only two weeks on the job. She was fired because she failed a "test"—the same test also failed by a white male co-worker who was not terminated. A laborer small in stature, Gloria was given a steel fork the length of a broom and told to flip a full length of railroad track, which she was unable to do. This task was not typically required of workers in the laborer classification, and, though laborers were occasionally asked to flip rail, they had the right to refuse. Gloria had not requested a transfer to a classification that might require that task. In addition, not everyone was given the test. Her union local expressed sympathy for Gloria, but since she was probationary, they gave her little hope of getting her job back. According to an article the *Bulletin,* "Probationary firings and discrimination are two sides of the same coin and the coin is in the U.S. Steel pocket. As long as the company can take away the right to representation of any union member whether on probation or not, everyone suffers" (*Bulletin* no. 5, n.d.).

The civil rights committee in Local 65 took up the cause of six black women probationary employees who were fired from U.S. Steel, South Works. In most of these cases, the supervisors claimed the women were not "equipped" to handle the jobs. The caucus, however, challenged the notion. "Black women were said to be equipped to pick cotton from 'can't see' in the morning to 'can't see' at night when their only pay was a lash across the back. But women are declared ill equipped to earn $7 an hour, and when they try U.S. Steel tries to break their backs, rather than assign them jobs commensurate with their physical ability. They insult and slander them rather than train and prepare them" (*Bulletin* no. 6, n.d.).

Making It "by Merit Alone"

In newspaper ads touting its commitment to equal opportunity, U.S. Steel made clear its position on affirmative action. A full-page ad featured a young, African American woman, Perla Little, holding the tools of her trade as a technician in the metallurgical laboratory at the South Works. Perla is no poster girl for affirmative action. The large bold headline proclaims, "I hold my job on my own, by merit alone." The text documents Perla's rise at U.S. Steel. She tells us, "When I started at U.S. Steel more than two years ago, there were very few women. But I stuck to my job, and I moved fast. *I haven't been hindered by being a woman,* and I'd like to think I haven't been given any tokenism, either. I hold my job on my own, by merit alone." Perla expressed gratitude for the job-training opportunities (much of it off the job and on her own time) provided by U.S. Steel. "You can always use more knowledge and at U.S. Steel it's available to those who want it." The ad copy suggests that the sky is the limit and that individual industriousness and hard work are the keys to achieving the American dream: "Training women for important satisfying careers in industry helps make America work" (*Chicago Sun Times,* 19 July 1977, 23).

The realities for black women at the South Works were far from the image painted in the company's public relations campaign. An EEOC complaint found that 95 percent of workers discharged from the South Works were black, though they comprised less than 50 percent of the workforce (*Bulletin* no. 6, n.d.).

Given the public discourse of equal opportunity and once the consent decree was put in place—prima facie evidence that discrimination no longer existed—it was hard for women and minority men to prove discrimination. Women and men of color were finally being given their chance, and now it was up to them to prove they were worth it. According to Dorreen, "Everyone can see discrimination is happening but the company 'keeps insisting it isn't there' and convinces the government and the union that it is not present" (*Bulletin* no. 6, n.d.).

The Women's Caucus was determined to make discrimination, in all its forms, visible. In addition, they used all the avenues for activism open to them—and created new ones. Through CLUW, they formed alliances with women from other unions who were working to address sexism and to increase the representation and participation of women. The caucus forged links with various organizations in the women's movement—despite the popular rhetoric that working-class women were not interested in the goals and activities of the women's liberation movement and were perhaps even hostile to it.

The caucus mobilized women Steelworkers to participate in the major campaigns of the day. At national, state, and local levels, women Steelworkers marched for passage of the ERA, lobbied Congress for passage of the Pregnancy Discrimination Act, and rallied to protect affirmative action and reproductive rights. They used whatever means were at their disposal—lawsuits and court briefs, grievances and complaints, marches and rallies, speak-outs, and quiet acts of persuasion. They worked within the labor movement and their union and, at the same time, challenged them to change. It took courage, but it also took patience.

Harassment

Company officials sometimes harassed women who complained of discrimination. Dorreen believed her union activism—particularly her work with the Women's Caucus—was the reason that she was threatened with the loss of her apprenticeship. "My immediate foreman charged me with being too critical of the company, of being a 'women's libber' and on a 'hate-authority' campaign." Although apprentices were union members, there was no contract language to protect them from being fired from an apprenticeship.

Dorreen was told by older workers to stay away from the union until she became a craftsman because "you are on probation all the years of your apprenticeship" (*Bulletin* no. 6, n.d.).

Other women reported similar experiences. Betty Dilworth and Patricia Smith of Local 1014 believed women's committees were needed to protect women and to end harassment and discrimination. According to Dilworth, she was harassed because she was involved in organizing and helping other women defend themselves against sexual harassment. The women's committee gave her the strength to fight back. "Because of the women's committee, I know what to look for, how to determine discrimination, when you file a grievance. A lot of women just sit back and take it" (*Bulletin* no. 6, n.d.).

Smith felt harassed for helping to organize a campaign to get adequate washroom facilities and came to understand the value of the women's committee: "I felt like I wanted to quit once because of all the harassment. But by the women's committee listening to women's problems—now I know where to go and how to get out of this harassment" (*Bulletin* no. 6, n.d.).

Women's Conferences

One important vehicle for bringing discrimination to the attention of the union, for networking with the broader women's movement, and for mobilizing women within the union was the District 31 women's conferences. These conferences brought women from different locals together with union staff and lawyers, with resource people from government and from the community, and with activists from the civil rights and women's liberation movements. The format of the women's conferences was similar to the standard union conference format—workshops, speak-outs, speeches, films, and social events—and planned by union staff with input from the constituency involved. The informal networking and the sharing that happened at these events were just as important as the formal agenda.

The first women's conference was held on 2 to 3 February 1978 and was claimed as an early victory by the Women's Caucus. They had made the women's conference a part of their demands and introduced the idea formally at the 1977 District 31 Conference, where their resolution to hold a women's conference passed unanimously. While the district director, Jim Balanoff, requested that each local send representatives to the conference, the caucus left nothing up to chance. They mobilized women to demand that they be sent to the conference as delegates. Because the conference was open to all members, women could participate even if they were not selected as official representatives of their locals. Wood said, "This is our Conference, we worked hard to get it, so let's be there" (*Bulletin* no. 7, n.d.). She was convinced that the way to get the union to serve as an advocate for women's issues was to increase women's participation and visibility. A good turnout at the conference was a way to do that. "We know that to best equip our Union to do the job for us, there is a big weakness to overcome—*lack of women's representation*" (*Bulletin* no. 7, n.d.).

By the time of the first conference, held at the Local 65 union hall in Chicago, the number of women Steelworkers in the district had reached about 10,000 out of 120,000 members. More than 200 women attended. They heard speakers from the International, such as attorney Barbara Hillman, who urged the women to organize on their own behalf. "Not until women organize themselves and organize their unions will they be able to force the trade union movement to change its direction and devote real attention to the problems of working women, both unionized and unorganized" (*Daily Calumet*, 3 February 1978, 6). In workshops, women were informed about their rights under the USWA contract and federal law, about how the union is structured and organized, and about health and safety issues.

Addie Wyatt, vice president both of the Meatcutters Union and of CLUW, told the women at the first conference to stay the course and to work at transforming their ideas into action. "This conference is a beautiful beginning for some, a continuation for others, but it must not be an end for any. The issues we are discussing today, so critical for the welfare of working women and all workers, must not remain on paper, but must be put into action"(*Daily Calumet*, 3 February 1978, 1). Stella Nowicki, featured in the documentary *Union Maids*,[9] was an honored guest at the conference, and she urged the women to run for union office and to get active in union affairs.

The conference culminated in the passage of a resolution calling on the International to establish a women's department, for District 31 to establish an official women's committee, and for locals to set up women's committees. Other resolutions called for full support of affirmative action and the ERA, for passing legislation that would end pregnancy discrimination, and for drastically shortening the probationary period. Support for every resolution was not unanimous. A group of conservative women opposed a resolution that called for the government to provide public funds for childcare expenses. They asserted that "public tax dollars shouldn't be used for the benefit of a few working mothers" (*Post-Tribune,* 9 February 1978, sec. C, 1).

In his welcoming remarks, District Director Balanoff attributed the convening of the conference to the rising visibility of women's activism. He told the audience that "the gathering was the hard work of the District 31

Women's Caucus and women throughout the area who realized it's the squeaky wheel gets the oil." He added that International attention to the special needs of women Steelworkers was long overdue and that the conference "will lay the groundwork for discussion in the International Executive Board, for an international union women's department" (*Daily Calumet,* 3 February 1978, 6).

Roberta Wood, a key organizer of the conference, recognized that while a good deal of work remained, the women had finally gotten the proverbial foot in the door—and a foot "with a metatarsal [protective] shoe. But we've got to get the women who are in the union to become active, to be involved. We've got to get them to go to union meetings, to speak up" (*Post-Tribune,* 9 February 1978, sec. C, 1). District 31 held additional women's conferences in 1979, 1980, and 1981 before they were folded into the bi-annual civil rights conference, which became the civil rights and women's rights conference.

Collective Action Frameworks

The caucus borrowed, extended, and modified the antidiscrimination and equal rights discourses that framed many of the demands of liberal feminism and civil rights and attempted to combine them with the political discourse of class that was more characteristic of the Left and of the trade-union movement. This proved very hard to accomplish in the United States because the individual-rights argument, framed by equal rights legislation, was discursively hard to reconcile with the group rights of workers, which were framed legislatively by the Wagner Act and the National Labor Relations Act and codified over time in collective-bargaining agreements.[10]

Official position papers and resolution language provide insight into how the caucus and the International framed the issues. For example, the caucus paired reproductive rights with maternity benefits and framed them not only as equity issues but also as economic or class issues. The caucus argued that women had the fundamental right to control their own bodies. For those who wanted to have children, it was the right to prenatal health care, for those who did not, it was the right to terminate a pregnancy—and they wanted insurance to cover both options. Women had the right to their own moral and religious views about abortion but not the right to restrict the rights of others. They believed the union was responsible for protecting them from pregnancy discrimination and for fighting right-wing political attacks on a woman's right to a safe and legal abortion. Equality for women and equal access to health benefits was seen as ways to strengthen working-class families. The *Bulletin* carried announcements of the activities of the reproductive rights movement and even helped to organize a boycott against the United Way when it denied financial support to Planned Parenthood (*Bulletin* no. 21, March–June 1981).

In 1981, the caucus published a special edition of the *Bulletin* on reproductive hazards in the workplace (no. 21). It featured an interview with Donna Hadley, a Steelworker who had given birth to a child with dextrocardia—a condition in which the heart is on the opposite side of the body. "I was a Motor Inspector apprentice in Cold Reduction maintenance, the pickle line, the five stands, and a new line called the Unikot, where they stripped the galvanize off one side of the coils for cars so the paint would stay on better." She had asked about exposure to carbon but had been reassured about her safety. Her physician had told her she could work as long as she wanted to during the pregnancy. After the birth, the company would not consider her exposure to chemicals a contributing factor. Donna suspected otherwise, but no one could pinpoint the exact cause of her son's medical problems. The union told her to document the chemicals to which she had been exposed, and she had a friend secretly remove dust from around the Unikot line for analysis. It was thick with sulfuric acid and zinc. A pediatrician suggested she had ingested a hallucinogen like LSD (acid) during the pregnancy. Donna was indignant. "The only acid I had come into contact with was sulfuric acid from work." According to Donna, "No doctor seems to want to have anything to do with work-related birth defects" (*Bulletin* no. 21, March–June 1981). Eventually the company replaced the line with a new process.

Some companies attempted to control their liability for environmental health risks by restricting the access of women in childbearing years to certain jobs or by forcing women to be sterilized in order to keep their jobs. The International saw this as a civil rights as well as a health and safety issue and held that workers should not have to choose between making a living and their health and safety. The position of the caucus and of the union was that "policies that remove women from jobs with known reproductive hazards while leaving men exposed should be opposed as discriminatory against both men and women. Companies must be forced to alter the workplace and not the worker" (*Bulletin* no. 20, October 1980). The caucus recommended that all Steelworkers become more informed about reproductive health hazards in the work environment, and they advised pregnant women to be especially careful. The International's position stated, "With very few exceptions, anything that will affect female reproductive systems will also affect male reproductive systems. Employer practices are extremely sexist and frequently deny females their livelihood, while denying men their health. Since the passage of the 1964 Civil Rights Act, Title VII, there has been a slow and gradual improvement in occupational opportunities for women. Workers now have equal work and equal hazards" (Wood Papers).

The caucus also framed the issue of sexual harassment in class-specific ways. On the one hand, they saw sexual harassment as a deterrent to building class solidarity between men and women and as an economic, bread-and-butter issue. "Sexual harassment is a form of discrimination which divides and weakens our union, and causes economic hardship through loss of job and stress-induced illnesses" (USWA District 31 Women's Conference Resolution; Wood Papers). But they also framed the issue as one of basic rights and responsibilities. "Many union members and officials are not aware of their rights and responsibilities in dealing with sexual harassment" (ibid.). The Women's Caucus demanded that all locals protect their membership against harassment by redefining discrimination in the collective-bargaining agreement as something that includes sexual harassment and by providing stewards and grievants training in how to handle sexual harassment complaints.

The caucus position on the ERA relied on the argument that the ERA would legally end sex discrimination and would close the wage gap between men and women. "The gap in wages between women and men gives employers incentive for dividing the workforce on the basis of sex" (*Bulletin* no. 17, February–April 1980). Lynn Williams, USWA president, noted that right-to-work states were, in many instances, the same states that had yet to ratify the ERA. He called the list of states that had not ratified the ERA the "dishonor" roll. The caucus called on the union to refuse to hold meetings in unratified states; to refuse to endorse candidates for public office who did not support the ERA; and to educate the membership on the merits of the ERA to counter the "lies and myths" of the antilabor, anti-ERA forces. The *Bulletin* provided extensive coverage of ERA activism in the district and published information to refute right-wing positions.

Ladies First: Gender and Job Loss

Deindustrialization and the deepening crisis in the steel industry took a significant toll on the women's activism and on the employment gains women had made in the steel industry. Plant closures and downsizing resulted in dismissals or layoffs of large numbers of women, including much of the women's caucus leadership. News about the formation of women's committees and about women being elected to local office was replaced with news about unemployment, food banks, and how to stem the tide of economic destruction.

In a letter to the *Bulletin* (no. 17, February–April 1980), the women's committee of Local 1011 at J&L Steel asked, "What is our future in the mill? As layoffs increase and the recession deepens we might become little more than a name on an unused locker." The women's committee could not get data on how many women had been laid off, but they estimated it to be about half. They discovered that some women had exhausted unemployment benefits, and some with families had turned to welfare. Others had given up hope of ever returning to their jobs but had difficulty finding replacement jobs. "One woman told us there are so many teenagers competing for jobs that even minimum wage jobs are hard to find." When the company needed temporary workers to work in the coke plant, they excluded women who were on furlough because they claimed they did not have "facilities." According to one woman, "If it comes to working in the coke plant or starving, I would gladly take the job."

Women were particularly vulnerable to the steel industry downturn. They were the most recently hired, and few had advanced to the better skilled and craft job classifications—jobs a little better protected during a recession. By 1980, only 2 women and 24 minorities out of 7,500 workers at J&L held craft jobs. The women's committee at J&L did not want to protect their jobs at the expense of other workers. "We want a solution that will put the burden on the company and not on our fellow male workers." The committee offered solutions like the extension of benefits, inverse seniority, and low-cost insurance for laid-off workers.

The next issue of the *Bulletin* (no. 18, May–June 1980), with a front-page headline that read "Lay Offs—Ladies First," was devoted to the topic of job loss. The photo on the front page showed a room full of women with their hands raised in the air with the caption: "Who's laid off? Almost everybody" (Figure 9). These women were attending a special Women's Caucus meeting on layoffs and the implications for women who were hired under the consent decree and who did not have the seniority to survive. This group, too, rejected super seniority for women and blacks as too divisive and proposed instead solutions that would spread the burden of job loss. They proposed novel solutions, such as a system of voluntary layoff by reverse seniority or of rotating layoffs, permanent recall rights, a shortened work week, extension of benefits, and skills training during layoff. The women at the meeting demanded data from the companies on the number of women laid off and suggested that every effort be made to make them live up to the terms of the consent decree.

Figure 9. "Lay Offs, Ladies First": special District 31 Women's Caucus meeting on layoffs, Gary, Indiana, 1980. Photograph by Dorreen Carey. Reprinted courtesy of Dorreen Carey and Bill Carey.

The caucus wanted the union to abandon concession bargaining and other efforts to cooperate with the industry and to fight harder for the jobs of all Steelworkers. "Certainly the concept of cooperation between the companies and the Steelworkers has been exposed as a lie by U.S. Steel's unexpected shutdown of the plants in Youngstown, Ohio, and the lack of concern the company has shown for the entire city whose jobs they have stolen. The Steelworkers union has to wage a fight to protect basic steelworkers' jobs. We are already well on the way to being an endangered species and the steel companies are acting like it is open season" (*Bulletin* no. 18, 1).[11]

In a dramatic speech before the Women's Caucus, Alice Peurala, president of Local 65 and the first woman president of a basic-steel local, told the audience that the issue was jobs for all workers not just women and minorities.

> When the layoffs and shutdowns are as extensive as they are, it affects everybody, and I think that the only way we can gain as women and as workers is to advance the proposition of Jobs for All. The important question to ask in looking for a long-term solution to the problem of jobs is whether or not private enterprise has the right to shut down a corporation or an industry that we're employed in, regardless of whether men or women are involved. (*Bulletin* no. 18, May–June)

She suggested that each local set up an unemployment committee to serve as a link between laid-off workers and the union. Such a committee could help to mobilize a fight for jobs and provide assistance with repossession of homes and belongings.

One woman responded to Alice's speech by suggesting that the caucus needed to take a stronger stand on affirmative action.

> Affirmative action gains have been modest. If we do not defend our affirmative-action gains today, we're not going to be around to change our union's lay-down-and-die approach. We must raise the proposal that the percentage of women and minorities in the workforce not be reduced as a result of layoffs. We saw our union successfully defend quotas in the *Weber* case. Should this victory be shelved until we win jobs for all? (*Bulletin* no. 19, July–November 1980)

According to this woman, the goal was not only to hire but also to keep women and minority men. "Don't be afraid to suggest seniority modifications. We can't accept 'Seniority is the most basic principle in our union.'"

In a *Bulletin* editorial entitled "State of Steel," Dorreen defended the workers from the charge that the union's wage demands had caused inflation and the problems in the steel industry. She reminded readers that the loss of 78,400 jobs was not the fault of worker's wage demands. "Wages only go up when inflation goes up. Wages respond to inflation. If you want to see inflationary wage raises, take a look at the wage increases these steel executives gave themselves in 1981. Bethlehem 97.9 percent, Inland 17.4 percent, LTV-J&L 47 percent and U.S. Steel 28.7 percent" (no. 23). In the end the caucus took a realist's stance: "Times are tough for everyone. We continue to uphold the principle and value of affirmative action but we understand that you can only have affirmative action when there are jobs" (*Bulletin* no. 23, June 1982).

The cutbacks had virtually eliminated women from the basic-steel mills, and the caucus wanted to tie the fight for jobs to the fight against the right-wing rhetoric about women's proper role in society. "As women we will fight against the 'normal' rights assertion that women must be pushed back into the well-to-do fantasy occupation of housewife and full-time mother. That's just an excuse to keep all the 'laid off' and 'fired' housewives from getting good paying jobs" (*Bulletin* no. 23).

Conclusion

The Women's Caucus had to find a way to forge feminism in the space between the two movements. Union feminists knew that liberal reform would not be enough. But, discursively, there was little else to go on. There simply was no social justice frame capable of resolving the tension between equal rights and collective rights in a way that could deliver immediate results, and immediate results were essential if women were to keep their jobs. The social movements that produced the legal tools to fight discrimination on the job eventually found themselves constrained by those successes.

The Women's Caucus and local women's committees were successful in solving many problems and in drawing attention to inadequate facilities, sexual harassment, and probationary firings. They also served to help integrate women into the life of the union local. Lorraine Springfield told me the caucus helped her to develop the confidence to run for union office, and, despite not liking politics, she won. She had gone into the mill under the consent decree because her job as a clerical worker on the shop floor paid more than any job she previously held, but she became an activist when she went to Washington to lobby for the passage of the Pregnancy Discrimination Act.[12]

Other women, like Dorreen Carey, who opted for a company buyout plan and left the industry when she became pregnant, and Joan Hac and Paula Dagman, who were displaced when their mill was closed, continued their activism in other causes and unions.[13] For Dorreen, it was the environmental movement, where she eventually found employment in a governmental agency responsible for environmental protection policies. For Joan, it was union organizing. After losing her job, Joan returned to school, earned a labor studies degree from Indiana University, and took a job on the staff of another union. Paula, who worked as a production assistant at *U.S. News and World Report* before taking a job in the mill as a janitor, returned to the world of the office at the University of Chicago, where she remained active in her new union.

Joan and Paula did not entered the industry thinking of themselves as feminists. Joan, a divorced, Arab American mother of three who had to rely from time to time on welfare before landing a job in the Blooming Mill at the Gary Works of U.S. Steel, told me, "If it wasn't for the women's movement, I never would have been in the mill. I don't like quotas but without quotas I wouldn't have been here. Quotas are the only way I know of to equalize things and get things right so they can stay right."[14]

Paula, a married, white woman and mother of one, never thought about the women's movement until she started to work in the steel mill. "I thought all those women were silly. That there wasn't a reason for all the commotion." She thought, "If somebody wanted to do something they should just go and do it," and that "anybody could do just about anything in this country." But working in the mill convinced her that not all women

could "just do it" and that they needed an advocate like the women's movement. In looking back over the five years she worked at Interlake, she talked
about the pride she took in doing a job that no one expected women to be
able to do. It was something I heard from many of the women I talked to
over the years. After telling me how important her family was to her, Paula
concluded the interview with these words:

> The thing that will be the most satisfying thing and the thing I am the
> most proud of in my whole life will be the fact that I worked in a steel
> mill, and I did it well. And I did it as good . . . as most of [the men]. I
> won't say all of them—there were certainly guys bigger, tougher, and
> stronger than I was—but I certainly was above average laborer in a steel
> mill, and I'm real proud of that.[15]

The defeat of the ERA, the ascendancy of the antifeminist backlash,
and the collapse of both the steel industry and the rank-and-file insurgency
movement presented formidable obstacles for women's organizing within
the Steelworkers. Many of the most active women in the caucus lost their
jobs. Balanoff was no longer the district director. Mary Elgin, one of the
last officers of the caucus, told James Lane (1996, 546) it was "too depress-
ing" to meet, and she decided it was "counterproductive" to hold caucus
meetings anymore. "The whole conversation would be, 'Are you still working?' 'No. I've been laid off.' And they'd talk about losing their house and
car. Over half the women at one point were not working." She came to believe that those who continued to work could do nothing to save the others.

Most displaced women returned to the type of low-wage, nonunion
jobs they held before finding jobs in the steel industry. After long periods of
layoff, some women, like Robin Rich, were called back to work and continue
to this day to be active in the union. She is currently a USWA staff representative in District 7. Her focus is different. The survival of the industry
became the primary issue and, according to Rich, "It was hard to think
about what we should be doing as women" (Lane 1996, 546). Although the
caucus disbanded, the tradition of women's activism in District 31 was carried forward by union feminists who were not employed in basic steel, like
Sharon Stiller. Women from the female-dominated locals possessed the experience and skills that had made the Women's Caucus successful, and they
were not going anywhere.

Against tremendous odds, the District 31 Women's Caucus accomplished a good deal in its short history. It brought attention to the concerns
of women entering a male-dominated occupation at a time when few of the

current legal supports were in place. Whether it was improving facilities or helping to win back a woman's job, the caucus did have concrete successes. A few women were mainstreamed into union office, and the important work they did laid the foundation for the reemergence of women's activism in the contemporary period.

7

Women of Steel Crossing the Border:
Union Feminism in Canada

> *The potential for forging a creative, productive partnership between working women and unions is greater now than at any other historic moment.*
>
> —Dorothy Sue Cobble, *Women and Unions*

> *Women concerned with labour force issues are no longer discussing whether unions have something to contribute, but how much and how best to do it.*
>
> —Julie White, *Sister and Solidarity*

The crisis in the steel industry during the 1980s and the conservative backlash against feminism and labor during the Reagan years inhibited the continued growth of union feminism in the Steelworkers in the United States. However, the crisis in steel did not have the same effect on union feminism in Canada, nor was the backlash against feminism and organized labor under the conservative Mulroney era as severe. Like their sisters in the Calumet region, women activists in the Steelworkers' District 6 (Ontario) were able to use institutional space, such as union conventions and conferences and union resources and programs, to construct and sustain a collective identity as union feminists. They put pressure on the Steelworkers to develop special initiatives to enhance the participation and representation of women. These included a leadership course, a sexual harassment policy, conference resolutions on gender equity, a campaign to prevent violence against women, women's conferences, and the formation of women's committees.

I view these initiatives, bundled under the title *Women of Steel,* as feminist organizing. Martin (1990) suggests that such efforts can be labeled feminist—whether the actors believe it to be or not—if they were founded as part of the women's movement or embrace feminist ideas, values, goals, or outcomes. The ideas of the *Women of Steel* initiatives as expressed in mission statements, conference resolutions, policy reports, educational curriculum, handbooks, and collective bargaining agreements are explicitly feminist by Martin's standards. Women are viewed as a disadvantaged group, and the expressed goals of these initiatives are to change the union, the workplace, and society. The *Women of Steel* documents emphasize the importance of changing consciousness and material conditions by constructing a discourse that blends trade-union principles and rhetoric with feminist ones. Women's committees are organized collectively around a consensus-building model—an important organizing principle of many feminist organizations.

Eventually, women in the United States lobbied the International to make these initiatives available to them as well. In this chapter I explain why union feminism in the Steelworkers reemerged in Ontario and how union feminism made its way back across the Canadian border to the United States. I analyze the meaning of union feminism to the participants in the *Women of Steel* initiatives, particularly in the *Women of Steel* leadership course. How do activists transform union resources and networks in their efforts to self-organize? What issues become important, and how do activists frame them in ways that resonate with the rank and file? Are the *Women of Steel* initiatives effective in mobilizing women on behalf of their self-defined "interests" as women? Is the *Women of Steel* leadership course effective? What impact are "Women of Steel" having on the union?

To survive the effects of deindustrialization and economic restructuring, the Steelworkers needed to organize outside their traditional jurisdiction. To do so they had to come to terms not only with the changing gender, racial, and ethnic composition of the workforce but with other changes as well. These changes included a steep decline in manufacturing and an increase in service-sector jobs, smaller and more decentralized work sites, a more mobile workforce, and a less favorable political climate for organized labor in both countries. It would not be sufficient simply to add "women's" issues, such as flex time, to the collective-bargaining agenda of unions (Cobble 1993). Whole new approaches to organizing and new forms of representation would need to be devised if there were to be a new more meaningful partnership between women and organized labor (Bronfenbrenner et al. 1998). This would require difficult changes in the organizational prac-

tices and policies of most unions but especially in a quintessentially industrial union like the Steelworkers. Would they be up to the task?

Political Opportunity Structure in Ontario (District 6)

Because of its dual-nation jurisdiction, the Steelworkers navigate within
and between two different political fields, each with a different set of political constraints and opportunities for union feminists. This dual location
has proven to be an asset to the growth and development of feminism within
the union. When opportunities were blocked in one nation, possibilities
opened up in another.

The political and legal environment in Canada, even during conservative times, was more favorable to the agendas of both labor and the women's
movement. The stronger presence in Canada of the social democratic Left,
particularly the New Democratic Party (NDP), enhanced the role of labor
in Canadian politics. The Steelworkers are one of the largest union affiliates
of the NDP and as such are well represented within the leadership of the
party.

The NDP serves as a vehicle for bringing labor together with other
popular movements, and this is particularly true in the case of the women's
movement (Bernard 1993). Women's committees were established in the
NDP as early as 1972, and since that time the party has required female
representation on all of its slates. In 1989, it became the first political party
in North America to select a women leader. Audrey McLaughlin was appointed to replace Ed Broadbent, who resigned as head of the party. In
1995, Alexa McDonough was elected in her own right to lead the party.
The presence of feminists and women activists within the NDP has allowed
feminist discourse to circulate more freely in Canadian labor circles than is
the case in the United States. For example, the American AFL-CIO did not
create a woman's department until 1995—one that has already been "mainstreamed" out of existence—but its Canadian counterpart, the Canadian
Labour Congress (CLC), has had a women's committee since 1974.[1] According to Bernard (1993), the CLC admits that the women's movement within
the NDP not only influenced the party to promote women but also had a
parallel effect within the CLC, pressuring it to promote women within the
labor movement.

The NDP and the CLC reevaluated their relationship and reaffirmed
their commitment to each other and to the struggle for social justice in 1989
after the party failed to do as well as predicted in 1988 federal elections.[2]
NDP political influence on the provincial level, where most of the laws
regarding labor are enacted, produced an impressive array of legislative

reforms favorable to labor. These reforms helped labor, during very difficult times, to maintain a relatively high rate of union density vis-à-vis the United States.[3] In 1990, the NDP secured its first victory in Ontario, winning 74 of 130 seats and capturing 38 percent of the popular vote (Bernard 1993, 150). This created very favorable political opportunity structures for the Steelworkers and for the feminists within the union. Unfortunately for labor, the NDP could not hold on to power and was replaced by the conservatives in 1996.

An NDP government in Ontario meant stronger equity laws as well. The Ontario Pay Equity Act stimulated the development of pay-equity experts and consultants, some of whom, like Sue Milling and Marlene Gow of the Steelworkers National Office, went on to play important roles in developing the union's equity agenda for women. The women's movement in Canada was successful in winning governmental support for women's rights, which were strengthened further as the NDP increased its political clout in Ontario. It was Ontario's Women's Directorate, a government equity office, that funded the research and development of the union's leadership course, *Women of Steel.* By contrast, government spending on gender-equity projects came to halt in the United States once Reagan was elected.

Women of Steel Leadership Course

The *Women of Steel* educational leadership course was originally designed and implemented in District 6. The purpose of the course is to develop leadership, broadly defined, among women in the union. It focuses on effective communication skills, on developing leadership styles and qualities, and on *critical analysis* of situations and obstacles women face. Topics include institutional barriers affecting women's advancement, sexual and racial harassment, history of women in the union, balancing work and family, health and safety, employment equity, forming women's committees, conflict management, and public speaking (Figure 10). The curriculum aims to demystify the union's power structure and union politics by having seasoned women union activists discuss how the union really works. The program also attempts to link the union's concern with these issues to other groups, organizations, or agencies in the community that are also concerned with equity issues for women.[4]

In 1986, Leo Gerard (then District 6 director and now international president) hired Michael Lewis to coordinate political action, human rights efforts, and women's programs for District 6 of the Steelworkers. Lewis is a long-time political activist in the NDP and son of David Lewis, one of the

Figure 10. Sue Milling, Education Department, Canadian Steelworkers National Office, conducting a Women of Steel *class in Toronto. Photograph by Lisa Blanchette.*

founders of the party. Gerard was keenly aware of the changes in the composition of the membership and in the need to target new groups of workers for organizing, and he wanted to know how the union should respond.[5] At that time, according to Lewis, women in the union—between 10 and 14 percent of total membership in Canada—were not being given the opportunity to get ahead.[6] He thought that without special programs nothing would change. He secured the support of the top leadership in the district and approached the Ontario Women's Directorate for funds to develop the *Women of Steel* leadership course.

The Women's Directorate awarded the union a substantial grant to develop the course but insisted that the union hire an outside expert to develop the project. The union hired Daina Green to design, pilot, and implement the new course. According to Green, a labor educator and pay-equity consultant with a background in public-service unions, the most innovative part of the project was the participant research.[7] The grant allowed her the time and resources to gain an understanding of the union culture, of how the union functioned, and of how the women perceived their status within the union. She conducted focus groups with the union's gender-equity committees to better understand the issues the women faced in a male-dominated union. She made the committees advisory groups so they would take more ownership in the project. As she developed materials for the course, she tried out her ideas on this group. "I gave them material they never thought about explicitly, on an analytical level, such as how they found out how things got done in the union, how power is brokered within the union." She talked with the women about how to build in things that would help women to increase their confidence and self-esteem. "They talked about how nervous they are when they talked in meetings, how shy they were to speak up—afraid none would care to listen—or how they were often singled out."

A key ingredient of the curriculum was the explicit attention given to racial and social diversity, and Green insisted that the participants from diverse backgrounds be selected to attend the course. "The union would submit names of women to participate, and I would ask, 'Are there any women of color, aboriginal women, or women with disabilities?'" If there were none, and usually there were not, she would send back the list and ask them to try harder. "At first they would say, 'We don't know them. They don't come to meetings.'" This recognition on the part of the staff that they might not know or be talking to a representative group of members was, in Green's words, "groundbreaking." "Asking them to take a chance on someone they didn't know, someone who wasn't already active was risky. But, of course, that was the point of the whole project. Sometimes they bought into it, and sometimes they wouldn't have anything to do with it."

When the participants were diverse, the discussions were more illuminating, and the sessions more controversial. According to Green, "We had difficult discussions about race. Some women, including black women, didn't want to talk about race or racism. They didn't feel safe. Some white women resented the word 'white'. They did not think of themselves as white, just as women. They tended to think of attention to race as divisive. They already felt outnumbered by men, and anything that further divided them was a problem."

At the same time, the Canadians acknowledge that power differences among union women require at times separate forms of mobilization for different groups of women, and they have conducted several separate *Women of Steel* courses for women of color—primarily immigrant women. Rusell Caracciolo, who participated in the special course, believed that women of color need separate space to talk about issues, such as abuse, in a culturally sensitive forum.

If you have a woman of color experiencing abuse, we would not talk about it. I find the average Canadian is willing to talk about it, they are more open, they are more willing to tell you openly about the things they experience in their families. We tend to keep that to ourselves and figure, well, already we are not that lucky (because of racism and discrimination) so let's keep that to ourselves.[8]

Others resisted the idea of any women having a separate course from men on the basis that it would divide men and women at a time when the whole union movement was under attack. This concern almost derailed the whole project. According to Green, "women who opposed the idea said things like, 'If we have a program just for women, then the men will say we can't go to their courses, we have our own courses' or 'We should be building solidarity with them. We shouldn't have secrets because they will think we are saying things behind their back. . . . We don't need that.'"

Some women did not want to be seen as getting somewhere solely because they were women. Some feared reprisals or thought they could make it "on the boys' terms." Green described one very tense session where a number of women changed their positions, "They heard each other's stories in a new way, and decided they did need a space of their own." There was conflict between those women whose goal was affirmative action within the union—particularly those who saw the union as a site of employment—and those women who wanted to build a women's movement within the union that would have a broader impact on women's rights in Canada. And, of course, there were women who thought the two goals were not incompatible.

Bringing *Women of Steel* to the United States

It would not be long before women in the United States became aware of the course and demanded that it be brought across the border. There were two precipitating events—Sandy Sutton's anger with the lack of female representation in the union and Nancy Lessin's response to sexual harassment at a union function—that facilitated the transfer. Sandy attended the union's legislative conference in Washington in 1991 and was upset by the lack of female representation and at the masculine symbolism of the whole event.

I remember walking into the legislative conference, and there was not one woman as a speaker the whole time we were there. And as we walk in . . . they were raffling off a Steelworker's watch, but they only had one— a man's watch—not the woman's version! Then, when I registered, they gave me a baseball cap and not a visor or a scarf or something. So, those three things alone—no woman speaker, a baseball cap, and only a man's watch that I could win—just kind of infuriated me![9]

Sandy brought her concerns to the attention of Marsha Zakowski, staff member of the International's Civil Rights Department, and told her, "You know, we've got to sit down with Lynn Williams, and we have got to talk to him about where we as women are going. We want women to feel welcome to come to something like this, and, if there, before they get in the god-damn door everything points to being for men, it just doesn't welcome them." Before the conference was over Sandy extracted a promise from Williams, then president of the Steelworkers, to meet to discuss women's issues. A few months later Sandy flew to Pittsburgh at her own expense because as she put it, "I wanted them to owe me, not me owe them." Sandy and Marsha met with Lynn for about five hours.

> He really asked a lot of questions on what we were looking for. Of course, we were prepared with a long list of things. He wanted us to come up with information for him and check on what other unions like the UAW were doing. And as . . . we were walking out the door, he kind of winked and he shook my hand. And he said, 'You know, Sandy, I'd really like to see a grassroots movement.' And I said, 'That sounds like a challenge.' And he laughed.

Sandy was very much up to such a challenge and began actively to mobilize other women. The second event that mobilized U.S. interest in the *Women of Steel* course was an incident of sexual harassment that occurred at a union-sponsored Health and Safety conference in the autumn of 1991. Nancy Lessin, one of the few women present at the conference, was sexually harassed in a hotel bar by an International staff representative. Inspired by the testimony of Anita Hill at the Clarence Thomas confirmation hearings and encouraged by a friend on the International staff, she wrote to Lynn Williams about the incident. I asked how she handled it in the moment and whether she knew that she would go to the top with a complaint when it happened.

> No, I didn't know what I was going to do. I was so angry. In the moment, I got stuck wanting to know how to break the bottom off of a beer bottle . . . I wanted to take one of the beer bottles that was on the bar, smash the bottom off it and put it in his face. And the thought, while this incident is going on, was, it would just be my luck that I'd hit it on the bar

and the bottom wouldn't come off. I'd hit it again. The bottom wouldn't come off, and I'd look like a fool.[10]

Nancy got in touch with Sandy, who advised her about how to approach the issue with the "big boys." Sandy told her about the *Women of Steel* course and sexual harassment policy developed by the Canadian Steelworkers. Nancy was invited to the International to meet with Lynn Williams, and brought with her a list of recommendations to improve the climate in the union for women. The recommendations included a uniform sexual harassment policy similar to the Canadian policy that would apply to union members and staff in nonemployment situations and the development of a leadership course for women in the United States. In addition, Nancy was given approval to organize a program at the 1992 USWA Constitutional Convention on "Women in the Union" in order to gain information on the unmet needs of women and to learn how the USWA could meet those needs. One demand not acted on was the demand to form an International Women's Task Force on the status of women to investigate discrimination and barriers to women's participation and to make recommendations to the International on what it will take to organize the workforce of the future— women, people of color, immigrants, and refugees.

The Canadian sexual harassment policy that so impressed the women from the United States was put into place in response to a sexual harassment case that had generated national media attention. Bonita Clark, a pump tender at the Stelco plant in Hamilton, filed a complaint with the Ontario Labour Relations Board in 1985. She charged, among other things, that sex discrimination and sexual harassment created a "poisoned work environment." Clark had been subjected repeatedly to sexual harassment by her foreman. "He was sexually insulting, physically grabbed her upper body and followed her around the plant continually for months" (Gray 1986, 16). She felt forced to bid on jobs she did not want to avoid certain areas of the mill with a reputation for harassment. The washroom facilities for women were inadequate, and "there was a constant imposition of intimacy with the men" (16). The company would not screen off the men's shower and change room, so Bonita had to see them naked. When she complained, she was told by supervision to "shut up and enjoy the free show" (16). Clark also filed a complaint with the Ontario Human Rights Commission, which accepted the complaint but did not investigate. Finally, she went to the media and to the Labour Board and charged that sexual harassment was a health and safety hazard. She claimed that she was being harassed because she had filed complaints about harassment and that, in general, harassment was being used as a tool by management to drive the few remaining women out of the steel mill. She asked for a number of remedies including construction of washrooms for women, enforcement of a policy on sexual harassment, and a declaration that sexual harassment was an unsafe working condition and as such was a violation of the Health and Safety Act.

As an outcome of the Clark case and a growing number of other sexual harassment complaints, the Canadian Steelworkers began to address the issue in more formal ways. According to Lewis, the Clark case was a crystallizing moment in the way the Clarence Thomas/Anita Hill hearings were in the United States. Though neither the local nor the company responded to Clark, the District 6 leadership under Gerard took the complaint seriously and commissioned the legal counsel to develop a position paper for the union on the topic of sexual harassment. A few years later, the union would develop a similar policy on racial harassment.

In June 1992, the International adopted a modified version of the Canadian harassment policy and invited the woman who originally lodged the complaint to attend the board meeting at which it was formally adopted. The union framed its opposition to sexual harassment on the basis that such actions violate "two basic trade-union principles—human rights and solidarity." The policy also established a committee on sexual harassment to develop educational programs on the topic.

Women of Steel Resolution

It soon became clear to the International that women had begun to mobilize across the U.S. and Canadian border and that they were very much up to Williams's challenge to organize a grassroots response to sex discrimination. In the months leading up to the 1992 Constitutional Convention of the union, women activists in the United States and Canada crafted their demands into a convention resolution *(Women of Steel Resolution)*. It was sent to women across the United States and Canada from a list of names gathered over the years by individuals concerned with women's issues. Sandy Sutton called in some political favors, and some of the biggest locals in the Calumet area endorsed the resolution. By the time it reached the convention floor, eighteen locals had endorsed some version of it. The resolution adoption process became an organizing tool for the women activists.

The growing group of women activists planned and organized a *Women of Steel* forum to take place at the 1992 Constitutional Convention in Pittsburgh. The forum was held the night before the *Women of Steel* resolution was introduced to the convention. Nancy Lessin, one of the event organizers, described how she felt when the next day convention delegates lined up at the microphones to support the resolution:

> We have organized for it, and it is very profound. The resolution is the most popular resolution on the floor. All the microphones on the convention floor are lined with people waiting to testify—sisters and brothers. We have organized well. One brother from Puerto Rico testifies in Spanish—it is the only time Spanish is heard officially at the Convention.

The body accepted the resolution, and the final version included the formation of a Women's Leadership Development Committee to modify the Canadian *Women of Steel* course for use in the United States. By November 1993, the course was finalized, and thirty-seven facilitators were trained. These facilitators soon formed the nucleus of an activist core around women's issues in the union.

At the 1994 Constitutional Convention, the women introduced another *Women of Steel* resolution, with its own unique history, and held the same type of women's forum and speak out. Some of the women who facilitated the *Women of Steel* courses in District 6 and District 31 were involved in organizing the speak-out event and introduced the speakers. The union's top leadership at the time—George Becker, President; Leo Gerard, Secretary-Treasurer; and Leon Lynch, Vice President for Human Affairs—all made brief remarks to the group. The women were concerned that some of their key issues were not being addressed by the convention. They left the convention with a commitment from Becker to establish an advisory body at the International level.

Union Feminism

As a result of these events, a mobilizing network open to the ideas of feminism was taking shape in the Steelworkers. I asked women at various union events between 1996 and 1998 if they considered themselves to be feminists and if so, what that meant to them. For most it meant taking a stand for equality and for dignity for women as a group. Some women, like Sandy, had no hesitation about identifying themselves as feminists:

> I don't think a feminist is a four-letter word. I'm very proud to be one. It means a lot of things. I think mainly it means to me that I'm going to stand up for what I believe in and fight for what I believe in and that I recognize that there has been a lot of double standards. And I have to do my part, or try to do my part, in changing those double standards.

Betty Wickie, a white Canadian and a twenty-seven-year employee of Inco Metals, the world's largest producer of nickel, was an active member of her local's women's committee and in her community in antiviolence efforts. Justice and equality are a part of her understanding of feminism.

> Well, of course, I'm a feminist. I really get tired of people who say, "I'm not a feminist." I get really ticked off. There was an article in the paper where the editor was talking about legal justice and social justice and going on about things that had to get done, but she concluded with "but, I am not a feminist." I felt like strangling her. That's exactly what feminism is! And she was an editor. . . . You want to tell her, "The only reason you are an editor is because of the women's movement." I just think that it is the dictionary definition [of feminism] . . . economic equality and legal equality, social equality.[11]

For Colette Murphy, acquiring a feminist consciousness was a gradual process.

> Yeah, at one time, if you had asked me if I was a feminist, I would have said, "Are you kidding?" But I really look at myself as a feminist now because I believe in, you know, equality for women, and I fight very hard for it. Because that's what it's all about—equality for women. And the more I learned about it, the more I could identify. My goals were their goals. We all had to fight together, you know, to achieve them.[12]

Nancy Hutchinson, a white gold miner from Western Ontario and now director of health and safety for District 6 of the Canadian Steelworkers, told me she was a feminist but said she did not fit the stereotype the men in the union have of feminists.

> I hold myself to the view that I support women's issues. I fight for women's issues at the mine. I try and promote the women that I know to get involved in women's issues. When I have an opportunity to be present at the women's forum, I would always take the opportunity to go, and I want to see women advance in the workforce and life, generally.[13]

Some of the women approached the label with caution. Loureen Evans, an African American hospital worker and course facilitator from California, told me:

> I think. A little bit. I'm not going to say, "No." I think I am. I keep saying, "Not a whole lot," but then I keep saying, "Yes, you are" (laughs). And it's not a drawback. But I think if you had asked me this maybe five

years ago, I would have said, "No." I would have definitely told you, "No." But now I think I am, because I see where women, we've come a long way, but we've still got a long way to go. So, I think I am. Not all the way, but I think I am.[14]

Neither Stephanie Stallings, an African American forklift operator and the chair of her unit in an amalgamated local of small fabricating plants, nor Valerie Thomas, an African American foundry worker, identified as feminists because of their perceptions that you could not be a feminist and enjoy life or be involved with men. About identifying as a feminist Stephanie said:

> We do our work. We take our work seriously. But you will still catch us in a bar or a club. When we're out there organizing—we're out there for our purpose. . . . But when we go out for fun, we don't dress like we're going out to unionize. We don't fit what men think a steelworker woman should be. We're gonna wear our makeup; we're gonna put our earrings on. We're going out to flirt. We're gonna get the job done, but we're doing it in our way.[15]

Valerie added, "I don't think we are feminists."[16] Yet, as we talked more about the dating scene, they seemed to reevaluate their position on feminism. Both women said that men were intrigued by their nontraditional, blue-collar occupations, but that it was harder for men to accept their union activism. Again, Stephanie:

> If you're out with a guy and he says, "So what do you do for a living?" "I work at the steel mill." "You work at the steel mill? Oh, OK, baby, you making some money." "I'm also an organizer." "You're what? (Oh, no, she's too powerful for me)." Then, "Gosh, he was the perfect guy. What happened to him?" It's the independence. Last boyfriend I had, he told me, "Your problem is you're too independent." That's where I guess the feminism comes in, we are viewed as independent plus!

Domestic Violence

Domestic violence is one of the issues that surfaced in the accounts of how Stephanie and Valerie became more involved in the union. The *Women of Steel* course addresses the issue and often has women from the community visit the class and talk about local resources for battered women. Yet neither woman originally made any direct connection between feminism and the antiviolence movement. Stephanie and Valerie were proud of the fact that they had left abusive marriages and felt empowered by their actions. Stephanie's parents had not wanted her to marry in the first place. She felt she had let them down, and it was hard for her to tell them about the abuse. But it was harder still to live with it, or worse yet, perhaps die from it:

> I was a victim of abuse. Finally I got tired of him hitting on me. One day, you know, I said, "I'm going to get my divorce." And he was like, "You get a divorce, I'll kill you." That's what he told me. So the second time he beat me up I was like, "Well, you're going to kill me any way it goes." And I say, "I'm going to get my divorce." And I got my divorce. Just the fact of getting my divorce, paying for my divorce, getting out of that relationship was like I can handle anything. I'm bad, now. And that's when, at the same time, because I didn't have a husband anymore, it left me with more time. I didn't have to worry about staying out past an hour or going somewhere without permission. So I was able to go to the union meetings and do different stuff. So I became more active. And this was high reroute of my life. And then I began to be effective.

Stephanie and Valerie discovered that they shared similar histories with abuse and bonded, in part, on that basis. "We tell the same stories, the same incidents." Valerie adds, "I went through so much with Stephanie. . . . Stephanie kept my furniture from getting slashed up. She kept me from getting killed."

The Canadian Steelworkers developed a unique educational campaign against domestic violence for the membership entitled *Let's Put It on the Table*. The campaign frames domestic violence as a serious form of gender discrimination that should be addressed at home, at work, and in society. The union's analysis of domestic violence is rooted in an understanding of power differentials and inequality and takes into account forms of disadvantage and discrimination such as class, disability, race, and sexual orientation.

> Our society, based on unequal wealth, status, opportunity, and power is a breeding ground for abusive behavior. Because of their lack of economic and political power, women are especially vulnerable to acts of violence. Doubly disadvantaged women—women with disabilities, lesbians, Aboriginal and visible minority women are doubly vulnerable to acts of violence. ("Let's Put It on the Table," 12)

Furthermore, the responsibility to end violence against women is placed squarely on the shoulders of the membership. "In order to change the behaviour of violent men everyone's behaviour needs to change. . . . We can no longer turn our backs. . . . So let's put it on the table. On our table, the bargaining table, the community table and the family table" (13). The Canadian approach consists of working with women's organizations representing battered and abused women, publishing fact sheets and lists of referral services, developing educational materials for use at union functions, and working with women's committees to create safe environments for victims to seek support and help through the union. They bring the issue of domestic violence to the bargaining table by developing contract language aimed at preventing violence and offering services to survivors. These measures include conducting workplace safety audits, allowing women the right to refuse work if they are being harassed, and finally, giving women who have been assaulted inside or outside of the workplace the right to take necessary medical leave, obtain paid legal assistance, and seek counseling of their choice insured by the employer. Contracts can specify sexual harassment training for every worker.

Through political action, the Canadian Steelworkers lobby the government for tougher enforcement of criminal laws related to sexual assault and other acts of violence against women and increased government spending for shelters and interval houses, for treatment centers, for counseling services, and for victim/witness assistance programs. Finally, the union also mobilizes its members to participate in the national campaigns that address violence against women, such as the National Day of Remembrance and Action on Violence against Women and to discuss their issue in their families. The Canadian Steelworkers also represent the staff of battered women shelters and counseling centers, which promises to bring a deeper understanding to the union's violence-prevention work.

The struggle against domestic violence and sexual harassment can and does empower women to challenge other forms of discrimination. The experiences of Valerie and Stephanie suggest that leaving a violent relationship can serve as a springboard to union activism and that union activism inspires women to leave violent and dangerous relationships. Some of the women activists reported they were inspired by Anita Hill in the United States and Bonita Clark in Canada to speak about their own experiences of sexual harassment and to press their union to do something about it. Whether or not individual women recognize the role of feminism in efforts to end all forms of violence against women, it is clear that the discourse of feminism circulates freely within the union in Canada on this issue and that women members have been influenced by it. In the hands of union feminists, the feminist discourse on violence against women is refashioned in class-specific ways that resonate more effectively with working-class women in the Steelworkers.

Solidarity and Diversity

Among the issues I have explored during my interviews is race. Women of color face situations that are the result of their multiple identities and their positioning in the complex intersection of race, class, and gender. Loretta Tyler experienced racism and sexism in ways that were difficult to sort out. She describes the following exchange during negotiations with a particular supervisor:

> When I first walked in there, his [company representative] attitude was so bad. And I couldn't understand what I had done to cause him to be so angry or so antagonistic. And I remember asking the staff guy, "What's wrong with him. You know, you worked with him a lot of years, what's wrong with him?" And he said, "Nothing, I always got along fine with him." And so I couldn't figure out what it was. I couldn't figure out if it was because I was black, because he wasn't from a plant that had a high concentration of blacks. It just never dawned on me that it was because I was a woman. And I remember we sat down at this meeting, and he was so angry and so just vicious across the table. And I'm trying to figure out where's this guy coming from. And I said something, and he said, "Well, look, *lady.*" And I said, "You know what? You've got a problem. And it's your problem, not mine. And it's something that you're going to have to get over, 'cause I don't intend to change anytime soon. I'm going to do this job for a while, and I'm gonna be a woman for as long as I live. So you need to get over that."[17]

According to Loureen Evans, building solidarity and cohesion across racial and cultural lines was crucial but painful at times. Because of the multiple diverse groups involved, the process was complex and often difficult for both the rank and file and the activists. The *Women of Steel* course attempted to address this issue, but it did not always have the intended outcome. She felt she had to battle the defeatist attitude that where race is concerned, nothing will ever change:

> Maybe California is a little bit different, you know. I think you have to want to bridge those differences. You have to want to work together. And it's not an easy road, but you work at it. But you have to, you still have to get out there and say, "OK, we're going to make a difference. We have to

work together to bridge racial discrimination." And, I find that the women I have come in contact with also want the same thing. And we know that if we're going to continue on, we have to—even at my job—we have to sit down with different cultures and say, "OK, how can we work together? What do we need to do to try to bridge the bridges?" And sometimes I've been told, "Well, there's no way to do it. Everybody is prejudiced, no matter what and that's never going to leave." Well, I say "What can we do to take that feeling away from you?"

Diversity work carries a higher cost for the women of color involved in the course than for white women. Loureen acknowledges that cost but says it is one she is willing to pay if it results in bridge building between women of different races and cultural backgrounds. During one particularly difficult session of the course on diversity, she told the women they could ask her anything about being black. She was surprised and caught off guard by the type of questions they raised. "Why are so many blacks on welfare?" or "Why is it OK for one black person to call another black person 'n—' but not OK for me?" I asked her how she felt about those questions. "I guess I was thinking they were going to ask me things about the job or the union. 'OK', I said to myself, 'I'm outta here. Let me go.'" But she didn't go. She patiently answered the question about welfare with statistics, with the reasons people in general go on welfare, and with the acknowledgment that it is wrong to take advantage of the system if you do not need assistance. The name-calling question was emotionally more difficult to address but Loureen persevered. "After all I said they could ask anything at all." She answered the question this way, "My mother named me Loureen. I don't like it when someone calls me something else, whether it's white, black, or green person or what. And it's not OK for them to do that, and it's not OK for you to do it." Loureen turned the table on the audience and asked them how they would feel if it happened to them? And then she listened.

> I go back to listening—and I'm very good at listening. Hispanics feel disrespected. Asians say that no one takes the time to listen through the accents. I guess what happened at that table was we began to network with each other. We began to understand . . . what is not acceptable, what is acceptable. And we went away networking among our co-workers, and we were able to bridge some bridges. Now I'm not saying we bridged all the bridges. I think we were kind of uncomfortable there a little bit, but we were able to sit there and work together. It showed all of us that we can go out there and work together. But you have to want to do, to do it.

One line of difference not regularly confronted in the course or in most of the other *Women of Steel* initiatives was sexual orientation. Green reported that lesbians often disclosed their identity to facilitators of the course but did not feel safe coming out to the group. The 1994 *Women of Steel* resolution originally referred to lesbians and indigenous women as a way to broaden the discussion of diversity and to better reflect the Canadian inclusion of sexuality and indigenous people in their human rights codes. The organizers of this idea were told it would not fly in the United States because most of the membership did not know what the terms "lesbian" and "indigenous" meant. Labor leaders in Canada often include reference to gays and lesbians when talking about human rights more generally and participate in gay pride activities in Toronto. The Steelworkers in Canada have negotiated same-sex benefits into some first contracts and have developed model contract language to cover such benefits—even before the recent Canadian Federal and Provincial Court ruling requiring such benefits be awarded to gays and lesbians. Lesbians and their allies within the union are working to get the Steelworkers to add sexual orientation to the antidiscrimination clause of the basic contract.

The Canadian Steelworkers have been active in diversity training with the membership and with the companies with which they bargain. Marlene Gow, who was severed from her job after twenty-two years because her plant moved its production facility to the United States, was hired by the Steelworkers (under an NDP government initiative) to coordinate employee-equity programs and antiharassment training. Legislation required that unions and companies work together on developing workshops that addressed sex and race discrimination and on setting up complaint procedures. "Equity committees with equal union and company representation would sit down and go through every employment policy and every employment practice and look for barriers and then decide what accommodations would be made." Marlene told me that what companies see as barriers and what workers consider to be barriers are two different things and that they are often very far apart in their thinking. Even among union members there were differences of opinion about how to ensure equity. Religion was one issue that sometimes made them "wild" and disability was the other. Workers hurt on the job had to be accommodated even if it violated seniority. Marlene believed that the membership from the dominant group needed more education about why equity was a union issue. I asked her what she tells workers. "Well, I mean it's not different than a whole lot of other fights we've had. We're always looking for a fair workplace. We want people to be treated equally, I mean, that's sort of the basis of unionism, right? We're saying what's good for one is good for all. Everybody should be treated the same. Accommodation is ensuring that everybody has equal access, right?" I asked, "Even if you have to take into account differences?"

> Yes, that's right. Sometimes in the equity course we use the example of the fox and the stork. We said if you were going to feed these two animals, obviously, if you use the same dish, if you used a long narrow dish the stork is going to have the advantage. If you use a round flat dish, you know, the fox is going to have the advantage. So in order to feed them both equally, you're going to have to use a different container to offer them, you know, the same access, right, so that's sort of a simple way of putting it. Sometimes you have to treat people differently in order to really treat them the same, in order to ensure that they have equal access. You have to treat them differently."[18]

Sexual harassment is defined as one of the barriers to employment equity, and Marlene has considerable experience in working with the Steelworkers harassment policy. She trains workplace counselors to help workers deal with harassment on the job. They, in turn, serve as a resource for resolving situations, particularly those involving co-workers, before they escalate and become formal complaints. They also serve as mediators. Marlene is a skilled facilitator for the *Women of Steel* course, who described the experience to me as a "blood transfusion." She relates to the course on a personal level and sees the way it has benefited women who might not otherwise discover their talents. "I was so shy, so insecure, and if it hadn't been for the union I never would have grown into the person that I am. And, that's what I see starting to happen when you get women in there (to the course), it's the hook sometimes, right? You get them started and then they build from there."

Women's Committees

Women's committees, once resisted in the United States during the 1970s, have been established or revitalized in both countries at local, district, national, and international levels. The goals of the women's committee are to educate women about their rights on the job, the union about women's concerns, and the community about the union. Typically, these committees display a collectivist form of decision making, rotating the division of labor so that women gain as much organizational experience as possible. Men can and do participate in activities and serve on subcommittees. The rationale for creating women's committees is predicated on women's minority status in a male-dominated union and on their experiences of sexual harassment and sex discrimination on the job. According to the reference guide for the Canadian women's committees:

> In many workplaces: mines, factories, and offices, women are in a minority. The work environment—from the physical layout of the office or plant, to the behavior of management and the traditional "shop talk"— creates barriers to women's employment and training. In the retail and service sectors, where work is traditionally undervalued and underpaid and hours of work vary tremendously, women struggle to organize and fight for job security and decent wages. In every sector across Canada, women continue to face workplace harassment and discrimination.[19]

Women's committees afford women separate, autonomous space where they can strategically mobilize on behalf of their emerging interests as women. The committees provide women with the opportunity to develop leadership skills and help to facilitate the integration of women into all of the activities and programs of the union. The concerns of the women's committees focus on many of the standard issues of the women's movement including pay equity, balancing work and family, sexual harassment, domestic violence, sex discrimination, training and promotion opportunities for women, organizational representation, and empowerment. The leadership course and the women's conferences emphasis the importance of women forming and/or participating in women's committees and provide practical support and guidance for their development. The local women's committees are linked through thirty regional women's councils and district-wide women's committees.

Assessing the Impact of the *Women of Steel* Course

Hundreds of women in the United States and Canada have taken the *Women of Steel* course since it was first offered in 1992. Sue Milling of the Canadian national staff who helped to develop the course believes that the success of the course can be measured by what the women do with the information. She told me, "The course helps to raise awareness about issues like family leave, harassment, childcare. Now, what have they done with that knowledge? Have they, with the support of their local, bargained for something? Have locals changed their meeting times to accommodate women? Is childcare available? Do the women take more educational courses? Are they running for office? Can they sustain networks? Or do they become more active in their church or at home but not taking it to the union?"[20]

I observed a one-week session of the course held at the union's retreat center at Bayview-Wildwood, Ontario, in April 1999, and I conducted a random telephone survey of the Canadians who took the course between 1992 and 1999. Over the years I have also interviewed *Women of Steel* graduates and facilitators at various union events held in both countries (see Appendix B).

Consciousness-Raising Effects

One focus of my interviews has been on the meaning of activism and feminism. I asked Sandy Sutton, who is also a facilitator for the course in the United States, what she thought the course accomplished. She believes that the course builds solidarity across various lines of difference.

> We've had courses where there are women that have come from hospitals, come from the shop floor, come from offices, bus drivers. And they get together, and they find they have so much in common. No matter what their job, no matter what their nationality, what their race, religion.... And they talked about racial harassment, racial discrimination, racial diversity, and sexual harassment. You could see the group blending. You see how much understanding was developing. And to me that's what it's all about. It's being able to understand somebody you have never met—totally different backgrounds, different race, different religion, whatever—how much you really have in common.

The course employs a broad definition of activism, consistent with feminist approaches to politics. According to Cuneo (1993), union activism includes a wide range of activities from speaking up at meetings, talking about an issue at work, volunteering for routine tasks around the union hall, and participating in organizing drives. "Activism is the capacity and willingness to act, and the practice of taking the initiative, of beginning new actions, of going on the offensive, of making things happen rather than waiting for them to happen" (111). Sutton echoes this sentiment:

> It's not necessarily about developing the next president of the Steelworkers—but hopefully someday that'll happen. It's activating the women and showing them that they have the skills already to become active.... The great thing about [the course], it's a work in process. It changes every time you do it. I mean you have certain guidelines, but the real knowledge comes from the people, not the instructors.

Stephanie Stallings, an early participant in the course, employed the metaphor of "joining the table" to describe the consciousness-raising effects of the course:

I guarantee you—no matter who you are, how much education, how much you think you know yourself—once you go through the *Women of Steel* course, you're a different person when you come out. If as women we go to a union meeting [and] every time we go we think that we're supposed to sit in the back and keep our mouths shut, then we don't open our mouths. We don't speak out against men, because we don't know what will happen. But once we cross those borderlines to speak out against the men, boom! You can't sit at the back of the room anymore. You want to sit in the first table, in their seats.

For Loureen Evans the metaphor that best described her experience was "moving to the front." She characterized the effect of the course's public-speaking exercise in the following way:

I want you to know that was the longest walk that I've had to take. And I was sick every step I took, you know, it was long. . . . I would not have been able to do that if had not been . . . for the program, letting me know that I can do it, that it wasn't just about education. It was showing me that I can do it, saying, "You can get involved. You don't have to take a back seat. You can sit up front." I think my classmates think they've created a monster. . . Because I've been on the go ever since. I've been able to do more. I'm able to tell women, "You need to get involved."

Nancy Hutchinson underscored the importance of the course for bringing together women who rarely have the opportunity to meet and talk and for building confidence:

The women are so outnumbered at work they often only encounter each other in the 'dry' or shower. . . . In my situation the course was the only mechanism that I could see to bring women together. . . . The only real link that we have to get together is these courses. I've always been a strong personality . . . so I can talk on the floor. But without a woman having confidence or self-esteem, it may not help the next woman. So I think that these forums for women are so important. I've seen at this convention how a woman, who a year ago wouldn't have gotten up and said "Boo" in public, is speaking at a microphone—which is fantastic—thanks to the *Women of Steel* and other courses.

Survey Results

In the summer of 1999, I conducted a telephone survey of Canadian women Steelworkers who had taken the *Women of Steel* leadership course to assess the impact of the course on increasing their level of union participation and activism. Participants in the telephone survey were selected at random and were similar to the general female membership of the union in Canada. Characteristics of the respondents are shown in Table 6. The typical respondent was white, middle age, and married; affiliated with the NDP; and living in a household with an average income of $48,000 (Canadian). Nearly a third of the women had some college education and, because of their age, few had children living at home. In general, the respondents were women with the time and political interest to participate in union programs and were the ones most likely to be open to union activism and feminist goals. These women were also more likely to come to the attention of the union and to be targeted for leadership development. While this is an important group of women, other less visible women are being left behind.

Women were asked in the survey to indicate the general level of change in their union participation after taking the course and their level of union participation before and after they took the course (on eight specific dimensions) and to identify those factors that facilitated or hindered their participation in the union (Table 7). In a general measure of change in participation (data not shown in Table 7), 51 percent said their involvement had increased after taking the course, 39 percent said it had remained the same, and only 10 percent said it decreased. Overwhelmingly, women reported that their participation had increased as a result of the course.

On five of the eight specific dimensions of participation, the women reported statistically significant differences in their level of union participation after taking the *Women of Steel* course—attending meetings, speaking at meetings, serving on committees, volunteering, and attending programs, workshops, or conferences. The largest positive changes in participation were speaking at meetings, attending meetings, and committee service.

Women already had high rates of union participation before taking the course for two of the items—attending union meetings (88 percent) and voting in union elections (81.9 percent). While these two items showed improvement, the item "speaking at union meetings" showed the greatest positive change, from 55.4 percent to 73.5 percent. The course gave some women the confidence to speak up at meetings. Before-and-after differences for voting in union elections, running for office, and being elected to office were not statistically significant. While there was an increase from 45.8 percent to 56.6 percent in the number of women who ran for office after taking the course, the number elected fell slightly, from 59 percent to 55.4 percent. However, a closer look at the offices to which women were elected after taking the course revealed that they were running for and being elected

Table 6

Demographics of Canadian participants in *Women of Steel* course

Demographic characteristic	Percentage
Education	
Less than high school	25.3
High school	42.2
Some college	32.5
Average	11.96 years
Age	
17–34	10.8
35–44	33.7
45–54	44.6
55+	10.8
Average	45 years
Marital status	
Married	66.3
Single	14.5
Separated or divorced	19.2
Number of children living at home	
0	48.2
1	28.9
2	13.3
3	7.2
4	2.4
Average	0.9 children
Race	
White	90.4
Minority or indigenous	9.6
Party affiliation	
NDP	56.6
Liberal	1.2
All other	42.1
Average household income (in Canadian $)	$48,000

Source: Telephone interviews, 1999.

Table 7

Significance of change before and after completion of the *Women of Steel* course by type of participation (N = 83)

Type of participation	Before (%)	After (%)	Z value	Significance
Attend meeting	88.0	97.6	2.339082	p ≤ .01
Vote	81.9	88.0	1.015257	
Serve on committee	61.4	73.5	1.366978	p ≤ .05
Attend program	51.8	65.1	1.324076	p ≤ .05
Speak at meeting	55.4	73.5	1.952798	p ≤ .001
Run for leadership	45.8	56.6	0.990736	
Elected to office	59.0	55.4	−0.35446	
Volunteer	44.6	59.0	1.324422	p ≤ .05

to more influential positions on the executive board. Overall, there was a net gain of ten executive-board positions for women in the sample (Table 8).

The largest gain in executive-level positions was six vice presidencies. Other positions registering a positive change were four presidencies, three recording secretaries, and one financial secretary. At the executive level, the losses in positions were three treasurers and three bargaining committee members. There was a net loss of fifteen seats in non–executive-board positions. The largest decline, from eighteen to nine, was for steward. It may be the case that women holding lower-level offices were more likely to run for higher offices after taking the *Women of Steel* course (Table 9). The shop steward position often serves as a stepping-stone to higher office.

Women who had taken the course were asked to identify the factors they thought were important to increasing women's participation in the union (Table 9). The respondents cited union-sponsored courses and training programs as the most significant factor: 83.1 percent said they were very important. Next was the presence of a mentor (79.5 percent) followed by encouragement from local president and other officers (75.9 percent). Convenient meeting time and location were slightly less important than opportunities for education and training and the encouragement of local officers (Table 10).

Respondents were also asked to assess the outcome of taking the *Women of Steel* course (Table 10). More than half of the participants, 53 percent, strongly agreed that the course helped them to better understand the importance of networking with other women, and 51.8 percent strongly agreed that the course helped them to understand the importance of building solidarity among women. Half of the participants said they felt more confident about their abilities after taking the course, and nearly 40 percent said the

Table 8
Type of office respondents held before and after *Women of Steel* course

Type of office	Before	After
President	2	6
Vice president	1	7
Treasurer	6	3
Recording secretary	7	10
Financial secretary	2	3
Executive board	3	2
Subtotal, executive level	21	31
Negotiating committee	3	0
Unit chair	5	2
Unit vice president	1	0
Unit secretary	2	0
Steward	18	9
Grievance	2	1
Health and safety	4	6
Other	6	8
Subtotal, non-executive level	41	26
Total	62	57

Table 9
Factors that facilitate women's involvement in unions

Factor	Very important (%)	Somewhat important (%)	Not too important (%)	Not at all important (%)	Don't know (%)
Union-sponsored courses and training	83.1	14.5	2.4	0.0	0.0
Presence of a mentor	79.5	16.9	3.6	0.0	0.0
Convenient meeting time	68.7	27.7	3.6	0.0	0.0
Encouragement from local president and other officers	75.9	18.1	4.8	0.0	1.2
Presence of other women at union meetings and events	63.9	30.1	4.8	1.2	0.0
Convenient meeting location	62.7	25.3	8.4	3.6	0.0
Daycare at union meetings and events	48.2	31.3	13.3	4.8	2.4
Shorter meeting time	25.3	41.0	21.7	9.6	2.4

Table 10
Outcomes of taking the *Women of Steel* course (N = 83)

Outcome	Strongly agree (%)	Agree (%)	Disagree (%)	Strongly disagree (%)	Don't know (%)
Understand the importance of networking with women	53.0	45.8	0.0	0.0	1.2
Learned new things about how the union works	47.0	45.8	6.0	0.0	1.2
Importance of solidarity among women	51.8	39.8	6.0	0.0	2.4
Better communicator of ideas	39.8	51.8	8.4	0.0	0.0
More confident about abilities	50.6	38.6	10.8	0.0	0.0
Want to become more active	42.2	41.0	15.7	0.0	1.2

course helped them believe they could be better communicators of ideas. Forty-two percent strongly agreed and another 41 percent agreed that the course made them want to become more active in their local. To an open-ended question asking for a description of what they gained from the course (data not shown in table), the most common response was confidence. Ranking next were consciousness about women's issues, new information or knowledge about the union, solidarity and networking, voice, and finally a sense of empowerment. Only three respondents in the eighty-three completed interviews said they had gained nothing from the course.

The women were so satisfied with the course that a very high percentage (96.4 percent) would recommend the course to others (data not shown in table). Large numbers of respondents (89.2 percent) would also like the union to develop a follow-up course that would cover topics such as how to advance in the union, how to resolve conflict with management, and how to build better links with other groups in the community working on women's issues.

There were, however, perceived obstacles to taking another union course (Table 11). The largest obstacle was the lack of financial support from the local, which 48.2 percent of the women said was very important. Women were concerned that once they had received the funding to attend a course, they would not get funding to attend another course. Another obstacle was the perception that there were few opportunities in the local to use the skills learned in the course, so taking another course would be futile. This was a very important issue for 33.7 percent of the respondents and a somewhat important issue for 39.9 percent. Family issues ranked next in terms of obstacles, with 25.3 percent of the women listing time away from home

Table 11

Obstacles to taking another union course (N = 83)

Obstacle	Very important (%)	Somewhat important (%)	Not too important (%)	Not at all important (%)	Don't know (%)
Lack of financial support from the local	48.2	34.9	14.5	1.2	1.2
Lack of opportunity to use skills in the union	33.7	39.8	19.3	3.6	3.6
Time away from home	25.3	25.3	36.1	13.3	—
Lack of support from spouse or partner	22.9	20.5	33.7	21.7	1.2
Only woman in class	14.5	15.7	42.2	27.7	—

and 22.9 listing the lack of support from spouse or partner as very important. The smallest obstacle was concern about being the only woman in the class. Only 14.5 percent listed this as an important obstacle.

Linking course participants with local women's committees is one way the union builds on the momentum of the course and creates a more permanent structure for activism. According to the results of the telephone survey (data not shown in table), the women who take the course tended to maintain contact with other women in their local who have taken the course (80 percent). Almost half (45.1 percent) joined the women's committee in their local. The majority (65.2 percent) said they were motivated to join because of their interest in pursuing the issues covered in the course, and 43.5 percent said the encouragement of a union official was very important in their decision to join the women's committee. Those who joined (91.3 percent) reported that they did so because they valued the work done by women's committees and because they believed there was the need for women to have separate arenas to discuss issues like sexual harassment. The course created an incipient network that could mobilize women around specific feminist issues and campaigns.

While there is strong support for the women's movement in general and for the goals of the women's movement among my Canadian respondents, there was less of an inclination to identify as feminists. In response to the question, "Has the women's movement made a difference to you personally?" 71 percent said yes, it had made a difference. However, in response to the question, "Do you consider yourself to be a feminist?" only 36 percent responded yes. Close to 40 percent (39.8 percent) of the women said they had experienced sex discrimination or harassment on the job, and a

Table 12
Political participation (N = 83)

Political activity	Yes	No	Don't Know
Have you ever written a letter to your MP?	41.0	59.0	—
Have you met or telephoned your MP or your provincial legislator about a problem or concern?	37.3	62.7	—
Have you contributed money to a party or candidate?	36.1	62.7	1.2
Have you worked for a party or candidate in an election campaign?	30.1	69.9	—
Have you ever used e-mail to contact an MP or provincial legislator about a problem or concern?	7.2	92.8	—

Note: 20.5 percent said they would like to be more involved in political campaigns and elections. MP = member of Parliament.

relatively high percentage (66.7 percent) reported such discrimination to the union.

The women also supported policy initiatives like affirmative action that create special opportunities especially for women. Seventy percent agreed that management should increase the proportion of women in male-dominated occupations through special training and hiring initiatives. In terms of their identification with other women as a group, 48.2 percent said they paid a great deal of attention to issues in the news that especially affect women. Women did not want to choose between their class interests and their gender interests. When asked, "Is it more important for women like you to fight for the rights of all working-class people or all women or both equally?" 82 percent said both equally.

Women who had taken the *Women of Steel* course reported high levels of political participation (Table 12). Eighty-five percent of the respondents reported that they had written, telephoned, e-mailed, or met with a member of Parliament or the Provincial Legislature about an issue or problem of concern in the past three years. Thirty percent said they had worked for a party or candidate in an election, and 36.1 percent said they had contributed money to a party or candidate. Women also said that they preferred to participate in the political process through their union (57.8 percent) rather than directly as an individual (31.3 percent). Twenty percent said they would like to be more involved in politics, and the number one reason they gave for not being more involved in politics was the belief that "politics is all talk and no action." The second most-cited reason for lack of involvement was that political activities did not fit with their schedule.

Women in the survey were already predisposed to political activism, and the course appeared to tap into that predisposition. Women reported that they spoke up more at meetings and were willing to run for executive board positions. Many were eager for new levels of participation but did not always believe their talents and interests would be utilized. They believed in the union (more than 30 percent wanted to help organize new workers) but refused to choose between the women's movement and the labor movement. Because women tended to keep in touch with other women who have taken the course and to join women's committees, the course also served as a mobilizing structure for future political action. While the majority did not identify as feminist, most believed they had benefited from the women's movement and supported many of the issues of concern to feminists. Their high level of political participation indicated that these women believed that they could be heard in public policy debates either as citizens or as union members. The course helped them to develop the skills and confidence to voice their opinions.

Conclusion

It is not surprising that union feminism would emerge in one of the few remaining international unions. The dual-nation status of the union provided activists with expanded political opportunity structures, and union feminists and labor activists in both countries took full advantage of these opportunities. Even though many were later repealed, the gender-equity initiatives enacted in Ontario when the NDP government was in power (1990–1995) gave feminists just enough resources and the leverage they needed to institutionalize a response to some of the long-standing demands of women Steelworkers in both countries. These initiatives created the infrastructure of resources—people with expertise in pay equity, women's leadership development, etc.—which had an impact on the union even after the NDP lost the next election.

Structural experiences of sex discrimination and sexual harassment did not in themselves raise women's consciousness about the need for political action. For some of the women, like Stephanie, the union taught her how to stand up for herself and, to use her word, "reroute" her life. This generalized sense of empowerment enabled her to leave a violent relationship and to help others do the same. This left her with more time for union work. Highly visible cases of sexual harassment in both countries galvanized key activists who put pressure on the union to take action. Through its violence-prevention campaign and its policy on sexual harassment, the Canadian Steelworkers are leading the way in transforming these seemingly private issues into more public workplace issues. Women Steelworkers in Canada are redefining what it means to be safe on the job. Responses to violence and sexual harassment through collective bargaining agreements have not been institutionalized in the United States because there is little legislation requiring unions and employers to do so.

Distinctions in equity discourses and law between the countries have created greater flexibility in developing collective action frames for union feminism. The Canadian discourse of multiculturalism and human rights has provided the space for activists and the union to think about equality and difference in more productive ways. Solidarity across lines of difference is mobilized by a human rights discourse that maintains that all people are entitled to basic rights by virtue of their membership in humanity. At the same time, the discourse of multiculturalism ensures that cultural differences are not suppressed. Unity through recognition of difference is at least a possibility in the Canadian context. The U.S. labor movement has never been able to reconcile group claims (affirmative action) with individual rights (seniority), and the government has actively turned against affirmative action as an important tool to end discrimination. This means that U.S. activists often turn to the elegant discourse of the civil rights movement. African American women Steelworkers framed their collective identity as "Women of Steel" and their activism in terms of "moving to the front from the back of the room" or as "taking a place at the front table." Civil rights activists in the United States have in turn inspired their Canadian sisters of color who find they must struggle to hold their nation and their union accountable to the ideals of human rights and multiculturalism. Canadian multiculturalism is not an uncontested concept and its meaning is highly context-specific depending on "who initiates it, on what theoretical and practical grounds, and why" (Bannerji 2000, 125).[21]

Understanding women's participation in the Steelworkers helps us to understand the ways in which gender consciousness and feminism are influenced by institutional location. These women form a collective identity as "Women of Steel" and as union feminists in the course of day-to-day struggles against sexism, racism, homophobia, and class inequities. Transforming these experiences into a political claim for rights occurs in the separate spaces that women have carved out for themselves in a male-dominated union. Gender equity is being framed for them in a particular way by their union—a union that is situated in two different political fields. Therefore, studying the lives of specific groups of working-class women and their struggles for dignity on the job can help us to understand the special forms and complex meanings of feminism for diverse groups of women. Such knowledge could prove useful to other unions interested in organizing women and in increasing the participation of women in union life. Such knowledge could be just as important to feminists who wish to create a more inclusive women's movement. A productive partnership between women and unions depends on it.

8

Building Feminist International Solidarity in the Age of Globalization

We think it is absolutely necessary to define human rights and labor rights from our own perspectives as women and rewrite international and national laws.

—Angeles Lopez

The words above are those with which Angeles Lopez, Women's Coordinator of the Frente Auténtico del Trabajo (Authentic Labor Front) of Mexico, opened the Canadian National Women's Conference of the United Steelworkers of America on 7 March 1999. The theme of women's international solidarity was chosen to celebrate the fiftieth anniversary of the United Nations Declaration of Human Rights, and the conference was organized to coincide with International Women's Day. The goal was to situate women's economic rights within the broader context of women's citizenship rights and human rights. But first, Lopez believed, it would be necessary to raise women's consciousness about their own human rights—their "rights to have rights" (Figure 11).

The Canadian Steelworkers' Conference was part of a larger campaign called "For Respect of Human and Labor Rights of Women" that was jointly developed by women labor activists and feminists from Mexico, Canada, Guatemala, Mozambique, Peru, and Bolivia. The campaign consisted of conferences, workshops, worker-to-worker exchange programs, posters, press conferences, testimonials, tribunals, pamphlets, flyers, buttons, stickers, and *fotonovelas* designed to raise political consciousness and to help women

Figure 11. Daina Green (left) and Angeles Lopez (right) talk with María de Jesús Sánchez Requñez, a metal worker from Mexico at the Canadian National Women's Conference, March 10, 1999, Toronto. Photograph by Lisa Blanchette.

become better advocates of their own rights.[1] The campaign was rooted in an analysis of sexism that attended to the cultural specifics and to the structural dimensions of inequality and emphasized the interconnections between public and private forms of discrimination and domination. According to the campaign's planning document, the "discrimination of women is produced, maintained and reproduced through social organization itself, via institutions, laws, educational systems, values, media and cultural patterns—particularly those that assume that women have principal responsibility for the family and for housework."[2]

One objective of the campaign was to reposition the issue of violence against women and the violation of women's labor rights as human rights violations. These rights include the right to be free of sexual harassment and domestic violence, the right to join unions, the right to participate in politics, the right to work in a safe environment, and the right to a decent standard of living. This re-reading of human rights laws and conventions from a woman-centered perspective is necessary, according to Lopez, because women have historically been excluded from many of the decision-making arenas and implementation structures of these human rights accords and covenants.

She believes women must become "active subjects" in the defining, exercising, and enforcing of their basic human rights. She told the audience of about five hundred that "there are conventions and laws that state women and men have the same rights, yet we, as women, experience the violation of those rights every day. We have been virtually excluded from the UN Declaration of Human Rights."

Discursive efforts to reframe women's rights (including their rights as workers) as human rights is consistent with the general strategy used by transnational feminists to expand political networks by linking the rights of women to human rights campaigns and organizations and to popular-democracy movements.[3] Recasting political rights as human rights opens up civic space where individuals can develop a sense of themselves as political subjects and can be mobilized to reclaim citizenship rights (Blacklock and Macdonald 1998; Naples and Desai 2002; Rowbotham and Linkogle 2001). By linking the violation of a woman's right to basic safety and bodily integrity in the privacy of her own home to the violation of her rights at work and in society more generally, feminists are helping to broaden the base of support for both women's rights and the rights of workers. By refusing to separate the public from the private, they are helping to demonstrate how international law and strategies for economic integration are often built on a foundation that tries to maintain a false separation of these mutually constitutive spheres (Blacklock and Macdonald 1998, 50).

Opportunities for working-class women and their advocates to come together across national borders are rare, and networks and events like the union's Canadian Women's Conference provide women the political space to discover common concerns and to forge strategic alliances in the face of remote and impersonal global forces. According to Lopez, "We are learning what the global economy looks like from where women walk. Women who bear the greatest burdens of globalization are building international connections to make sure that social issues stay on the agenda. Women are fighting for their rights and searching for alternatives. We are not where we started, but we are not where we want to be. It is important not to just reject but to propose alternatives—to recover our right to imagine the kind of society and world and family we want" ("Women of Steel Go Global").

The global economy and the geopolitics it has spawned constitute the political environment in which feminists and other social movements concerned with social justice and economic redistribution must operate—an environment that simultaneously produces constraints and opportunities for collective action. My goal in this chapter is to analyze how women labor activists and feminists in Mexico, Canada, and the United States are using transnational union networks and resources to construct a feminist political response to the pressures of globalization and economic restructuring. Women's activism within the cross-border labor networks of the Steelworkers has become a site for the emergence and construction of feminist international solidarity—an important site for building transnational coalitions for women's rights. International feminist solidarity is being socially constructed through union networks of struggle and political action. Organizational identity as "Women of Steel" serves as the basis for that solidarity.[4]

The success of social movements seeking to mobilize working-class women within the context of globalization will depend on the ability of such movements to develop culturally specific frames of action, collective identities, and mobilizing structures that connect the local with the global. Their efforts to build solidarity across various lines of cultural and social difference will have to be achieved without suppressing the political significance of these differences. What are the issues, discourses, organizing strategies, and structural formations that facilitate this type of solidarity work? What is the potential impact of women's activism on the union's efforts to mediate the effects of globalization and economic restructuring on workers in Canada, the United States, and Mexico?

Gender and Globalization

Globalization is a gendered process—although often in very contradictory ways. "Gender appears to be less important in understanding the global political economy and at the same time, more of a determining factor in its transformation. On the one hand, it is widely recognized that restructuring means a relative increase in the proportion of women exposed to direct market forces" while also "harmonizing" the work experiences of some men and women (Bakker 1996, 7). Women's labor-force participation has increased worldwide because of the growth of the service sector and because of the growing significance and expansion of the informal sector and non-standard forms of labor. By contrast, gender convergence occurs because more men (some of whom were displaced from manufacturing jobs) are moving into the service sector—the traditional domain of women. This is even more pronounced in Mexico, where masculinization of the maquiladora sector is occurring as men find employment in the same sector as women, though they typically perform different jobs. The growing participation of men in the maquiladora workforce is the outcome of growing product diversity and the use of high-tech equipment, which requires more managers and technicians (La Boltz 1992).[5]

The gendered dimension of globalization and restructuring is also reflected in the increasing growth of female-headed households on a world scale and in the accompanying feminization of poverty. In addition, women are more likely than men to curtail consumption and to increase their domestic workload to compensate for household-income loss. Women are also more directly affected by reductions in social welfare spending and public programs. The privatization of public services often means that these services are shifted from the paid work of women in the public sector to the unpaid labor of women in the domestic sphere, thus cuts in public employment also disproportionately affect women. Finally, labor flexibility—a hallmark of globalization—has resulted in the proliferation of nonstandard jobs, which are disproportionately filled by immigrants and women of color (Brodie 1995; Jamal 1998; Ng 1998).

Although often painted as an economic imperative, economic restructuring and the structural adjustment policies that accompany globalization have a differential impact on countries, regions, and different groups of workers whose gender, race, nationality, education, etc., have structured their location in the labor market in different ways (Bakker 1996; Cohen 1997). Because gender exists in relation to other determinants of power, not all women experience the effects of restructuring in the same way. Some women benefit from globalization while other women (and men) are victimized by the process (Gabriel and Macdonald 1994; Ng 1998; Jamal 1998). Sector location—which is already structured by race, class, and gender—plays an important role in determining how workers will fare in both the domestic and the global economy. For example, the flight of capital encouraged by free-trade agreements (like the North American Free Trade Agreement) has resulted in the loss of jobs in manufacturing and textiles for workers in Canada and the United States and in an increase in the exploitation of girls and young women in the maquiladoras of Mexico.[6] There are now nearly one million maquiladora workers, the majority women, employed in thousands of factories throughout Mexico. Alongside the explosion of low-wage factory jobs in what were once peripheral countries has come the reperipheralization of the core—the coming home of sweatshops to take advantage of the home market and cheap immigrant labor. "Global capitalism has meant the feminization of labor worldwide and the ethnicizing of labor on the home front" (Appelbaum 1996, 298). Fewer restraints on trade and the easier flow of capital back and forth across borders has contributed to a situation where workers from the South migrate North only to find jobs in the same kind of sweatshops they left behind.[7]

Feminism and Trade Activism

As a political environment, globalization has reconfigured the opportunities for politics and the repertoires for collective action available to social movements. For that reason, it is important to situate the emergence and development of transnational forms of feminist solidarity within this ever-changing social, cultural, and political environment. Union feminists with structural ties to organized labor and to the women's movement are in a unique position to mobilize within both movements in response to the issues and concerns that rapid economic globalization raises for women workers. Union and feminist advocacy networks provide working-class women with the opportunity to participate in this ongoing construction of transnational labor solidarity. Union feminists challenge the traditional notions of class-based solidarity of the labor movement by acknowledging the differences of gender and race within class and of the gender-based solidarity of the women's movement by acknowledging the class differences among women. The formation and articulation of gender-specific, class-based political claims changes the boundaries of those included and excluded in the process of class formation, thus creating new types of political claims and new solidarities—what Curtin (1999) labels contingent solidarities (160). In the case of union feminists, these contingent solidarities are mediated through organizational affiliation and collective identification with a specific union.[8]

Because of globalization, the opportunities for political action and the sites for feminist class-based activism are increasingly transnational and more varied. Some feminists and other social activists are paying closer attention to the changing role of the state in regulating and managing the economy and to the emerging transnational sites where these decisions are made. Transnational union networks as well as the global feminist networks (strengthened by the UN Conferences on Women, the United Nations Development Fund for Women, Ford Foundation, etc.) are being coopted by union feminists who are struggling to have a policy impact on both nation states and on the increasingly powerful but less transparent, supranational private institutions like the World Trade Organization (WTO), the World Bank, and the International Monetary Fund.

The Canadian women's movement has been very attuned to the domestic consequences of trade agreements in restructuring the global economy and to the constitutive relationships between globalization, race, culture, and gender. If Canadian feminists wanted to protect gender-equity gains, particularly for working-class women, from downward harmonizing pressures of U.S. corporations operating in Canada, they had to be attuned.

Tension between Canadian feminists who lobbied the state for liberal reform measures against sex discrimination and those who saw the interests of women more in terms of class inequities came into sharp focus during the mid-eighties. According to Bashevkin (1991), the liberal reformers held sway as long as they could get results from the state. However, once their successes made the women's movement more visible, conservatives in Canadian politics began to challenge state funding for feminist projects. Radical feminists began to question the effectiveness of a women's movement that was so closely allied to the state. Could the women's movement's critical edge be coopted by the state? Would institutionalization transform a radical protest movement into another interest lobby or pressure group? Globalization and economic restructuring, which had already begun to jeopardize important social democratic and gender-equity advances that feminists and labor had wrestled from the state, exacerbated these tensions. They came to a head within the Canadian women's movement when the National Action Committee (NAC) attempted to carve out a position on "free trade."[9]

The NAC based its position on the research of feminist economist Marjorie Cohen (1997), who served as the vice president of NAC and whose work is respected within labor circles, including the Steelworkers. NAC argued that the costs of "free trade" would be higher for workers who were already at a disadvantage in the workforce. Women workers who were disproportionately segregated in light-manufacturing industries such as textiles, clothing, and electronics were much more vulnerable to job loss caused by the flight of capital to markets such as Mexico where labor costs were lower. It would also be difficult for displaced women with little mobility to find new jobs paying manufacturing wages—this was particularly true for immigrant women. Finally, the incursion of multinationals into the female-dominated service sector might affect Canadian women in ways that were not even predictable. NAC was successful in linking women's issues to economic policy by showing that equality gains for women in the workplace were being undermined by the reduction in spending for the social-welfare policies that had made it possible for women to balance work and family. Threats to the Canadian welfare state were framed as threats to women's liberation and to a decent standard of living for working-class families.

The NAC's participation in coalitions against free trade brought a gender analysis of globalization to the debates surrounding trade issues. Likewise, NAC was able to strengthen its understanding of global economic issues and to share its new wisdom with its member groups and organizations. Fears that NAC would lose its focus on women by participating in more general political networks, such as the Ontario Coalition against Free Trade and the Pro-Canada Network, did not materialize. NAC's participation in the Pro-Canada Network placed it in closer contact with organized labor, including the Steelworkers, and did much to challenge the notion that feminists were indifferent to the needs of working-class women. It also helped labor to see that trade was indeed a feminist issue. According to Bashevkin (1991), NAC anticipated the possibility of feminist interests being coopted by its strategic partners in the new alliances formed in opposition to free trade. NAC astutely maintained its traditional alliances with smaller feminist coalitions and protected its independent identity as the leading representative of the Canadian women's movement.

Canadian anti-free-trade activism, at first, was centered on the Canadian–United States Free Trade Agreement—the precursor to NAFTA—and was nationalist in tone. Much of its energy was directed at the United States—not an optimal situation for building transnational solidarity. The acclaimed writer and feminist Margaret Atwood compared the domination of the Canadian economy by U.S. economic interests to male domination of women. She wrote in the *Globe and Mail*, "Canada as a separate but dominated country has done about as well under the United States as women, worldwide, have done under men; about the only position they've ever adopted toward us, country to country, has been the missionary position, and we were not on top" (quoted in Bashevkin 1999, 141). According to Bashevkin (1999) there was a 20-point gender gap in support for NAFTA, with women much more likely to oppose it.

However, with NAFTA, it became more apparent to both labor and the women's movement that trade was a transnational issue requiring oppositional strategies that reach across borders. As one of the few remaining internationals, the Steelworkers—a union well aware of the implications of globalization—was poised to play a leading role in the growing opposition to free trade developing in the United States. The understanding of globalization that the Canadians brought to the union had been informed by feminist arguments about the gendered nature of globalization. In addition, the Canadian Steelworkers already had well developed ties with anti-NAFTA forces to the south—particularly in Mexico. Some of these networks had been influenced by class-conscious feminists working in nongovernmental organizations (NGOs) and in popular movements for democracy.

Few if any feminist organizations in the United States took up the issue of free trade as a core feminist issue, and most did not address the issue until the mid-nineties.[10] Nevertheless, U.S. feminists were attuned to women's status in other parts of the world. In fact, the active and deepening participation of U.S. feminists in transnational feminist networks is perhaps one of the major positive developments in the U.S. women's movement of the last decade. The growth of these international ties has been facilitated by technology and by a number of international forums sponsored by the United Nations. These conferences and forums on women were magnets for bringing together feminists from grassroots campaigns and from nongovernmental agencies. These conferences have produced new discourses on global feminism and a common language for addressing women's rights as human rights.

The Ford Foundation was "light years ahead of other major foundations" on funding for women's projects devoted to improving women's status in various parts of the world. Their work began in 1974, when at the insistence of feminists, the International Division of the Ford Foundation created a Committee on Women. The mission of the committee was to develop programs to promote social justice for women both as an end in itself and as a means of furthering economic development by utilizing women's resources more fully (Hartmann 1998, 170). Ford began to fund a range of far-reaching activities geared toward this end involving research, public information, policy reports, conferences, women's leadership training, and experimental development projects.[11]

A few of these projects are detailed in a special report, "Now It's a Global Movement," published by Ford (2000). Feminists argue that linking economic rights to human rights is essential as global feminism moves into the next millennium. Charlotte Bunch, director for the Women's Global Leadership at Rutgers University, contends that in light of the growing economic disparity between nations and between classes of workers within nations it would be hard to ignore the globalization of the economy as a feminist issue. She sees economic justice and human rights as interconnected. "In the human rights arena, we see that as hard as it is to stop torture, it's a lot harder to stop economic exploitation because it is more complicated. But this is also the one place where human rights principles can be useful, as they demand that economic systems be held responsible for their impact on people's lives" (Thom 2000, 32). Gita Sen, an activist and economics professor at the Indian Institute of Management in Bangalore and founding member of Development Alternatives with Women for a New Era (DAWN), argues that feminists must hold governments accountable for the impact of economic and political decisions on the lives of women. "We have to recognize that the levers of economic power have shifted, yet we in women's organizations can't ignore the need to work to transform our own states so that they become more responsive to our demands" (32).

However, scholars of feminists politics are also aware that an exclusive focus on the state as the site of politics excludes the majority of women's political activity as well as the politics of the private sphere (Naples 1998; Randall and Waylen 1998; Shanley and Narayan 1997). Working-class women, particularly women of color, have always had a different relationship to the state, and their activism and movements have been more mobile (Sandoval 2000). Union feminists extend their activism beyond the workplace and the state to the homes and neighborhoods of working-class families. This "bread-and-roses" approach to activism still resonates with contemporary union feminists around the world as they attempt to bring issues like domestic violence, reproductive and sexual freedom, and women's empowerment into the international debate about workers' rights and human rights. This is particularly true in Latin America, where feminism is more intertwined with popular movements for democracy that focus on a broader range of issues. Union feminists are in a position, structurally, to convey to the labor movement the value of feminist analysis for understanding politics in terms of the need for both gender-specific and gender-neutral approaches and for ways in which the role of the everyday is ripe for mobilization. Thus, women's increased activism in unions has the potential of expanding the labor movement beyond the workplace to include community-based organizations and allies (Cobble 1994; Needleman 1998).

Globalization, Fair Trade, and the Steelworkers

Labor is also increasingly turning to the discourse of human rights as a device to frame the rights of workers internationally and turning to transnational forms of opposition politics (Gordon and Turner 2000; Turner et al. 2001). The Steelworkers have adopted and, in some cases, modified the demands and rhetoric of the International Labor Organization (ILO) and human rights organizations to frame international solidarity. The Steelworkers are very active in the transnational campaign to build labor standards, environmental accords, and basic human rights protections into trade agreements and their regulatory bodies. The Steelworkers, who played a prominent role in organizing opposition to the WTO, frame their opposition to globalization in class terms. They seek not to eliminate trade but to change the rules for trading.

> Unless the WTO is fundamentally changed to include core labor rights and environmental accords, workers must call on their government to take whatever steps are necessary to replace it with a set of global trading rules that work for working families. No working person should be forced to sacrifice their hard-earned economic security or occupational safety to satisfy the greed of global corporations. No citizen should have to surren-

der their rights to advance the power grab of international financiers. To prevent further injustices like these, our government must radically reorder its priorities. It must incorporate worker rights, rising living standards and the protection of our environment as fundamental elements of the global trading regime. ("Globalization—Making It Work for Workers")[12]

The Steelworkers and the labor movement are fashioning a more transnational response to the economic pressures of the global economy.[13] To be effective these strategies will have to be informed by an understanding of how gender, race, culture, and nation situate men and women differently (Bakker 1996; Gibson-Graham 1996; Sassen 1998).[14] The Steelworkers— who have become more aware of the need to look to alternative forms of political activism, to construct new alliances, and to develop new sites for organized politics—have become somewhat more open to the women's movement and feminist ideas. Through worker exchanges, conferences, educational programs, and development projects, union feminists in the Steelworkers are helping their union to understand the implications of the global economy for women.

The Steelworkers' efforts to build international solidarity and transnational forms of politics occur at multiple sites, some of which are more accessible to women and feminists than others. These sites include international labor federations and secretariats such as the International Confederation of Free Trade Unions, the International Metalworkers' Federation, and the International Federation of Chemical, Energy, Mine, and General Workers' Union (which have their own women's committees); UN forums and organizations such as the ILO and the People's Summit; regional trading structures created to arbitrate the side agreements under NAFTA; and international and national NGOs.

Within the labor movement, the Steelworkers are playing a leading role in pushing the AFL-CIO to develop new approaches to politics that recognize the changing political climate brought by globalization. These include participation in mass mobilizations like the one at the WTO meeting in Seattle, the construction of ongoing internal education and organizing about international solidarity, pursuing corporate campaigns that transcend national boundaries, devising pension investment strategies and stakeholder initiatives that challenge corporate practices that abandon workers and their communities, and building and strengthening ties with international labor bodies.[15]

In transnational political opportunity structures, feminists may actually have more experience than labor (Waterman 1998). Union feminists, who have organizational links in transnational feminist networks and who have participated in the campaigns and forums that address gender-specific concerns internationally, can mobilize women within the union to participate in the union's solidarity-building efforts. They are also in a position to advise the union on how to work in broader transnational networks—some of which will be feminist. Increasingly, these structures for unions include international law, NGOs, UN tribunals, conferences and resolutions, human rights campaigns, and cross-border organizing (Keck and Sikkink 1998; Sassen 1998; Smith 1997b).

To maximize their impact on fair trade, on the U.S. front the Steelworkers have developed a new political-action structure called Rapid Response that engages in direct forms of political action on issues of concern to Steelworkers and mobilizes support for these issues among the membership. These actions range from conventional petition and letter-writing campaigns to mass rallies in protest of trade policy. The Steelworkers have also created a program to train the rank and file to lobby, and some Steelworkers are running for office at state, local, and national levels. According to Jim English, Secretary-Treasurer of the International, this initiative came about in part because of the unresponsiveness of the U.S. government to the concerns of labor, in part because of the pace of globalization, and in part because of the need to educate members about the effects of economic policy on their work life. In some cases the membership was allowing conservative social issues like gun control and abortion to obscure their understanding of broader class issues like trade.[16]

Because of technology, the pace of politics has quickened and the emphasis of the Rapid Response is on speed—how quickly the membership can be mobilized to respond.[17] Whether these new approaches to politics and mobilizing structures can accommodate the gender-specific interests of women is yet to be seen. There are, however, some promising developments. One of the two national coordinators of Rapid Response is an African American woman, Glenda Williams, who brings a history of civil rights activism and much energy to the task. In addition, four of seven Rapid Response district coordinators in the United States are women.

Labor and NGO Networks: The Steelworkers Humanity Fund

One site where women are playing a significant role in building transnational solidarity is the Steelworkers Humanity Fund in Canada. The Humanity Fund is a labor NGO established by the union in 1985 that supports thirty-one international aid and development projects in thirteen countries located throughout the Third World—including seven women's NGOs in Bolivia, Mexico, Peru, Nicaragua, Bangladesh, South Africa, and Guatemala.[18] The Humanity Fund is involved in development education and in policy and advocacy work in the areas of workers' rights, food self-sufficiency, structural adjustment, and north/south relations. Their educational activities include a labor course called "Thinking North-South," mini-schools, and worker-to-worker exchange programs. Workers from Canada visit participating programs and projects in the south. According to the Humanity Fund's newsletter, "Each program becomes a window through which Canadian steelworkers can get a glimpse of the lives, issues and struggles of working people in another part of the world" ("Steelworkers Humanity Fund at a Glance," 1998, 2). The worker-to-worker exchanges create opportunities for direct interaction between workers and encourage discovery of common concerns and sharing of information. All projects sponsored by the fund are required to reflect principles of gender equity, democratic participation, and environmental sustainability. While the fund is expanding programs with other labor NGOs and worker organizations in Latin America and in southern Africa, it continues to support indigenous NGOs working on basic needs and in policy areas relevant to popular/social movements. The fund's advocacy work attempts to bring the problems of developing countries back home to Canada, helping its members to understand that responsibility for poverty and suffering in the south rests with policies of governments and of institutions in the north. The fund has formed working relations with other transnational advocacy campaigns and networks concerned with economic justice and fair-trade relations between the north and south ("Steelworkers Humanity Fund at a Glance," 1998, 2).

The Steelworkers have joined a growing network of labor NGOs involved in developing a new, more extensive approach to international solidarity work. Because they are organically linked to large, membership-based organizations, labor NGOs are different from standard, constituency-based NGOs. Labor NGOs have a large resource base from which to draw support and can also use preexisting communications networks to disseminate information about the lives of workers in other parts of the world and to raise consciousness about international solidarity. For example, Steelworkers and their employers contribute to the Humanity Fund through a payroll-deduction plan negotiated into collective-bargaining agreements. The integration of the Humanity Fund into the ongoing work of the union builds a more active and knowledgeable membership base that can be mobilized into international solidarity work. Union members receive regular reports

on Humanity Fund activities at union meetings, at conferences and workshops, and through union publications and the Web site.

As an active member of the Canadian Council for International Cooperation, the main umbrella group of NGOs in Canada, the Humanity Fund
is in a position to network with other NGOs and to raise issues concerning
labor rights and standards before a broader audience. The Steelworkers Humanity Fund maintains a presence in Common Frontiers—an interagency
network that engages in research and in policy and advocacy work on economic integration, free-trade agreements in the Americas ("Steelworkers
Humanity Fund: Partner Profile," 1998, 9). The Humanity Fund also supports projects undertaken by its partners in the "third world" that are linked
with regional and international advocacy networks.

At the insistence of feminists and women activists within the Steelworkers, gender must be addressed in each organization's proposals for project
funds. Projects must demonstrate how the design, implementation, and
evaluation of the project incorporates the involvement of women and how
projects will affect gender and the division of labor, property relations, and
access to education and training opportunities. The Steelworkers' District 6
women's committee helped to produce the Steelworkers Humanity Fund
Gender Statement. They collaborated with women in the south through
letters, visits, and direct interviews and learned that development activities
may affect women differently than men and that these activities may in
fact reinforce inequality, women's invisibility, or marginality. "Development
activities have historically affected women differently than men. This reflects
the greater poverty and dependence women experience in most parts of the
world and the inequality of women relative to men in their political, economic and social power." In order to be proactive, the gender equity statement encourages projects that

> bring women together to identify their practical and social needs in a
> way that considers women's additional reproductive and productive re-
> sponsibility;
>
> ensure the active participation of women in needs assessment, in project
> design, delivery, and monitoring and in the evaluation and dissemina-
> tion of project outcomes;
>
> contribute to the social, political, and educational advancement of women
> as they define such progress for themselves;
>
> enhance women's economic stability and self-sufficiency; and promote
> women's freedom from violence and other forms of oppression. ("Gen-
> der and Solidarity")

The Humanity Fund encourages projects that help women to discover their own unique approaches to empowerment and to develop leadership and communication skills through their participation in community-based organizations serving women. For example, the Women's Integral Training Institute (IFFI) received money from the Humanity Fund for an educational program involving about 750 women from more than forty women's organizations working in poor urban neighborhoods in Bolivia. "Using participatory techniques and activities" the curriculum seeks "to increase the capacity for women to exercise and influence power in both their private and public lives" ("Gender and Solidarity"). According to Carmen Zabalaga, IFFI's Director, "We're involved in teaching women about their rights, and have been successful in our campaign to enact legislation prohibiting domestic violence. Unless we get involved politically, our work won't be self-sustaining. We have to institutionalize change if we want it to endure."[19] In Lima, Peru, the fund supports an NGO working to develop communication skills among women in working-class and poor neighborhoods by training them to become "popular" communicators and "neighborhood journalists." The women learn to produce pamphlets, newsletters, and leaflets and to use local radio and video to publicize issues that affect women, such as domestic violence ("Gender and Solidarity"). Other projects have a strong economic component and seek to help women produce, market, and manage their own economic activities. For example, the Humanity Fund supported a program providing credit, training, and technical assistance to five hundred women in various grassroots organizations in Nicaragua. The program's goal was to help "women find alternative means of economic survival and sustainability for themselves and the families they support" ("Economic and Political Empowerment of Poor Women in Nicaragua"). Many of the projects combine support for women's activities in the community with support for their activities in the workplace.

Women of the Authentic Labor Front

Women Steelworkers have formed a partnership with the Women of the Authentic Labor Front (Frente Auténtico del Trabajo [FAT]). Although now a secular organization, FAT was founded in 1960 as a social justice project of the Catholic church with an emphasis on internal union democracy, freedom from political parties, and autonomy from the state and from employers. Structurally the federation is divided into four sectors—unions, cooperatives, peasants, and neighborhoods—and prefers to operate at the local or regional level. According to Dave Mackenzie, executive director of the Humanity Fund, this model of alliances across sectors is instructive for the labor movement in the United States and Canada.

The general goal of FAT is to create a society organized along the principle of *autogestión* or worker self-management. *Autogestión* is simultaneously a goal and a method for reaching that goal. The principles of *autogestión* are direct democracy and direct action, based on a consensus of those with a direct interest in the decision; mutual support or solidarity as an ethical principle; extension of *autogestión* to the community and to personal relations with family members, friends, and co-workers; and commitment to education and consciousness-raising *(formación)* (Hathaway 2000, 104–5).

Projects and activities of FAT are organized to develop and promote self-management and class consciousness and include union organizing, strike support, credit unions, marketing coops for farmers and other producers, community kitchens and other neighborhood services, and support of land-tenure struggles. FAT has been very active in the campaign against neoliberalism, has been educating and mobilizing workers to participate in decisions about economic development, and has built strong ties with American unions concerned with the same issues—particularly the United Electrical Workers.

Women have been involved with FAT since its founding, but it was not until 1993 that women began a process of "reflection on the work with and by women." In 1994, the FAT constitution was changed to encourage an increase in the active participation of women in all sectors of the organization. After much discussion and debate, the women at the First National Encounter of Women of the Frente Auténtico del Trabajo decided against establishing a separate formal sector for women and instead opted for creating separate "organizing space" within the federation "to push our gender agenda in all organizations and sectors." According to a document produced for the Second National Encounter of the Women of the FAT, "Women have much to contribute to the strengthening of each sector," and creating a separate sector would siphon off that activity. Within the existing structure, "There are opportunities to grow and strengthen the organization of the women of FAT which would then grow and strengthen the FAT itself." The integration of women reinforces the notion that "women can contribute new things to all aspects of the work of the FAT and that women were always a part of it, of its history, life struggle, and ideals."[20]

Women in the FAT recognized the need for their own space and established an office for La Coordinación Nacional de Mujeres del Frente Auténtico del Trabajo to coordinate the FAT's work with women. The Center for the Organization and Essential Development of Women (CODIM) in León was chosen as the location of the new office to demonstrate its commitment to reaching grassroots women who reside outside of Mexico City. This women's center, an NGO, is a member organization of FAT and is open to any individual or organization involved in the effort to end discrimination against women. It offers legal counseling to unions and to individual workers concerning the rights of women on the job and offers practical assistance on pressing charges in cases of sexual harassment and other forms of workplace discrimination. The center also offers family counseling and legal assistance to women who have experienced sexual violence, programs for the development of women's self-esteem and leadership, and education about the human rights of women. The center has a lending library of media materials and documents on topics of interest to women to be used as consciousness-raising tools. Consistent with the FAT principle of *autogestión*, emphasis is placed on women's developing the skills to analyze their own experience and on the construction of a sense of self as a democratic subject—"autonomous women, with self-esteem, self knowledge, and our own identity that would allow us to value ourselves." Giving women the their own space "for exchange, reflection, and formation" leads to a new consciousness of their role as agents of change.[21]

The mission of the Women's Coordinating Office of the FAT is to "transform unequal and unjust relations between men and women; in couples, families, work, and society" and to build "a more solidary and just world" compatible with the philosophy, goals, and activities of the CODIM. Their goals can be summarized as follows:

1. Develop and facilitate organizing, training, and consciousness-raising on gender issues within the FAT

2. Coordinate the work on women between sectors, regions, and zones of the FAT

3. Build relations, alliances, and formations among women within the FAT

4. Develop informational and training programs for women

5. Conduct research on the status of women

6. Monitor the progress of women in the FAT and in society.[22]

The coordinating office organizes conferences, workshops, and meetings, helps participants develop their own programs of action for women's rights, and trains women for leadership roles.

Women of the FAT actively collaborate with other women's groups and organizations that seek to eliminate gender inequality. Their understanding of inequality covers a wide range of practices from job sex segregation, the wage gap, sexual harassment, and the double day to the low quality of health care for women, lack of educational opportunities and social security, and the feminization of poverty. They view as violence any "social structure that excludes half of humanity." The FAT's strategic plan for women includes the formation of women's leadership teams for each sector, zone, and region and the preparation and training of female leaders to defend the rights of women within their own organizations. The plan also called for the development of a target-leadership program for unions that pushes them "to transform the functioning, sensibility, and perspectives of unions so that they act on the participation and demands of their women, and incorporate them into the movement, collective contracts, training, and mobility." Unions are called upon to create and promote "encounters, formations, and denouncements of the life and working conditions of women" and to engage in the "fight against sexual harassment, for equal pay, and for positive actions in favor of women."[23]

These women activists view the labor movement as "a space in which women can discuss their problems and channel their demands." They believe it desirable "that men in the labor movement view the elimination of sex discrimination as their responsibility and not just the responsibility of the women."[24] Equality between the sexes is valued at work and within intimate relations. Women of the FAT actively seek alliances with feminists in other unions in Mexico as well as in the United States and Canada and view the struggles around NAFTA and free-trade issues as an opportunity to form strategic alliances. They also participate in community coalitions concerned with broader economic issues and with border relations, such as the Southwest Network for Economic Justice and Mexican Network for Action on Free Trade.

Women of the FAT are utilizing women's networks—including feminist ones—throughout the region and internationally. They have adopted the Beijing platform and the human rights rhetoric of various UN resolutions and conferences. But, they also maintain a strong presence at the local level where activists reframe women's equality and women's rights in terms that resonate with local workers.

Transnational Advocacy Networks and Feminist Solidarity

The Steelworkers' network spans national borders and serves as a resource for building international feminist solidarity, thus it can be classified as a transnational advocacy network. According to Keck and Sikkink (1998) a "network that includes those relevant actors working internationally on an issue, who are bound together by shared values, a common discourse, and dense exchanges of information and services" (2) constitute such a network. Activists in these networks are linked by a shared commitment to a set of principled ideas or values—such as women's rights, human rights, or sustainable environments—that motivate the formation of the network. These networks can be understood as "political space" that provide the opportunity for social actors to apply new approaches to international politics. Because not all actors are equally situated in the same political space, the cultural meaning and practices of politics, of building coalitions and alliances, and of constructing international solidarity have to be constantly negotiated.[25]

Transnational advocacy networks, like feminist networks in unions, are not the inevitable outcome of greater global integration of the economy (Khagram et al. 2002; Smith 1997). These networks and their resources have to be mobilized, and participants have to develop a sense of themselves as political actors who can make change happen. Unions and their networks provide structure and opportunity for action but, in order for the membership—or a segment of it—to be politicized or mobilized to the point of action, organizers and activists must develop collective frames of action that resonate cognitively and culturally with potential participants (Gordon and Turner 2000; Klandermans 1997; Turner et al. 2001). These frames help to give action its meaning. According to Tarrow (1992), the political culture provides leaders with a reservoir of symbols with which to construct a cognitive frame for collective action. "Enterprising individuals and groups draw upon existing mentalities and cultures to create action-oriented frames of meaning . . . [and] use widely shared symbols for their instrumental ends but they manipulate these symbols in order to mobilize others on behalf of their political goals" (186). For Tarrow, the ideas and discourses embedded in collective action frames function to signal a movement's goals; to communicate messages among leaders, supporters, and outsiders; to build solidarity and cohesion among participants; and help to make the situation more comprehensible to the rank and file.

Given the current assault on group rights and the organizations that advocate for them—particularly unions, which are often seen as a damper on competition and as obstacles to flexible work rules and increases in productivity—unions are turning to human rights as a master frame for addressing labor rights. Internationally, feminists are doing the same with women's rights, moving from a discrimination frame to a human rights frame.[26]

Neoliberal discourse on citizenship has also been coopted by transnational activists. According to Alvarez (1998), social movements in Latin America are expanding the discursive space created by the neoliberal discourse about capitalism and democracy. By reconfiguring new forms of citizenship, rights, and democratic participation, these social movements are challenging what counts as political. In the same political space, neoliberal modernization rhetoric about individual rights and responsibilities contends with oppositional redefinition of rights to mean the inclusion of previously excluded and marginalized groups. For women, the urban poor, peasants, indigenous peoples, and racial minorities the "right to have rights" becomes a radical demand (Dagnino 1998). "Movements attempting to promote the protection of human rights, women's rights, and self determination—movements that essentially assert the political rights of excluded groups—are among the top transnational movement industries" (Smith 1997b, 57).

Conclusion

Union feminists are a part of a process of redefining the political, but their concerns are not particularly new. By linking quality-of-life issues—housing, health, education, etc.—and equalitarian relationships between the sexes with workers' rights, these women continue the tradition of demanding "bread and roses." Union feminists are bringing the issue of violence against women before the labor movement, often recasting the right to bodily integrity as each worker's right, one solidly grounded in basic human rights. Union feminists are also using the Beijing platform for women's rights as a legitimizing frame for their demands. Women activists in the United Steelworkers of America and in the Frente Auténtico del Trabajo of Mexico combine separate autonomous space for consciousness raising and leadership development with the integration of institutional structures that seek to bring women into the mainstream of their organizations. Participants are learning about their rights. They are defining that to which they are entitled as women, as workers, and as citizens—while at the same time, demanding those rights through political action.

Union feminists are not just demanding that the union help to fund democratic projects that enhance women's rights. Through the principle of *autogestión,* they are also demanding and achieving more democratic unions. The labor union and its federation are as much a target of political action as they are a structural vehicle through which to organize that action. Women activists and feminists are playing an important role in internationalizing the labor reform movement. Moreover, the women of the Frente Auténtico del Trabajo of Mexico and of the United Steelworkers of America are participants in what is rapidly becoming a transnational mobilization of workers who seek the achievement of global justice through the advancement of human rights. This is an international demand of all laborers for "bread," for "roses," and for "rights."

The pressures of globalization have brought feminists and trade union-ists in Mexico, Canada, and the United States together politically in new ways—particularly in the aftermath of NAFTA. Being similarly situated in world markets as workers is not sufficient to generate the type of transnational working-class solidarity necessary to challenge the gendered and racialized forces of globalization. Not until the institutional frameworks that stimu-late and support economic integration become sites for feminist politics will the possibility of new opportunities for collective action be opened up (Marchand 1994). If women are to be mobilized to make something of these opportunities, organized labor and the women's movements will need to develop culturally specific frames of political action, collective political identities that acknowledge difference, and diverse strategies for change.

Working-class women confront globalization on a daily basis at the local level, and it is here according to Emmett (1998) that they learn to make use of globalization. Women draw on sex and gender as the raw materials in their encounters with economic transformation, and women use their daily struggles with the forces of globalization to expand the demand for equality in the public and domestic spheres and to create solidarity across lines of so-cial and cultural differences. Because local conditions structure citizenship, local networks can be mobilized into transnational campaigns for women's rights as workers and can serve as the site of struggle for the rights of citi-zenship and for social movements. "The practices that regulate women, nation and state can be subverted by local community networks and relations," and out of these emerges "a civil arena to counter masculinist nationalist agendas" (Alarcón et al. 1999, 12).

The link between the local and the global and the efforts of activists to mobilize women in their communities and in their labor organizations to defend and expand their rights as workers in the global economy is com-plex. My study of women's activism in the Steelworkers is an effort to provide a "geographically anchored" case study (Mohanty 1997). Mohanty con-tends that the "local and the global are connected through parallel, contra-dictory, and sometime converging relations of rule which position women in different and similar locations as workers" (6). She suggests the need for a comparative methodology of geographically anchored case studies that would unearth the interconnections and discontinuities of globalization. Without attention to cultural contexts and historical specificity, the refram-ing of the rights of women workers as basic citizenship rights can become a recolonizing gesture. The discourses of democracy and of human rights must be analyzed and problematized before they can be used to create transna-tional forms of feminist struggle.

Cross-border organizing in the NAFTA bloc has radical potential that can only be realized when women's strategic interests (in all specificity) as workers in the global economy become the foundation for transnational feminist solidarity rather than abstract universal appeals to women's rights as citizenship rights (Mohanty 1997; Ong 1999). The strategic interests of women workers are situated differently in both the labor movement and the women's movement in all three countries, and this has important implications for building alliances between movements and across borders. International labor unions like the Steelworkers have resources and networks that can be mobilized by the feminists in their ranks to construct new strategic alliances between workers in Mexico, the United States, and Canada.

9

Forging Union Feminism and the Fight for Social Justice

Our ultimate success of beating back corporate attacks on our living stan-dards will depend on our ability to forge strategic alliances and create a broad-based movement committed to fighting for social justice.
—"Reaching Out to Build a Movement for Social Justice," Resolution 29

For most of its history, the Steelworkers had been a man's union, and, in many ways, it was not very well prepared to deal with the issues of sex dis-crimination and women's rights. Union feminists understood that it would be up to them to make their union understand that women's rights were le-gitimate trade-union issues. To do so they would need the support of the emerging body of civil rights and human rights law and the energy and for-ward momentum of the women's movement.

Women steelworkers from different racial and cultural backgrounds and from a variety of working-class occupations have been forging a unique collective identity within their union as feminists and as trade unionists during the past twenty-five years. They continue to do so at a time when solidarity across lines of difference is more difficult to construct and main-tain (Colgan and Ledwith 2002; Form 1995).

The groundwork for the growth and development of union feminism was laid in the 1970s when women gained access to the steel industry and its union in the midst of great social movement activity in the United States and Canada. Globalization and the economic restructuring policies of more conservative governments have taken its toll on the steel industry, placing the union and its feminists on the defensive. Yet neither their identity as unionists nor as feminists withered away. After a period of abeyance, feminist organizing within the Steelworkers has resurfaced and in fact has developed at a relatively fast pace throughout the 1990s and into the early part of the twenty-first century. Women are beginning to have a significant impact on the union, and their mobilization will be crucial if the Steelworkers are to become a vital force for economic justice and social change.

Mobilization and Collective Identity

Women of Steel is more than a name given to a set of initiatives and activities designed to increase women's representation and participation in the union. "Women of Steel" is also a politically constructed collective identity forged within the constraints and opportunities of the union. Women members become "Women of Steel" in the course of participating in the *Women of Steel* programs and activities. Over time they came to see themselves as part of a larger more politically effective group.

The union's networks, structures, and discourses designed to mobilize members to act on behalf of the organization's goals and objectives can and do become coopted and refashioned by women Steelworkers as they construct a collective identity based on a more particularized set of interests. While collective definitions of interests are articulated by discourse, political identities emerge and movements ensue because collectives consciously coordinate action. Collective identity is thus both a source of mobilization and a product of it (Cerulo 1997).

Union conventions, conferences, workshops, and schools serve as important sites for women's activism and for the ongoing formation of union feminism. They are the sites at which women from all over the United States and Canada come together to meet each other, to share experiences, to talk about their issues, and to develop strategies to effect change. Union resources make it possible for working-class women, who would otherwise not have the finances, to participate in the construction of union feminism. It is at these events that women activists build mobilizing structures, construct an agenda of gender specific issues, and forge a sense of collective identity.

It is within these spaces and networks that women identify their concerns and translate them into specific issues and campaigns that can in turn mobilize more "Women of Steel." Campaigns, like the Canadian Steelworkers campaign to prevent violence against women, help build links between the women's movement and the labor movement, thus expanding the mobilizing networks of women in both movements. The extent to which unions will broaden their agenda beyond wages and working conditions to include

Table 13

Percentage of respondents who indicate it is very important for the union to be concerned about key issues

Key issue	Canadian (N = 192)		United States (N = 625)	
	Percentage	Rank	Percentage	Rank
Violence against women	86.5	1	55.2	9
Sexual and racial harassment	86.7	2	70.6	2
Pay equity	84.9	3	75.9	3
Women's health	80.7	4	70.2	6
Exploitation of women and child labor	77.6	5	74.6	5
Declining standard of living (NAFTA)	75.5	6	80.6	1
Affirmative action for women and minorities	71.9	7	60.8	8
Contract proposals on balancing work and family	69.8	8	75.5	4
Organizing women	68.8	9	62.1	7
Rise in part-time and temporary jobs	66.7	10	53.8	10

issues such as affirmative action, childcare, sexual harassment—issues not typically thought of as industrial issues—depends on the presence of union feminists (Cobble and Michal 2002).

According to a nonrepresentative sample of women who responded to the union's "Tell Us What You Think Survey," women Steelworkers in both countries believe their union should be concerned with social issues that are traditionally thought of as gender specific (Table 13).[1] The survey, conducted in preparation for the First International Women's Conference held 6 to 9 February 2000, revealed that women thought their union should be concerned about violence against women, women's health, pay equity, sexual and racial harassment, and attacks on affirmative action. While there is strong support for union involvement on both sides of the border, Canadian women feel somewhat stronger about the need for union involvement. There is some divergence between the two groups concerning which issues are most important. Canadian women list their top three issues as violence against women, sexual and racial harassment, and pay equity, and women in the United States rank declining standard of living due to NAFTA followed by sexual and racial harassment, and pay equity. Although 55.2 percent of the women in the United States said the union should be involved with violence against women as a social issue, it ranked ninth overall. A considerably high percent (86.5 percent) of Canadian women believe the union should be concerned with this issue, which may indicate that the union's campaign against domestic violence, a Canadian-only initiative, has made domestic violence more salient to Canadians.

Political Opportunities

Union feminists have maximized their effectiveness by taking advantage of the political opportunity structures in two very different political fields, and this explains why union feminism has survived such difficult and challenging times for organized labor and for the Steelworkers in particular. Dual nation location affords activists greater flexibility in the selection of strategies for achieving their goals. Attention to variation in political fields helps us to understand the specific ways in which collective identity formation and activism are not only historically situated but rooted in geography—time and place *do* matter. Union feminists in the United States were able to mobilize a collective identity as women steelworkers in the 1970s but not during World War II, and in the Calumet and the Ontario districts but not in Pittsburgh or in the surrounding small steel towns like Steubenville until very recently.

Movement Outcomes

The success of feminist mobilizing within the Steelworkers is not easy to measure, but there are important signs that activists are increasingly effective and that the union has become more representative of women and more responsive to women's issues. Women are the fastest growing segment of new union members and are 20 percent of the total membership. About a third of the female membership are women of color. Women are concentrated primarily in manufacturing, but increasing numbers are located in service sector jobs. One of the largest new groups to join the Steelworkers is the administrative and technical staff at the University of Toronto in District 6. According to District 6 Director Harry Hynd, the 3,500 (mostly female) new members represent the largest unit organized in the past forty years in Canada. They were officially granted their charter on International Women's Day, 7 March 1999 (Figure 12).

Women workers at the University of Toronto told me they decided to join forces with the Steelworkers because they were the only category of workers on campus who were without a union. Without an official place at the university's bargaining table they were losing ground in wages and benefits under restructuring. The workers interviewed five different unions and decided on the Steelworkers because they wanted the strength of a big union behind them. They also felt comfortable with the diversity of workers represented by the Steelworkers. Carolyn Egan, a long-time activist in both the

Figure 12. Members of Local 1998 at the University of Toronto receiving their union charter, March 9, 1999. Left to right, Marjorie B. Hola-Swami, Allison Dubarry, Margaret Martin. Photograph by Lisa Blanchette.

labor movement and the women's movement and the president of a large amalgamated local in Toronto, was assigned by the Steelworkers to assist in the organizing drive. Egan, a *Women of Steel* course facilitator, told me that the university organizing campaign was run from the bottom up. "I think probably at the height, about a hundred inside organizers were there, most of whom were women. And we had an open steering committee that met every week to plan the strategy and the tactics of the campaign."[2]

Fil Falbo from the union's organizing staff told me, "What was ironic was that once you took away what I call the gloss of the university what you would find are workers that had the same concerns as people working in manufacturing or in the health care system. These workers were concerned about whether or not they were going to have a job after restructuring. Everybody had a title. Everybody was a manager. Everybody was a supervisor, but at the end of the day nobody had security, something they could depend on in case something went wrong." The union employed a different organizing model, more like those used at Harvard and other universities. According to Falbo, "We used different tactics 'cause we didn't have to hide behind the pop machine or meet in a doughnut shop. We could do the organizing in public. We took advantage of the fact that the university had a reputation to protect."[3]

The network of feminist activists developed through the *Women of Steel* initiatives in Canada demonstrated the ability to mobilize large numbers when feminists organized more than 1,000 Steelworkers to participate in the World March of Women 2000. Steelworkers from all across Canada, including Calgary, Sudbury, Kimberley, Vancouver, Halifax, Toronto, Montreal, and Ottawa joined the march of 50,000 to end poverty and violence against women. Canadian National Director Lawrence McBrearty, who authorized union resources for the march and rally, was there in person to lend his support (Figure 13). Carolyn Egan, who was assigned by the union to help mobilize Steelworkers' participation in the march, reported, "The World March brought together the incredible strength of the women's movement and the labour movement. It showed real potential for the change that's possible."[4] Lee Edwards of District 3 said, "I'm proud to be one of the thousands of Steelworkers participating in the March. I'm extremely proud to be part of the women's committee. It means something to be a 'Woman of Steel.' It also made me proud to be a New Democrat. We're very lucky to have a political party that addresses the needs of working people."

As a researcher who has followed the efforts of women to gain voice and visibility in the Steelworkers for more than twenty-five years, symbolically the most dramatic moment for me came on 6 February 2000, at the International's first Women's Conference—a demand the women had first articulated in 1976. I walked into the ballroom at Pittsburgh's historic William Penn Hotel, site of the conference, and saw a standing-room-only crowd of eight hundred energized "Women of Steel." Women who only a few years earlier told me that they were terrified to speak in public were on the podium introducing dignitaries and giving their own speeches. They talked about their activism—from supporting workers who had been locked out of their jobs in Ravenswood, West Virginia, to walking the halls of the U.S. Congress to lobby for worker's rights as part of the union's legislative internship program. Some talked about taking part in the World Trade Organization demonstration in Seattle, and the Canadian women talked about what they had learned about international solidarity from their exchange program with women labor activists in Frente Auténtico del Trabajo of Mexico. The facilitators for the *Women of Steel* course conducted workshops, greeted delegates, and, with the help of Catherine Glen, a cultural worker

Figure 13. Lawrence McBrearty (center), national director of USWA-Canada, with "Women of Steel" at the World March of Women 2000, Ottawa, Ontario, October 17, 2000. Photograph by Lisa Blanchette.

and artist from Toronto, brought the house down with a performance of a play they crafted about the role of women in the labor movement.

Women of Steel coordinators from the districts organized meetings of delegates with their respective district directors so that the directors could have the opportunity to hear what was on the minds of the women in their districts. I attended the meeting of District 1 (Ohio) where the *Women of Steel* coordinator, Michelle Laghetto, led her group (the largest delegation to attend the conference) in a discussion of women's issues with Director Dave McCall. Michelle believes she has the ear of her director, and women's committees and conferences have grown in Ohio. The *Women of Steel* initiatives, which grew up as a grassroots effort, have been institutionalized by the top leadership and are now beginning to push themselves back down through the districts, though unevenly.

At the convention I met women who worked at utility companies, in uranium mines, steel mills, and nursing homes, and even some—like the delegation from the Virgin Islands—who worked on oil rigs. They were welders, pipefitters, shipbuilders, tire builders, health care workers, clerks, and telemarketers. I talked to women who were attending a union function for the first time and with seasoned trade unionists, like Carol Landry, who were presidents of their locals. Carol joined the Steelworkers in the mideighties when she went to work as a planning clerk at Highland Valley Copper in the interior of British Columbia—at that time the world's second largest open-pit copper mine.[5]

Carol was one of only a handful of women who worked at the mine, but, like Sandy Sutton and Loretta Tyler, she worked her way up to the presidency of her local of about 1,100 workers. While she is the first woman to serve as president, she did not start at the top. She became active in her local when the office and technical workers who were unhappy about their contract asked her to serve on the bargaining committee—the only woman to do so. Her district director, Ken Neuman, invited her to attend the first *Women of Steel* course offered in her district (District 3) and then to be an instructor. From there she went on to other programs and courses and ran for office. She was elected treasurer, vice president, and eventually president, and she was a part of a Canadian delegation that went to Buffalo, New York, to train the U.S. women to facilitate the *Women of Steel* course. Carol attributes her success to role models and mentors like Susan Carrigan, Steelworkers Organizing Coordinator for District 3, and to the support she received from her family and from the staff and leadership in her district. The Steelworkers recognized Carol's talents and offered her a staff position in

Burnaby, British Columbia, and eventually a position on the International staff.

Much has happened in the Steelworkers since that day in 1976 when a small group of women Steelworkers meet in Roberta Wood's hotel room to carve out an agenda for women. While the demand for an International Women's Conference has recently become a reality, other issues, like a women's department and constitutionally mandated women's committees in each local, are still being debated. No woman has yet been elected to any of the top four International offices or to the position of district director; consequently, no women serve as voting members of the executive board. However, they do attend board meetings. There has been progress in appointing women as department chairs and to staff positions at the International. Four women serve as department heads at the International: Maxine Carter for civil rights, Melena Barkman for membership development, Karen Hoffman for purchasing and travel, and Mary Ann Westion for accounting and finance.

The *Women of Steel* initiatives were further institutionalized when in 1998 George Becker appointed Sharon Stiller to a new position—assistant to the president for women's issues. Stiller has long been an advocate for women's rights in District 7 and was a part of the original District 31 (now District 7) Women's Caucus. She, too, worked her way up through the ranks, first holding office in a large office and technical local at the Northern Indiana Power Company, then being appointed to staff representative in District 31, and now serving as assistant to the president. I asked Sharon to assess the growth and development of women's activism in the Steelworkers.[6]

Many of the successes are hard for her to measure. She sees women having an impact on the organization as a whole, on local leadership, on the community, and on each other. "It's not a straight line, and it's also not grafted onto a flat surface. It's spiral. It's like going on in, among, themselves." Sharon believes that when women do good work, like the campaign against domestic violence in Canada or the U.S. support for the locked-out workers at AK Steel in Ohio, they will get the attention of the organization and of the community. Other organizations, seeing their work, join with them, and the events get bigger and the women gain a broader perspective. It works like this. "In the U.S., the issue was solidarity for the workers locked out of AK Steel in Mansfield, Ohio, in District 1. 'Women of Steel' throughout the district were involved in a number of rallies to demonstrate their support for the workers in the local. Then, they expanded their work to build support in other districts and then were able to organize a much larger rally and to raise a significant amount of financial support. The highly visible work of the 'Women of Steel' got the attention of the International leadership and coverage in the union and regional press" (Figure 14).

Sharon believes this event built a sense of sisterhood and solidarity among the women who organized it and participated in it and that it showed the community and the male membership that the women had something important to offer the union and the community. According to her, the impact of what happened was felt at every level. The women involved told Sharon, "It was really nice, marching with other women. We were recognizing each other and building our network." Sharon believes the women start to feel pretty good about not just the things that they are doing, but the possibility that there might be other women out there that they could get involved with.

"Women of Steel" are forging feminism within their organization, and they are positioned to mobilize working-class women in both the labor and the women's movements. Sharon believes that the Steelworkers are beginning to see women's issues as union issues. "But to be effective, women's activism within the organization has to be built at the grassroots level. When the labor movement and the women's movement 'get it together', we, as 'Women of Steel,' will be in the forefront rather than trying to run behind the movement."

Strategic Alliance

I opened this chapter with a quote from a conference resolution adopted at the Steelworkers 30th Constitutional Convention in 2000. The Steelworkers are beginning to understand the necessity of building alliances and coalitions with other unions, other social movements, student groups, and community-based organizations. They also acknowledge that successful alliances are based on reciprocity:

> Keeping allies means being an ally. If we expect community, religious, student, women's and civil rights, environmental groups and organized workers in other countries to support us in opposing a workplace closing or conducting an organizing drive, then we need to reciprocate when it is time to pass a civil rights ordinance or march for child care or deliver a message to a corporation. (Resolution 29)

Steelworkers see their interests more allied with other social movements and their organizations and seek to form coalitions and strategic alliances with such groups. "Labor's quest for justice and dignity in the workplace overlaps with the social justice agenda of an array of groups, but our goals

Figure 14. Leo Gerard (center), president of the United Steelworkers of America, with Ohio State University women's studies students. Left to right (on Gerard's left), Sheri Davis, Zakiyyah Jackson, and Alice Chen at a solidarity rally for locked-out Steelworkers at AK Steel, Mansfield, Ohio, 9 September 2000. Courtesy of the United Steelworkers of America.

are not always identical. Alliances must be based on unflinching honesty, agreeing to work together where we stand on common ground, while respecting our differences." The union realizes that these differences cannot be suppressed or "sugarcoated" nor can they be viewed as "insurmountable" (Resolution 29).[7]

Their goal in seeking strategic partners is to change the political environment in which they must function as a union. The union is talking much more like a social movement these days. "In actively seeking alliances within our communities we are committing ourselves to building an economic and social alternative to a system which only values corporate profits. Our goal is to construct an economic and political democracy in contrast to the secretive dealings of the elite who seek to buttress a world order rooted in inequality" (Resolution 29).

The Steelworkers have formed a strategic alliance with the California Nurses Association (CNA), an organization whose militancy has been described in the press as "Mother Theresa with brass knuckles." The Steelworkers and the CNA will work on a joint, union-organizing project. Ninety percent of the health care industry lacks union representation, and the newly forged Health Care Workers Alliance will try to change that by organizing workers at various levels of the health care system. The alliance will focus not only on the health care worker but also on the right of everyone to quality health care. This includes a universal health care system in the United States, preserving the system in Canada, and assuring that patient needs are the primary component in health care decision making. According to recently retired Steelworkers president George Becker, "Health care is a vital resource and public service, not a commodity to be exploited for profit by a few. We need a model that will protect workers but also the public well-being by giving patients an improved health care system with a genuine health care safety net."[8] Rose Ann DeMoro, executive director of CNA, believes that the industrial approach to organizing makes sense because of the corporate character of the private health care system. In addition to organizing, the two organizations will provide mutual support for collective-bargaining strategies and will work together to build public and legislative support for issues of mutual concern, such as universal health care.

Globalization presents new and difficult challenges to the Steelworkers as the steel industry has been racked again with bankruptcies, plant closings, and downsizing. Eighteen steel companies filed for bankruptcy in the first half of 2001, including Wheeling-Pittsburgh Steel and other mills in my study, and employment levels are at record lows. Only a union revitalized and energized by an active and politically informed rank and file can meet those challenges. The Steelworkers and the labor movement cannot meet the challenges ahead without forging coalitions with other progressive forces around the world.

Globalization presents new and difficult challenges to all social movements concerned with social justice. It also presents new opportunities for protest and new networks for social action. Now more than ever, labor needs new forms of coalition that recognize the usefulness of (and do not fear) multiple and intersecting forms of collective identity. This new coalition will have to be built across borders and across lines of social and cultural difference. The Canadian Steelworkers, through the work of the Humanity Fund, lead the way. Constructing such alliances and coalitions will not be easy. Union feminists who serve as a bridge between the women's movement and the labor movement can be a catalyst for social change. It is up to both movements to capture and harness the activism and energy of "Women of Steel."

Methodological Appendixes

Appendix A

The Study

I collected the data for this study in three distinct phases over the past twenty-five years. The first phase of the research (1975–77) was my dissertation project in the Department of Sociology at The Ohio State University under the direction of Professor Laurel Richardson (Fonow 1977). I conducted a case study of the first group of women hired at Wheeling-Pittsburgh Steel Corporation in Steubenville, Ohio, under a court-directed, affirmative-action order issued in 1975, the consent decree. I wanted to understand the links between social-movement formation and mobilization, public policy, and sex discrimination.

I grew up in Steubenville, Ohio, and my best friend, Cecelia (Sissy) Humienny, was a member of the first group of women who went to work in the mill. She talked endlessly about working in a male-dominated industry. The more she talked about her life in the mill, the more I wanted to study this particular group of women. I entertained the idea of getting a job in the mill myself and doing a classic participant-observation study. Fortunately, there was a long layoff period, and my willingness was never tested. I settled for a more conventional approach. I interviewed women about their jobs, about their attitude toward the women's movement and feminism, and about their participation in the union. Sissy was elected to union office during this period, and with her I attended informal meetings, workshops, and conferences—any event where labor was addressing women's issues. She provided me with access to a rich and complex field and with much of the information that was crucial to my understanding of that field. At each of these events I collected documents, interviewed participants, and made observations.

The second phase of the research (1983–86) involved studying the impact of deindustrialization on the work lives and union activism of the women who had been hired into what soon became a declining industry. The women, like the men, were being laid off and for longer and longer periods, and their activism turned to assisting the unemployed and to lobbying an unresponsive federal government to save their jobs and communities. Eventually, Wheeling-Pittsburgh Steel filed for bankruptcy, and the workers went on strike rather than work without a contract. During this period I attended solidarity rallies in Washington, D.C., fund-raisers for the unemployed, and strike-support activities for the workers at Wheeling-Pittsburgh Steel. I interviewed the women involved in these events, collected documents, and made observations, and I have written more extensively about these events elsewhere (Fonow 1998). Although some of the women pioneers eventually returned to their jobs after the strike, my friend Sissy decided to leave the steel industry and move out west.

I resumed the final and the longest phase of my research (1992–2001) about women steelworkers after the 1992 Annual Meeting of the American Sociological Association held in Pittsburgh. The program committee organized a "redevelopment" tour of the Mon Valley—a region of tightly packed steel towns along the Monongahela River in Pennsylvania that was very much like my hometown. I boarded the air-conditioned bus with much anticipation, mostly because I wanted to believe that there had been some significant redevelopment in the region. The bus rolled past one devastated site after another, and the tour director called out the names of all the small steel towns along our winding route: Braddock, Duquesne, Homestead, and McKeesport. I was stunned by the devastation and rubble that lay on the ground.

We got back to the convention hall just in time to hear Lynn Williams, then the president of the Steelworkers, address an audience of three hundred academics. He challenged us to work with labor in trying to understand what was happening to workers in the "new economy" and how labor could best respond to those circumstances. He invited us to study steelworkers, their union, and their communities, and I decided to take him up on that invitation.

My grandfather Nicholas Villies, a Greek immigrant, held his last job as a laborer in the 60-inch mill at Wheeling-Pittsburgh Steel. He never intended to be a steelworker, and he worked in the mill a mere ten months. In his day, men gathered at the plant gate to be hired as needed. Some days there was enough work, and some days there was not. There was no union yet to protect the worker's interests, and my grandfather, who was afraid to miss an opportunity to work, did not seek treatment for an injury he received on the job. On 29 April 1934, he unexpectedly died of a cerebral hemorrhage at the age of forty-seven though he had been in good health.

Growing up, I believed that his death and the untreated injury were related. My grandfather's autopsy report does not explicitly indicate an injury serious enough to have caused his death, yet it does note that "over the right elbow was a reddish blue area about 5cm in diameter. Over the left knee was a similar area." He is described in the report as "robust" and "muscular." My uncle Gus remembers a large and ugly gash on his father's leg. Perhaps our theory is wrong, but the story of why he died has been passed down from one generation to the next. I do not know if it is true. I do know that the injury and death rate among unskilled, non-English-speaking immigrant steelworkers was quite significant. Even today almost everyone growing up in a steel town knows of an industry-related injury or death, whether in their own family or someone else's family. My grandmother Belle Karantza, like many other widowed immigrant women of her time, struggled to raise her family of seven children before there was a union or the benefits it made possible. I did not want people to forget what it means to working-class people to have the protection of a union.

I have augmented my fieldwork during these twenty-five years with an analysis of the union's historical records, housed at the Calumet Regional Archive at Indiana University Northwest and at the Historical Collections and Labor Archives at Penn State University. I was also fortunate to meet Roberta Wood, one of the founders of the District 31 Women's Caucus, who turned over to me all of her personal records concerning this organization. These included correspondence, newsletters, memos, flyers, leaflets, court briefs, and meeting minutes. In addition, I interviewed Dorreen (nee Labby) Carey and Steffi Domike, former steelworkers and rank-and-file activists, who served, respectively, as editor of the District 31 Women's Caucus newsletter and producer of the video *Women of Steel.*

Because activism is an emergent phenomenon, evasive and hard to capture, I have used a variety of methods. I followed the women's activism wherever it led me, and I made detailed descriptions of events, settings, participants, rhetoric, symbols, and ephemera. I talked to people formally and informally; did a close reading of union documents, resolutions, newsletters, press accounts, and historical records; and participated—attending conferences, workshops, picket lines, and rallies. Finally, I designed and analyzed data from two surveys. The first survey was designed with input from the Canadian National Women's Committee and was a random telephone survey of Canadian women who have taken the *Women of Steel* course.

This survey was conducted by the Survey Research Center at The Ohio State University (questionnaire available from the author on request). The second survey (also available from the author) duplicated much of the first survey and responses were collected on the union's Web site, through the union's magazine, *Steelabor,* and at union events. The nonrandom survey of women Steelworkers in the United States and Canada was designed to help the union assess the interests of its female members. I have treated the results of each survey separately.

Interviews

Between 1976 and 1977, I conducted in-depth interviews with women who worked at Wheeling-Pittsburgh Steel. Each interview was tape recorded (lasting between 1.5 to 2 hours), and I took notes and identified relevant quotations from the audiotapes. I used a "snowball" sampling technique where those I interviewed identified other women whom I might interview. I supplemented these interviews with interviews of women delegates at a union convention and with a select number of male members of union Local 1190. Between 1994 and 2001, I interviewed fifty-five women at various union events and activities and a select number of union officials in Canada and the United States. Seventy-five percent of these interviews were tape recorded and transcribed.

Observations

I recorded observations and collected documents at the following labor events.

Constitutional Convention of the Coalition of Labor Union Women (Detroit), 1975

Women's Conference of the Ohio AFL-CIO (Columbus), 1975

International Steelworkers Convention (Las Vegas), 1976

Steelworkers Convention (Cleveland), 1984

Midwest School for Women Workers (Columbus), 1985

District 7 Civil Rights and Women's Conference (Gary), 1996

Canadian National Women's Conferences (Toronto), 1996

Canadian National Women's Conference (Toronto), 1999

Board meeting of District 6 Women's Committee (Toronto), 1995

Board meeting of the Canadian National Women's Committee (Toronto), 1998

Women of Steel course at Bayside, Ontario, 1999

First International Women's Conference (Pittsburgh), 2000

Union-Related Documents

I collected documents at various union events and reviewed union records at the Calumet Regional Archive at Indiana University and at the Labor Archive at Penn State University. I also arranged to have documents from the Frente Auténtico del Trabajo of Mexico translated into English. These documents are listed at the end of the reference section.

Appendix B

Telephone Survey of *Women of Steel* Course Participants

With the help of the Survey Research Center at Ohio State, I designed a random telephone survey of 286 women who had taken the *Women of Steel* course to evaluate its effectiveness in increasing women's participation in the union. Data collection for this project commenced 29 June 1999, and was completed on 31 July 1999. Collection was conducted through telephone interviews using a list of participants; 191 potential respondents were randomly selected to participate, representing women from the provinces of Ontario, British Columbia, Alberta, Manitoba, Saskatchewan, and New-foundland. Only current union members were eligible to participate in the survey.

Interviews were executed using CATI process based upon CASES software. Many participants were called ten or more times to try to find a convenient time to talk. Of the 191, 83 completed interviews were obtained. Forty-four were invalid telephone numbers; 39 respondents were unavailable during the field period; 2 respondents were not interviewed due to language; 1 did not complete the interview; 10 respondents refused to be interviewed; and 13 were no longer union members. In the 112 cases in which an interviewer spoke with the eligible prospective respondent, interviews were completed in 73 percent of the cases. With 83 completed interviews, the margin of sampling error is plus or minus 9 percent. In 19 of 20 cases, results will differ due to sampling error by no more than 9 percent in either direction from what would have been obtained by interviewing all 286 women. The project was supervised by Karen Ehrhardt-Martinez of the Center for Survey Research within the College of Social and Behavioral Sciences at The Ohio State University, Paul Lavrakas, Director.

Appendix C

Interview Guide for Activists

Name:

Age:

Company:

Job title and description of work:

Family member in unions and USWA:

1. How long have you been with _____ company?

2. How did you become involved with USWA?

3. Describe the history of your involvement with the union.

4. Does your family support your activism in the union? Are other members of your family Steelworkers? Other unions?

5. How would you describe an activist in your union?

6. How would you compare yourself with men in your local/regional in terms of opportunities for leadership?

7. What kinds of organizing efforts have you been a part of? Why did you participate in them?

8. Please describe the kinds of problem you feel you run into at work and in the union because you are a women.

9. Please describe your ideas and thoughts about feminism.

10. Would you describe yourself as a feminist? Why or why not?

11. How do you describe yourself racially and ethnically?

12. Has this definition hindered or benefited your participation and activism in the USWA? How?

13. Please describe the race, gender, and ethnic relations at your workplace and in union membership.

14. What are your goals as an activist (leader/feminist) in USWA?

15. Any other comments?

Notes

1. Union Feminism, Social Movements, and Gender

1. Loretta Tyler. Interview by the author, Las Vegas, Nevada (30 August 1994). Tape recording.

2. For an analysis of this campaign and Sandy's role in it, see Needleman (1990).

3. Sandy Sutton. Interview by the author, LaPorte, Indiana (8 September 1994). Tape recording.

4. Colette Murphy. Interview by the author, Las Vegas, Nevada (29 August 1994). Tape recording.

5. Ferree and Roth (1998) and Klandermans (1997) decry the lack of serious theoretical attention given to social-movement interaction.

6. Here I use Omi and Winant's definition of race to mean "a concept which signifies and symbolizes social conflicts and interests by referring to different types of bodies" (1994, 55).

7. For a detailed discussion of racial politics in the USWA, see Hill 2002; Hinshaw 2002; Lynd 1997; Needleman 2003; Nelson 1997, 2001; Nyden 1984; Stewart 2001; Stein 1998.

8. The rationale for the separate program reflects the Canadian preference for accommodating difference rather than requiring assimilation. In the U.S. context, special treatment evokes memories of "separate but equal" for an older generation of black women.

9. This is particularly true for Quebec. During the 1981–82 recession, the USWA experienced substantial membership loss in all districts. However, the losses were not as great in Canada as they were in the United States, and within Canada

there was variation in loss across districts. Membership fell by 32 percent in District 6 (Ontario), while it fell by 16 percent in District 5 (Quebec). By 1990, Quebec had not only recovered the losses but also started to show real gains in membership. And, while District 6's recovery was better than districts in the United States, it did not match the situation in Quebec. For a discussion of the explanation and implications of this phenomenon in Quebec, see Murray (1998).

10. Labor-union density is higher in Canada, where 30 percent of workers are members of unions compared to only 13 percent in the United States in 2000. The proportion of women in unions is about the same as men in both the United States and Canada. In the United States, the percent of women in unions is 11 percent, with higher rates for black women at 15.4 percent (U.S. Bureau of Labor Statistics, press release, 18 January 2001, "Union Members in 2000" [on-line]. Available from stats.bls.gov/newsrels.htm). In 1999, 31 percent of Canadian women were in unions (Women in Canada 2000, Statistics Canada).

11. The ability of Canadian politics to accommodate differences stems in part from ongoing, long-standing debates about separatism and autonomy for Quebec and, to a lesser extent, from the discussion about the rights of the indigenous population.

12. The extent to which gender inequality is reproduced in social institutions suggests that changes in the gender regime of the institutional context should be understood as part of the broader set of political constraints and opportunities that impinge on social movements (Taylor 1999).

13. Bashevkin (1991) does an excellent job of explaining how trade emerged as a feminist issue in Canada, and I will pursue this topic more fully in chapter 8.

14. In her study of gender framing in the Pittston coal strike of 1989, Beckwith (2001) contends that gender is so embedded in the "common sense" notion of how to do a strike that it can neither be taken for granted nor assumed away as irrelevant. Examples of collective repertoires that are based on cultural assumptions about gender differences include placing all women on the front lines of a demonstration, using language and metaphors of struggle that are sports or military based, and assigning movement tasks along gender-differentiated lines.

2. Women in the Workshop of Vulcan

1. For an analysis of the cultural politics of deindustrializaion and representation, see Linkon and Russo's (2002) study of Youngstown.

2. *Danny* (1987), Stashu Kylartas, no. 2 of "Video Against AIDS. *The Deer Hunter* (1978), Michael Cimino, Universal Pictures, Universal City, California. *Heart of Steel* (1983), Donald Wrye, Beowulf Productions, ABC Movie of the Week.

3. See Demarest 1992.

4. *The Full Monty* (1997), Peter Cattaneo, Fox Searchlight Productions.

5. Downs (1995) shows how the gender division of labor in the French and British metalworking industries prior to World War I rested on cultural assumptions about gender and skill. "Here femaleness meant dexterity and speed within a 'scientifically' ordered work process, whereas maleness signified a clumsier brute strength but also an exclusive capacity to gain mechanical understanding of the overall labor process, and so to rise to positions of technical and moral authority on the shop floor" (4). Sex typing of skills lay at the center of inequality within the industry itself.

6. Theresa Ogresovich. Interview by the author (1977). Tape recording.

7. Peggy Piazza. Interview by the author (1977). Tape recording.

8. According to Stevens in *Women Remember the War* (1993), the majority of women who went to work during the war did not find employment in industrial settings but in traditional service and clerical occupations. Though women did make inroads in manufacturing, their real importance lay in the way they challenged cultural stereotypes about gender. Thus, the attention given to Rosie the Riveter was all out of proportion to her actual numbers.

9. In the Detroit war industries, according to Honey (1999), black women and men were 6 percent of all employees in aircraft, whereas white women were about 40 percent. The biggest gains for African Americans were in heavily male-dominated industries such as foundries, shipbuilding, blast furnaces, and steel mills. "Black women went into dangerous munitions factories, did heavy labor for the railroads, or were hired as washroom attendants and cleaning women in war plants" (7).

10. Hartmann (1982) also documents that black women faced the racial animosity of white women co-workers and the discriminatory policies and practices of the government, the unions, and the companies. In some situations, white women refused to work with black women and engaged in sit-down strikes over integrated lunchrooms and bathhouses (81).

11. See Cooper (1991) for a discussion of workplace practices during the Depression that adjusted the sexual boundaries of job classifications within the electronics industry. Her analysis of workers at Philco suggests that "sexual difference was something men and women knew and understood but life experiences could alter their conceptions of their gender roles and blur or shift the boundaries between men's and women's responsibilities" (335). The act of crossing gender-traditional occupational boundaries is not in and of itself a violation of gender norms because a variety of formal and informal occupational rules operate to realign workers to gender normative standards (Williams 1989).

12. I am extending the insights of Nelson (2001) and Roediger (1991) concerning the wage premium associated with white privilege.

13. Women's Bureau, U.S. Department of Labor, "Women in Unions in a Midwest War Industry" (World War II), RG 86, National Archives (hereafter, "Women

in Unions"). This is a study conducted at Carnegie-Illinois Steel Corporation, South Works. The United Steelworkers of America represented workers.

14. "Women in Unions," 2.

15. Women's Bureau, U.S. Department of Labor, Records of Women's Bureau of Labor, 1918–1965, pt. 2, reel 5.

16. "Women in Unions," 20.

17. Lola Murrin. Interview by the author (1977). Tape recording.

18. Women workers did not necessarily view their war work as temporary. Of the 19.5 million U.S. women who were employed in 1945, 15.9 million were working before the war mobilization (Goldfarb 1976, 12). War production gave some women who were already in the workforce the opportunity to move into higher paying industrial jobs from low-paying, nonunion, female-intensive jobs. After the war the majority returned to jobs in the expanding service sector but at considerably lower wages. New hiring partially offset the separation of women from wartime jobs (*Pidgeon* 1947, 667).

19. For a brilliant analysis of the social, cultural, and historical factors associated with how wages are gendered, see Kessler-Harris (1990). Her new book (2001) provides more extensive coverage of how the ideological and practical relationships of race and gender shape conceptions of fairness in economic policy more generally.

20. It was modeled after the U.S. Women's Bureau and concentrated on gathering and disseminating information on all aspects of women's employment.

3. Bread, Roses, and Rights

1. As Hartmann (1998) argues, with their direct access to workers and to employers, unions are uniquely situated to become key players in the implementation of antidiscrimination laws—if they choose. In part, what makes some unions choose such a path is their own vulnerability to lawsuits under Title VII, which holds unions liable if they do not challenge discriminatory practices of the employers with whom they have developed a collective-bargaining agreement.

2. See Crenshaw (1988) for a discussion of DeGraffenreid v. General Motors. In this case the courts ruled that black women could not receive compensation for their experiences of discrimination that were a result of being both black *and* female.

3. There are contradictions in the two bodies of law that place the individual's right to equal representation in conflict with majority or group rights spelled out in collective bargaining agreements. The practical implication of these contradictions in law, according to Iglesias (1997), is "to imprison minorities in institutional arrangements in which they can hold no effective power" (321). Since women of color will never be in the majority in either predominantly black work settings or predominately female work settings, they are caught in an incommensurable situation.

4. This information comes from O'Farrell and Kornbluh (1996).

5. For an understanding of the significance of the EEOC battle, see Betty Friedan (2000) and Rosen (2000).

6. Stone (1975) argues that this deliberate pattern of fragmentation promoted competition and blunted class-consciousness and solidarity.

7. Ethnic stratification magnified the advantages of the initial job placement within the mill. Each European group had their own place in the mill. Unlike race, the adverse effects of ethnicity tended to diminished over time.

8. Minority workers were allowed to retain their old wages if transferring to a new department to take advantage of better promotional opportunities resulted in a pay cut.

9. See Kleiman (1975) and Fischer (1975) for detailed account of the consent decree from the union's perspective.

10. Teamsters v. United States, 431 U.S. 324.

11. For conflicting interpretations of *Weber,* see Hill (2002) and Stein (1998).

12. Audit and Review, b3f6.

13. Mary Kearney. Interview by the author, Wheeling, West Virginia (1977). Tape recording.

14. Ibid.

15. Audit and Review, b30f6.

16. Robert Moore. Interview by the author, Washington, D.C. (9 November 1998). Tape recording.

17. Gloria Reehill. Interview by Mary Lu Foote, HCLA, Penn State University, University Park (6 July 1971). Tape recording.

18. United Steelworkers of America, Local 1104 v. United States Steel Corp., 479 F. 2d 1255 (6th Cir. 1973).

19. Audit and Review, b6.

20. See the film *Struggles in Steel: The Fight for Equal Opportunity* (Tony Buba [1996], California Newsreel). For an analysis of the film see Lynd (1997).

21. Audit and Review, b6.

22. For a much fuller discussion of the case see Luxton and Corman (1991); Easson et al. (1983); and Gray (1986).

4. What's a Nice Girl Like You Doing in a Place Like This?

1. In 1976–77 when I conducted these interviews, the political climate was such that I believed that identifying respondents would place them at risk. The passing of time has made it impossible to locate the original subjects to secure permission to use their names.

2. Given the nature of racist stereotypes, the representations of black women, particularly in situations that challenge normative cultural scripts for femininity, may not function the same ways as representations of white women. The black

press might be more sensitive to the hypermasculinizing of black women by the dominant media.

3. This is particularly startling because this plant was known for its union militancy and radical labor politics and for the role the union local played in the civil rights movement in Detroit (Stepan-Norris and Zeitlin 1996).

4. Theresa Ogresovich. Interview by the author (1977).

5. Conway Owens. Interview by the author, Steubenville, Ohio (1977). Tape recording.

6. Peggy Piazza. Interview by the author (1977).

5. Mobilizing Women Steelworkers for Their Rights

1. The Calumet region includes the following counties in Illinois: Cook, DuPage, Grundy, Kankakee, Kane, Kendall, and Will; and in Indiana: Lake, Porter, LaPorte, and St. Joseph.

2. For a discussion on the significance of place in understanding union culture, see Herod (1998).

3. See Weigand (2001) for a fascinating account of the role communist women played in the 1950s and 1960s to keep feminism alive.

4. International Socialists moved to other heavily industrialized regions of the country, such as Chicago, Baltimore, Detroit, Pittsburgh, and Buffalo, targeting steel and auto as part of a deliberate political program to move workers to the Left.

5. See Horowitz's (1998) political biography of Friedan, particularly on her work as a labor journalist for UE and her familiarity with united-front politics.

6. See Nancy Seifer's (1976) interview with Bonnie Halascsak for details about the conflict between the community chapter of NOW and the union chapter.

7. See Mansbridge (1986) for detailed account of why the ERA lost in Illinois.

8. See Evans (1979), Freeman (1975), Rosen (2000), and Strobel (1995) for an understanding of the link between the women's movement and the New Left, with particular attention to Chicago.

9. Dorreen Carey. Interview by the author, Gary, Indiana (4 August 1999). Tape recording.

10. Ola Kennedy. Interview by James Lane (21 March 1991).

11. For the definition of bridge leadership and for an analysis of the various types of bridge leadership, see Robnett's (1997) discussion of the role of African American women in the struggles for civil rights.

12. For an analysis of the ways in which the civil rights infrastructure mobilized for the election of Hatcher, see Nelson and Meranto (1977) and Greer (1979). For a discussion of the role of the Ad Hoc Committee in District 31, see Needleman (2003), Nyden (1983), and Wilson (1980).

13. Steffi Domike. Interview by the author, Pittsburgh (9 January 2001).

14. According to Hammonds (1997, 296), "The conference is at once a discursive field, a pedagogic apparatus, and a site of cultural reproduction." While she makes this point about feminist conferences, I think the same can be said for labor events.

15. Issues of autonomy, control, and building solidarity across the many lines of difference among women continued to perplex the organization (Balser 1987; Roth 1997).

16. Anonymous delegate. Interview by the author, Las Vegas, Nevada (2 September 1976).

17. Anonymous delegate. Interview by the author, Las Vegas, Nevada (2 September 1976).

18. Group interview (included Sissy Humienny, Diane (nee Gumulauski) Kaczocha, Alice Peurala, and Roberta Wood) by the author (Las Vegas, Nevada, 2 September 1976). Tape recording.

19. See discussions in Bruno (1999) and Metzgar (2000) about the meaning and political significance of shop floor struggles regarding work rules.

6. Making Waves

1. Wood Papers, Annual Officers Report (1977). Handwritten.

2. For a discussion of the dilemma pregnancy presented to the women's movement, see Vogel (1993) and Greenwald (1978).

3. See Greenwald (1978) and Vogel (1993) for a more extensive analysis of *Gilbert* and of pregnancy discrimination more generally.

4. See Crenshaw (1988) for a discussion of the contradictory nature of anti-discrimination legal discourse.

5. A complete set of the *Bulletin* is located in Gary, Indiana. Newsletters, USWA 31 Women's Caucus, 1978–1982, Dorreen and William Carey Papers, Calumet Regional Archives, Indiana University Northwest Library, Gary, Indiana.

6. Ola Kennedy. Interview by James B. Lane (21 March 1991). Calumet Regional Archives, Gary, Indiana.

7. Robin Rich. Interview by James B. Lane (24 March 1991).

8. Dorreen Carey. Interview by the author, Gary, Indiana (4 August 1999). Tape recording.

9. *Union Maids* (1980), James Klein, Julie Reichert, and Miles Mogulescu, New Day Films.

10. For a detailed discussion of this contradiction and for other ways in which equity law fails to address the type of discrimination faced by women of color at work, see Iglesias (1997), Smith (1991), and Crenshaw (1988).

11. See Metzgar (1984) on the Steelworkers' approach to concession bargaining.

12. Lorraine Springfield. Interview by the author, Columbus, Ohio (6 August 1985). Tape recording.

13. Interview by the author (1985). Tape recording.

14. Joan Hac. Interview by the author, Columbus, Ohio (6 August 1985). Tape recording.

15. Paula Dagman. Interview by the author, Columbus, Ohio (6 August 1985). Tape recording.

7. *Women of Steel* Crossing the Border

1. The functions of the AFL-CIO's Working Women's Department have been absorbed into other departments, and its former director, Karen Nausbaum, serves as assistant to the president on women's issues.

2. See Canadian Labour Congress (CLC). 1989. *Report of the Task Force on the Labour/Party Relationship.* Ottawa: CLC.

3. In Canada, union density slipped from 40 percent in 1983 to 36.2 percent, and in the United States it fell to below 20 percent (Jenson and Mahon 1993, 81).

4. *Women of Steel* Development Course: Leaders' Manual (1998). USWA Canadian National Office, Toronto.

5. Leo Gerard. Interview by the author (10 January 2001).

6. Michael Lewis. Interview by the author, Etobicoke, Ontario (21 August 1995). Tape recording.

7. Daina Green. Interview by the author (21 August 1995). Tape recording.

8. Rusell Caracciolo. Interview by the author, Pittsburgh (5 August 1996). Tape recording.

9. Sandy Sutton. Interview by the author, LaPorte, Indiana (8 September 1994). Tape recording.

10. Nancy Lessin. Interview by the author, Las Vegas, Nevada (29 August 1994). Tape recording.

11. Betty Wickie. Interview by the author, Etobicoke, Ontario (21 August 1995). Tape recording.

12. Colette Murphy. Interview by the author, Las Vegas, Nevada (29 August 1994). Tape recording.

13. Nancy Hutchinson. Interview by the author, Las Vegas, Nevada (30 August 1994). Tape recording.

14. Loureen Evans. Interview by the author, Las Vegas, Nevada (30 August 1994). Tape recording.

15. Stephanie Stallings [pseud.]. Interview by the author, Merrillville, Indiana (21 October 1994). Tape recording.

16. Valerie Thomas [pseud.]. Interview by the author, Merrillville, Indiana (21 October 1994). Tape recording.

17. Loretta Tyler. Interview by the author, Las Vegas, Nevada (30 August 1994). Tape recording.

18. Marlene Gow. Interview by the author, Toronto, Ontario (22 August 1995). Tape recording.

19. Women of Steel Development Course: Building Solidarity, section 1, p. 1.

20. Sue Milling. Interview by the author, Etobicoke, Ontario (21 August 1995). Tape recording.

21. There is a growing body of feminist writing about race and nation in Canada. See Agnew 1996, Andrew and Rodgers 1997, Bannerji 2000, and Pierson and Cohen 1995.

8. Building Feminist International Solidarity in the Age of Globalization

1. The use of media to frame movement issues and strategies for social change is characteristic of transnational social movement organizations (McCarthy et al. 1996).

2. *For Respect for the Rights of Working Women: Authentic Labor Front and Women of Steel,* n.d.

3. Observers and activists have noted that the convergence of human rights discourses and citizenship-rights discourses (around themes of democracy and globalization) has created and expanded networks across national boundaries that are organized. Participants in these networks develop a sense of themselves as political subjects who can be mobilized to reclaim citizenship rights (Blacklock and Macdonald 1998).

4. See Rupp and Taylor (1999) for an excellent discussion of the ways in which organizational identity can become the basis for solidarity.

5. Maquiladoras employ about one million workers throughout Mexico, though most of the employment is concentrated in towns and cities along the Mexico and U.S. borders. Women are 65 percent of employees in this sector of the Mexican economy (Enrique Rangel, "Mexican Women Breaking Free of Restraints," *Houston Chronicle,* 11 January 1998, sec. J1). There are several good references for understanding women's employment in the maquiladoras. See Prieto (1985), Cravey (1998), and Fernandez-Kelly (1983).

6. The amount of job loss in the United States and Canada as a direct result of NAFTA is hard to measure. The U.S. government's General Accounting Office claims that statistics are unreliable and that results from various studies range from job losses of 420,000 to job gains of 160,000 (*El Financiero Weekly International,* 11 January 1998).

7. United Electrical (UE) brought organizers from the Frente Auténtico del Trabajo to Milwaukee to organize Mexican workers who had migrated to the city looking for better jobs but had only found more of the same. With the help of the Frente Auténtico del Trabajo, UE won the union election at Ace Co., an aluminum foundry (Davis 1998). Ng (1998) argues that the restructuring of the garment industry has resulted in the recolonization of third world women in the first world.

8. As a tool of analysis, the concept of contingent solidarities provides a framework for identifying how and why women have defined their political interests the way they have within particular political fields. This concept "allows for a cross-national analysis of the ways in which class, welfare state, labor market and cultural discourses have included or excluded women and how women trade unionists themselves have influenced the construction and formulation of claims, strategies and solidarities" (Curtin 1999, 160).

9. "This weakening in the liberal feminist leadership within NAC occurred at the same time as socialist and radical feminists were working both to strengthen their representation and to re-organize NAC along more grassroots lines. By the fall of 1985, the stage was set for a potentially very significant confrontation between NAC and the policies of the federal Conservative government" (Bashevkin 1991, 140).

10. The CLUW addressed the issue at its 1994 convention, followed in quick succession by the Beijing Conference on Women, National Council for Research on Women, NOW, and Feminist Majority.

11. For an excellent discussion of the role of the Ford Foundation in financing feminism in general, see Hartmann (1998).

12. The full text of their demands includes the following item as the number one demand: Incorporate core workers' rights and environmental accords—with strong enforceable procedures—into the WTO rules. These rights must include prohibition against the use of forced or compulsory labor, specific prohibitions against the use of forced child labor, worker supported standards for wages, hours of work and occupational safety and health, and requirements for nations to enforce their existing laws—including those that bar discrimination. Other demands include harmonizing these standards up to the level of the nation with higher standards; eliminating all WTO rules that undermine national regulations protecting public health, the environment, and social programs; WTO membership criteria pegged to compliance with core workers rights and environmental protections in home nation; access for unions and NGOs to WTO dispute settlement process; and a mechanism for strengthening safeguards against import surges that threaten domestic industries.

13. Although the capacity and willingness of states to intervene to ameliorate the social dislocations and disruptions caused by increased international competi-

tion for capital investments vary by regime type, in almost all cases it has been weakened (Breitenfellner 1997).

14. Unfortunately, the focus has been too often on women as victims—forced abortions, rape, prostitution.

15. See Juravich and Bronfenbrenner (1999) for an interesting account of how the Steelworkers employed an international campaign to win a protracted labor dispute at an aluminum plant in Ravenswood, West Virginia.

16. Jim English. Interview by the author, Pittsburgh (8 January 2002).

17. The Steelworkers claim that Rapid Response is responsible for stopping the fast-track authorization initiative of President Clinton.

18. For a discussion of NGOs as sites for feminist politics, see Alvarez (1998) and Lang (1997).

19. *Steelabor*, Winter 1999, 24. *Steelabor* is the union's official membership magazine, published every two months. It is also published on the Web.

20. *"Estrategias Programa De Trabajo Del Authentic Labor Front 1998–2000,"* XI Congreso Nacional, Frente Auténtico del Trabajo, 13–14 (n.d.). Translated by Norma Juarbe-Franceschini.

21. "Mujer: Una presencia esencial para desarrollo," (CODIM, n.d.).

22. "Mujer: Una presencia esencial para el desarralla" (Coordinación Nacional de Mujeres del Authéntic Labor Front, n.d.). Translated by Norma Juarbe-Franceschini.

23. "XI Congreso Nacional Frente Auténtico del Trabajo: Estrategias y Programa de Trabajo del FAT 1998–2000," n.d. Translated by Norma Juarbe-Franceschini.

24. Ibid.

25. For an excellent discussion of unequal power relations and their effect on feminist efforts to build international solidarity, see Ong (1999).

26. This has been stimulated, in part, by two highly visible, international conferences sponsored by the United Nations—the World Conference on Human Rights in Vienna in 1993 and the Fifth International Women's Conference in Beijing in 1995. For a complete discussion of the emergence of international women's rights networks and their links to human rights issues, see chapter five in Keck and Sikkink (1998).

9. Forging Union Feminism and the Fight for Social Justice

1. See the USWA Website for the complete results of the "Women of Steel" survey at www.uswa.org.

2. Carolyn Egan. Interview by the author, Toronto, Ontario (8 March 1999). Tape recording.

3. Fil Falbo. Interview by the author, Toronto, Ontario (8 March 1999). Tape recording.

4. Quotes by Egan and Edwards are from the USWA Website (www.uswa.ca), "USWA Canada Steelworkers 72 Hours on Parliament Hill for the World March of Women 2000."

5. Carol Landry. Interview by the author, Pittsburgh (February 2000). Tape recording.

6. Sharon Stiller. Telephone interview by the author (9 September 2001). Tape recording.

7. Ibid.

8. *Steelabor,* March/April 2001, 11.

References

Abella, Rosalie. 1987. "The Dynamic Nature of Equality." In *Equality and Judicial Neutrality*, edited by S. L. Martin and K. E. Mahoney, 3–9. Toronto: Carswell.

Acker, Joan. 1995. "Feminist Goals and Organizing Processes." In *Feminist Organizations: Harvest of the New Women's Movement*, edited by Myra Marx Ferree and Patricia Yancey Martin, 137–44. Philadelphia: Temple University Press.

Agnew, Vijay. 1996. *Resisting Discrimination: Women from Asia, Africa, and the Caribbean and the Women's Movement in Canada*. Toronto: University of Toronto Press.

Alarcón, Norma, Caren Kaplan, and Minoo Moallem. 1999. "Introduction: Between Woman and Nation." In *Between Woman and Nation: Nationalisms, Transnational Feminisms, and the State*, edited by Caren Kaplan, Norma Alarcón, and Minoo Moallem, 3–16. Durham: Duke University Press.

Alvarez, Sonia. 1998. "Latin American Feminisms 'Go Global': Trends of the 1990s and Challenges for the New Millennium." In *Cultures of Politics/ Politics of Cultures: Re-visioning Latin American Social Movements*, edited by Sonia E. Alvarez, Evelina Dagnino, and Arturo Escobar, 293–324. Boulder: Westwood.

Andrew, Caroline, and Sandra Rodgers. 1997. *Women and the Canadian State/Les Femmes et L'Etat Canadien*. Montreal: McGill-Queen's University Press.

Appelbaum, Richard P. 1996. "Multiculturalism and Flexibility: Some New Directions in Global Capitalism." In *Mapping Multi-Culturalism*, edited by Avery F. Gordon and Christopher Newfield, 297–316. Minneapolis: University of Minnesota Press.

Bakker, Isabella. 1996. *Rethinking Restructuring: Gender and Change in Canada.* Toronto: University of Toronto Press.

Balser, Diane. 1987. *Sisterhood and Solidarity: Feminism and Labor in Modern Times.* Boston: South End Press.

Bannerji, Himani. 2000. *The Dark Side of the Nation: Essays on Multiculturalism, Nationalism, and Gender.* Toronto: Canadian Scholars Press.

Baron, Ava. 1991. "Gender and Labor History: Learning From the Past, Looking to the Future." In *Work Engendered: Toward a New History of American Labor,* edited by A. Baron, 1–46. Ithaca: Cornell University Press.

Bashevkin, Sylvia. 1991. *True Patriot Love: The Politics of Canadian Nationalism.* Toronto: Oxford University Press.

———. 1998. *Woman on the Defensive.* Chicago: University of Chicago Press.

Beckwith, Karen. 1996. "Lancashire Women against Pit Closures: Women's Standing in a Men's Movement." *Signs: Journal of Women in Culture and Society* 21: 1034–68.

———. 2001. "Gender Frames and Collective Action: Configurations of Masculinity in the Pittston Coal Strike." *Politics and Society* 29 (2): 295–328.

Bernard, Elaine. 1993. "Labour, the New Democratic Party, and the 1988 Federal Election." In *The Challenge of Restructuring: North American Labor Movements Respond,* edited by Jane Jenson and Rianne Mahon, 137–53. Philadelphia: Temple University Press.

Bensman, David, and Roberta Lynch. 1988. *Rusted Dreams: Hard Times in a Steel Community.* Berkeley: University of California Press.

Blacklock, Cathy, and Laura Macdonald. 1998. "Human Rights and Citizenship in Guatemala and Mexico: From 'Strategic' to 'New' Universalism." *Social Politics* 5 (2): 132–57.

Blum, Linda M. 1991. *Between Feminism and Labor: The Significance of the Comparable Worth Movement.* Berkeley: University of California Press.

Boswell, Terry, and Dimitris Steves. 1997. "Globalization and International Labor Organizing." *Work and Occupations* 24 (3): 288–308.

Breitenfellner, Andreas. 1997. "Global Unionism: A Potential Player." *International Labour Review* 136: 531–55.

Briskin, Linda. 1993. "Union Women and Separate Organizing." In *Women Challenging Unions: Feminism, Democracy, and Militancy,* edited by Linda Briskin and Patricia McDermott, 89–108. Toronto: University of Toronto Press.

Briskin, Linda, and Patricia McDermott. 1993. *Women Challenging Unions: Feminism, Democracy, and Militancy.* Toronto: University of Toronto Press.

Briskin, Linda, and Mona Eliasson. 1999. *Women's Organizing and Public Policy in Canada and Sweden.* Montreal: McGill-Queen's University Press.

Brodie, Janine. 1995. *Politics on the Margins: Restructuring and the Canadian Women's Movement.* Halifax: Fernwood Publishing.

Brody, David. 1987. *Labor in Crisis: The Steel Strike of 1919.* Urbana: University of Illinois Press. ?

Bronfenbrenner, Kate, Sheldon Friedman, Richard W. Hurd, Rudolph A. Oswald, and Ronald L. Seeber. 1998. *Organizing to Win: New Research on Union Strategies.* Ithaca: Cornell University Press.

Brown, Lawrence A., Linda M. Lobao, and Anthony Verheyen. 1996. "Continuity and Change in an Old Industrial Region: The Case of the Ohio River Valley." *Growth and Change* 27: 175–205.

Brown, Wendy. 1995. *States of Injury: Power and Freedom in Late Modernity.* Princeton: Princeton University Press.

Bruno, Robert. 1999. *Steelworker Alley: How Class Works in Youngstown.* Ithaca: Cornell University Press

Burns, Barbara. 1977. "Why I Decided to 'Go Underground.'" *McCall's,* September, 69, 73, 82.

Carter, Dan T. 1995. *The Politics of Rage, the Origins of the New Conservatism, and the Transformation of American Politics.* New York: Simon and Schuster.

Cerulo, Karen A. 1997. "Identity Construction: New Issues, New Directions." *Annual Review of Sociology* 23: 385–409.

Clarke, Paul F., Peter Gottlieb, and Donald Kennedy. 1987. *Forging a Union of Steel: Philip Murray, SWOC, and the United Steelworkers.* Ithaca: ILR Press.

Cobble, Dorothy Sue. 1990. "Rethinking Troubled Relations between Women and Unions: Craft Unionism and Female Activism." *Feminist Studies* 16 (3): 519–47.

———. 1991. *Dishing It Out: Waitresses and Their Unions in the Twentieth Century.* Urbana: University of Illinois Press.

———. 1993. *Women and Unions: Forging a Partnership.* Ithaca: ILR Press.

———. 1994. "Recapturing Working-Class Feminism: Union Women in the Postwar Era." In *Not June Cleaver: Women and Gender in Postwar America, 1945–1960,* edited by Joanne Meyerowitz, 57–83. Philadelphia: Temple University Press.

———. 2003. *Transforming Work: Lost Traditions of Feminism in Modern America.* Princeton: Princeton University Press.

Cobble, Dorothy, and Monica Bielski Michal. 2002. "On the Edge of Equality? Working Women and the U.S. Labor Movement." In *Gender, Diversity, and Trade Unions: International Perspectives,* edited by Fiona Colgan and Sue Ledwith. London: Routledge.

Cockburn, Cynthia. 1997. "Gender in an International Space: Trade Union Women as European Social Actor." *Women's Studies International Forum* 20 (4): 459–70.

Cohen, Marjorie Griffin. 1997. "What Women Should Know about Economic Fundamentalism." *Atlantis* 22 (1): 97–107.

Colgan, Fiona, and Sue Ledwith. 2002. *Gender, Diversity, and Trade Unions: International Perspectives.* London: Routledge.

Colker, Ruth. 1998. *American Law in the Age of Hypercapitalism: The Worker, the Family, and the State.* New York: New York University Press.

Collins, Patricia Hill. 1990. *Black Feminist Thought: Knowledge, Consciousness, and the Politics of Empowerment.* New York: Routledge, Chapman, and Hall.

Cook, Alice, Val R. Lorwin, and Arlene Kaplan Daniels. 1984. *Women and Trade Unions in Eleven Industrialized Countries.* Philadelphia: Temple University Press.

Cooper, Patricia. 1991. "The Faces of Gender: Sex Segregation and Work Relations at Philco, 1928–1938." In *Work Engendered: Toward a New History of American Labor,* edited by A. Baron, 320–50. Ithaca: Cornell University Press.

Cornfield, Daniel. 1989. *Becoming a Mighty Voice: Conflict and Change in the United Furniture Workers of America.* New York: Russell Sage Foundation.

Cornfield, Daniel, and Melinda D. Kane. 1998. "Gender Segmentation, Union Decline, and Women Workers: Changes in the AFL-CIO Policy Agenda, 1955–1993." Paper presented at 93rd annual Meeting of the American Sociological Association, San Francisco, California.

Crain, Marion. 1994. "Between Feminism and Unionism: Working Class Women, Sex Equality, and Labor Speech." *Georgetown Law Journal* 82: 1903–2001.

Cravey, Altha J. 1998. *Women and Work in Mexico's Maquiladoras.* Lanham, Md.: Rowman and Littlefield.

Creese, Gillian. 1996. "Gendering Collective Bargaining: From Men's Rights to Women's Issues." *Canadian Review of Sociology and Anthropology* 33 (4): 437–56.

Crenshaw, Kimberlee. 1988. "Race, Reform, and Retrenchment: Transformation and Legitimation in Antidiscrimination Law." *Harvard Law Review* 101 (May): 1331–87.

Crimp, Douglas. 1992. "Right On, Girlfriend." *Social Text* 33: 2–18.

Cuneo, Carl L. 1993. "Trade Union Leadership: Sexism and Affirmative Action." In *Women Challenging Unions: Feminism, Democracy, and Militancy,* edited by Linda Briskin and Patricia McDermott, 109–36. Toronto: University of Toronto Press.

Curtin, Jennifer. 1999. *Women and Trade Unions: A Comparative Perspective.* Brookfield, USA: Ashgate.

Dagnino, Evelina. 1998. "Culture, Citizenship, and Democracy: Changing Discourses, and Practices of the Latin American Left." In *Cultures of Politics/*

Politics of Cultures: Re-visioning Latin American Social Movements, edited by Sonia E. Alvarez, Evelina Dagnino, and Arturo Escobar, 33–63. Boulder: Westwood.

Davis, Terry. 1998. "Cross Border Organizing Comes Home: UE and Frente Auténtico del Trabajo in Mexico and Milwaukee." *Labor Research Review* 23: 23–29.

Deaux, Kay, and Joseph C. Ulman. 1983. *Women of Steel: Female Blue-Collar Workers in the Basic Steel Industry.* New York: Praeger Publishers.

Deitch, Cynthia, Thomas Nowak, and Kay Snyder. 1991. "Manufacturing Job Loss among Blue-Collar Women: An Assessment of Data and Policy." In *Gender and Public Policy,* edited by Mary Lou Kendrigan, 33–66. Westview, Conn.: Greenword.

della Porta, Donatella, Hanspeter Kriesi, and Dieter Rucht. 1999. *Social Movements in a Globalizing World.* New York: St. Martin's Press.

Demarest, David, Jr. 1992. *"The River Ran Red," Homestead 1892.* Pittsburgh: University of Pittsburgh Press.

Deslippe, Dennis. A. 2000. *Rights Not Roses: Unions and the Rise of Working-Class Feminism, 1945–80.* Urbana-Champaign: University of Illinois Press.

Devinatz, Victor G. 1993. "From Industrial Unionism to General Unionism: A Historical Transformation?" *Labor Law Journal* 44 (April): 252–56.

Dickerson, Dennis. 1986. *Out of the Crucible: Black Steel Workers in Western Pennsylvania, 1980.* Albany: State University of New York Press.

Downs, Laura Lee. 1995. *Manufacturing Inequality: Gender Division in the French and British Metalworking Industries, 1914–1939.* Ithaca: Cornell University Press.

Easson, J., D. Field, and J. Santucci. 1983. "Working Steel." In *Hard Earned Wages: Women Fighting for Better Work,* edited by Jennifer Penny, 191–218. Toronto: Women's Educational Press.

Emmett, Ayala. 1998. "Sex and Gender as Raw Material: Local Women Negotiate Globalization." *Sex Roles* 39 (7/8): 503–13.

Erickson, Ethel. 1944. *Women's Employment in the Making of Steel.* Washington, D.C.: Government Printing Office.

Evans, Sara. 1979. *Personal Politics: The Roots of Women's Liberation in the Civil Rights Movement and the New Left.* New York: Random House.

Faludi, Susan. 1991. *Backlash.* New York: Crown Publishing.

———. 1999. *Stiffed: The Betrayal of the American Man.* New York: William Morrow and Company.

Fantasia, Rick. 1988. *Cultures of Solidarity: Consciousness, Action, and Contemporary American Workers.* Berkeley: University of California Press.

Faue, Elizabeth. 1991. *Community of Suffering and Struggle: Women, Men, and the Labor Movement in Minneapolis.* Chapel Hill: University of North Carolina Press.

Fernandez-Kelly, Maria Patricia. 1983. *For We Are Sold, I and My People: Women and Industry in Mexico's Frontier.* Albany: State University of New York Press.

Ferree, Myra Marx, and Patricia Yancey Martin. 1995. *Feminist Organizations: Harvest of the New Women's Movement.* Philadelphia: Temple University Press.

Ferree, Myra Marx, and Silke Roth. 1998. "Gender, Class and the Interaction Between Social Movements." *Gender and Society* 12 (6): 626–48.

Fischer, Ben. 1975. "Evaluating the Steel Industry Consent Decree." b21, f22, HCLA, Penn State University, University Park, Pennsylvania.

Fitch, John. 1969. *The Steel Worker.* New York: Arno and the *New York Times.*

Flain, Paul O., and Ellen Sehgal. 1985. "Displaced Workers of 1979–83: How Well Have They Fared?" *Monthly Labor Review* 108 (6): 3–16.

Fonow, Mary Margaret. 1977. "Women in Steel: A Case Study of the Participation of Women in a Trade Union." Ph.D. diss., Ohio State University, Columbus.

———. 1998. "Protest Engendered: The Participation of Women Steelworkers in the Wheeling Pittsburgh Steel Strike of 1985." *Gender and Society* 12 (6): 710–28.

Form, William. 1995. *Segmented Labor, Fractured Politics.* New York: Plenum.

Forrest, Anne. 2001. Connecting Women with Unions: What Are the Issues?" *RI/IR* 56 (4): 647–74.

Franzway, Suzanne. 2000. "Sisters and Sisters? Labour Movements and Women's Movements in (English) Canada and Australia." *Hectate* 26 (2) 31–46.

———. 2001. *Sexual Politics and Greedy Institutions: Union Women, Commitments, and Conflicts in Public and Private.* Annandale, NSW: Pluto Press.

Fraser, Nancy. 1997. *Justice Interruptus: Critical Reflections on the "Postsocialist" Condition.* New York: Routledge.

Freeman, Jo. 1975. *The Politics of Women's Liberation: A Case Study of an Emerging Social Movement and Its Relation to the Policy Process.* New York: David McKay.

———. 1999. "A Model for Analyzing the Strategic Options of Social Movement Organizations." In *Waves of Protest: Social Movements since the Sixties,* edited by Jo Freeman and Victoria Johnson, 221–40. New York: Rowman and Littlefield Publishers.

Freeman, Joshua B. 1993. "Hard Hats: Construction Workers, Manliness and the 1970 Pro War Demonstrations." *Journal of Social History* 26 (Summer): 726–32.

Friedan, Betty. 2000. *Life So Far: A Memoir.* New York: Simon and Schuster.

Gabin, Nancy F. 1990. *Feminism in the Labor Movement: Women and the United Auto Workers, 1935–1975.* Ithaca: Cornell University Press.

Gabriel, Christina, and Laura Macdonald. 1994. "NAFTA, Women and Organising in Canada and Mexico: Forging a 'Feminist Internationality.'" *Millennium: Journal of International Studies* 23 (3): 535–62.

Gamson, William A. 1997. "Constructing Social Protest." In *Social Movements: Perspectives and Issues,* edited by Steven M. Buechler and F. Kurt Cylke Jr., 229–44. Mountain View, Calif.: Mayfield.

Gamson, William A., and Gadi Wolfseld. 1993. "Movements and Media as Interacting Systems." AAPSS *Annals,* July, 114–25.

Gamson, William, and David S. Meyer. 1996. "Framing Political Opportunity." In *Comparative Perspectives on Social Movements,* edited by Doug McAdam, John D. McCarthy, and Mayer N. Zald, 275–90. Cambridge: Cambridge University.

Gerstel, Naomi, and Dan Clawson. 2001. "Union Response to Family Concerns." *Social Problems* 48 (2) (May): 277–97.

Gibson-Graham, J. K. 1996. *The End of Capitalism (As We Knew It): A Feminist Critique of Political Economy.* London: Blackwell.

Goldfarb, Lyn. 1976. *Separated and Unequal: Discrimination against Women Workers after World War II (The U.A.W. 1944–1945).* Silver Springs, Md.: The Women's Work Project.

Gordon, Michael E., and Lowell Turner. 2000. *Transnational Cooperation among Labor Unions.* Ithaca: ILR Press/Cornell.

Gray, Stan. 1986. "Fight to Survive—The Case of Bonita Clark." *Canadian Dimension* 20 (3): 15–20.

Greer, Edward. 1979. *Big Steel: Black Politics and Corporate Power in Gary, Indiana.* New York: Monthly Review Press.

Greenwald, Carol Schiro. 1978. *Women's Rights, Courts, and Congress: Conflict over Pregnancy Disability Compensation Policy.* New York: Social Studies/Social Sciences Education. September 3. Microfiche.

Hammonds, Evelynn. 1997. "When the Margin Is the Center: African-American Feminism(s) and 'Difference'." In *Transitions, Environments, Translations: Feminisms in International Politics,* edited by Joan Scott, Cora Kaplan, and Debra Keates, 295–309. New York: Routledge.

Haraway, Donna. 1991. *Simians, Cyborgs, and Women: The Reinvention of Women.* New York: Routledge.

Hartmann, Susan M. 1982. *The Home Front and Beyond: American Women in the 1940s.* Boston: Twayne Publishers.

———. 1998. *The Other Feminists: Activists in the Liberal Establishment.* New Haven: Yale University Press.

Herod, Andrew. 1998. "Geographic Mobility, Place, and Cultures of Labor Unions." In *Organizing the Landscape: Geographical Perspectives on Labor*

Unionism, edited by Andrew Herod, 123–28. Minneapolis: University of Minnesota Press.

Hathaway, Dale. 2000. *Allies across the Border: Mexico's "Authentic Labor Front" and Global Solidarity.* Cambridge, Mass.: South End Press.

Hewitt, Nancy A. 1991. "The Voice of Virile Labor: Labor Militancy, Community Solidarity, and Gender Identity among Tampa's Latin Workers, 1880–1921." In *Work Engendered: Toward a New History of American Labor,* edited by A. Baron, 142–67. Ithaca: Cornell University Press.

Hill, Herbert. 1991. *Black Labor and the American Legal System.* Washington, D.C.: Bureau of National Affairs.

———. 1993. "Black Workers, Organized Labor, and Title VII of the 1964 Civil Rights Act: Legislative History and Litigation Record." In *Race in America: The Struggle for Equality,* edited by Herbert Hill and James E. Jones Jr., 263–344. Madison: University of Wisconsin.

———. 2002. "Race and the Steelworkers Union: White Privilege and Black Struggle. A Review Essay of Judith Stein's *Running Steel, Running America.*" *New Politics* 7 (4): 1–58.

Hinshaw, John. 2002. *Steel and Steelworkers: Race and Class Struggle in Twentieth Century Pittsburgh.* Albany: State University of New York Press.

Honey, Maureen. 1984. *Creating Rosie the Riveter: Class, Gender, and Propaganda during World War II.* Amherst: University of Massachusetts Press.

———. 1999. *Bitter Fruit: African American Women in World War II.* Columbia: University of Missouri Press.

Horowitz, Daniel. 1998. *Betty Friedan and the Making of the Feminine Mystique: The American Left, the Cold War, and Modern Feminism.* Amherst: University of Massachusetts Press.

Hymowitz, Carol. 1985. "Layoffs Force Blue-Collar Women Back into Low-Paying-Job Ghetto." *Wall Street Journal,* 6 March, 39.

Iglesias, Elizabeth M. 1997. "Structures of Subordination: Women of Color at the Intersection of Title VII and the NLRA. Not!" In *Critical Race Feminism: A Reader,* edited by Adrien Wing, 317–32. New York: New York University Press.

Jamal, Amina. 1998. "Situating South Asian Women in the Canadian/Global Economy." *Canadian Woman Studies/Les Cahiers de la Femme* 18 (1): 26–34.

Jenkins, J. Craig, and Kevin Leicht. 1997. "Class Analysis and Social Movements: A Critique and Reformulation." In *Reworking Class,* edited by John R. Hall, 369–98. Ithaca: Cornell University Press.

Jenson, Jane, and Rianne Mahon. 1993. "Legacies for Canadian Labour of Two Decades of Crisis." In *The Challenge of Restructuring: North American Labor*

Movements Respond, edited by Jane Jenson and Rianne Mahon, 72–91. Philadelphia: Temple University Press.

Johnston, Hank, and Bert Klandermans. 1995. *Social Movements and Culture.* Minneapolis: University of Minnesota Press.

Johnston, Hank, Enrique Laraña, and Joseph R. Gusfield. 1997. "Identities, Grievances, and New Social Movements." In *Social Movements: Perspectives and Issues,* edited by Steven M. Buechler and F. Kurt Cylke Jr., 274–94. Mountain View, Calif.: Mayfield.

Jones, Amelia. 1992. "Feminism, Incorporated: Reading 'Postfeminism' in an Anti-Feminist Age." *Afterimage,* December, 10–15.

Juravich, Tom, and Kate Bronfenbrenner. 1999. *Ravenswood: The Steelworkers' Victory and the Revival of American Labor.* Ithaca: Cornell University Press.

Kanter, Rosabeth Moss. 1977. *Men and Women of the Corporation.* New York: Basic Books.

Katzenstein, Mary Fainsod. 1990. "Feminism within American Institutions: Unobtrusive Mobilization in the 1980s." *Signs: Journal of Women in Culture and Society* 16: 27–55.

———. 1995. "Discursive Politics and Feminist Activism in the Catholic Church." In *Feminist Organizations: Harvest of the New Women's Movement,* edited by Myra Marx Ferree and Patricia Yancey Martin. Philadelphia: Temple University Press.

———. 1998. *Faithful and Fearless: Moving Feminist Protest inside the Church and Military.* Princeton: Princeton University Press.

Keck, Jennifer, and Mary Powell. 1996. "Working at Inco: Women in a Down-sizing Male Industry." In *Changing Lives: Women in Northern Ontario,* edited by Margaret Kechnie and Marge Reitsma-Street. Toronto: Dundurn Press.

Keck, Margaret, and Kathryn Sikkink. 1998. *Activists beyond Borders.* Ithaca: Cornell University.

Kelley, Robin. 1997. *Yo Mama's Disfunktional: Fighting the Culture Wars in Urban America.* Boston: Beacon Press.

Kessler-Harris, Alice. 1975. "Where Are the Organized Women?" *Feminist Studies* 3 (no. 1–2): 92–110.

———. 1990. *A Woman's Wage: Historical Meanings and Social Consequences.* Lexington: University of Kentucky Press.

———. 2001. *In Pursuit of Equity: Women, Men, and the Quest for Economic Citizenship in 20th-Century America.* Oxford: Oxford University Press.

Khagram, Sanjeev, James V. Riker, and Kathrynn Sikkink, eds. 2002. *Restructuring World Politics: Transnational Social Movements, Networks, and Norms.* Minneapolis: University of Minnesota Press.

Klandermans, Bert. 1997. *The Social Psychology of Protest.* Oxford: Blackwell.

Kleiman, Bernard. 1975. "Seniority Remedies under Title VII: The Steel Consent Decree—A Union Perspective." b10, f9, HCLA, Penn State University, University Park, Pennsylvania.

Kriesi, Hanspeter. 1996. "The Impact of National Contexts on Social Movement Structures: A Cross-Movement and Cross-National Comparison." In *Comparative Perspectives on Social Movements: Political Opportunities, Mobilizing Structures, and Cultural Framing,* edited by Doug McAdam, John D. McCarthy, and Mayer N. Zald, 185–204. Cambridge: Cambridge University.

Krupat, Kitty, and Patrick McCreery. 2001. *Out at Work: Building a Gay-Labor Alliance.* Minneapolis: University of Minnesota Press.

Kubasek, Nancy K., Jennifer Johnson, and M. Neil Browne. 1994. "Comparable Worth in Ontario: Lessons the United States Can Learn." *Harvard Women's Law Journal* 17: 103–32.

Kumar, Pradeep. 1993. "Collective Bargaining and Women's Workplace Concerns." In *Women Challenging Unions: Feminism, Democracy, and Militancy,* edited by Linda Briskin and Patricia McDermott, 207–230. Toronto: University of Toronto Press.

Kurtz, Sharon. 2002. *Workplace Justice: Organizing Multi-Identity Movements.* Minneapolis: University of Minnesota Press.

Kymlica, Will. 1996. "Three Forms of Group-Differentiated Citizenship in Canada." In *Democracy and Difference,* edited by Seyla Benhabib, 153–170. Princeton: Princeton University Press.

La Boltz, Dan. 1992. *Mask of Democracy: Labor Suppression in Mexico Today.* Boston: South End.

Lane, James. 1996. "Feminism, Radicalism, and Unionism: The Calumet District Women's Caucus and Its Fight against Sex Discrimination in American Steel Mills." Proceedings of the International Oral History Conference, 9: 541–48.

Lang, Sabine. 1997. "The NGOization of Feminism." In *Transitions, Environments, Translations: Feminisms in International Politics,* edited by Joan W. Scott, Cora Kaplan, and Debra Keats, 101–20. New York: Routledge.

Laughlin, Kathleen A. 2000. *Women's Work and Public Policy: A History of the Women's Bureau, U.S. Department of Labor, 1945–1970.* Boston: Northeastern University Press.

"Let's Put It on the Table." 1997. United Steelworkers' Guide to Violence Prevention. Toronto: Canadian National Office of the USWA.

Linkon, Sherry Lee, and John Russo. 2002. *Steeltown U.S.A.: Work and Memory in Youngstown.* Lawrence: University of Kansas Press.

Lipset, Seymour Martin. 1990. *Continental Divide: The Values and Institutions of the United States and Canada.* New York: Routledge.

Livingstone, David, and Meg Luxton. 1996. "Gender Consciousness at Work: Modification of the Male Breadwinner Norm." In *Recast Dreams,* edited by David Livingstone and J. Marshall Mangan, 100–130. Toronto: Garamond Press.

Livingstone, David, and J. Marshall Mangan. 1996. *Recast Dreams.* Toronto: Garamond Press.

Lorber, Judith. 1994. *Paradoxes of Gender.* New Haven: Yale University Press.

Luxton, Meg. 1997. "Feminism as a Class Act: Working Class Feminism and the Women's Movement in Canada." Paper presented at Annual Meeting of the American Sociological Association, Toronto, Ontario.

Luxton, Meg, and June Corman. 1991. "Getting to Work: The Challenge of the Women Back into Stelco Campaign." *Labour/Le Travail* 28 (Fall): 149–85.

Lynd, Staughton. 1997. "History, Race, and the Steel Industry." *Radical Historians Newsletter* 76 (June): 13–16.

Mansbridge, Jane J. 1986. *Why We Lost the ERA.* Chicago: University of Chicago Press.

Marchand, Marianne H. 1994. "Gender and the New Regionalism in Latin America: Inclusion/Exclusion." *Third World Quarterly* 15 (1): 63–76.

Martin, Patricia Yancey. 1990. "Rethinking Feminist Organizations." *Gender and Society* 4 (2): 182–206.

McAdam, Doug. 1992. "Gender as a Mediator of the Activist Experience: The Case of Freedom Summer." *American Journal of Sociology* 97: 1211–40.

———. 1994. "Culture and Social Movements." In *New Social Movements: From Ideology to Identity,* edited by Enrique Laraña, Hank Johnston, and Joseph R. Gusfield, 36–57. Philadelphia: Temple University Press.

———. 1997. "The Political Process Model." In *Social Movements: Perspectives and Issues,* edited by Steven M. Buechler and F. Kurt Cylke Jr., 193–210. Mountain View, Calif.: Mayfield.

McAdam, Doug, John D. McCarthy, and Mayer N. Zald, eds. 1996. *Comparative Perspectives on Social Movements: Political Opportunities, Mobilizing Structures, and Cultural Framings.* Cambridge: Cambridge University Press.

McCarthy, John D. 1996. "Constraints and Opportunities in Adopting, Adapting, and Inventing." In *Comparative Perspectives on Social Movements: Political Opportunities, Mobilizing Structures, and Cultural Framings,* edited by Doug McAdam, John D. McCarthy, and Mayer N. Zald, 141–51. Cambridge: Cambridge University Press.

McCarthy, John D., Jackie Smith, and Mayer N. Zald. 1996. "Accessing Public, Media, Electoral, and Governmental Agendas." In *Comparative Perspectives on Social Movements,* edited by Doug McAdam, John D. McCarthy, and Mayer N. Zald, 291–311. Cambridge: Cambridge University Press.

Metzgar, Jack. 1984. "The Humbling of the Steelworkers." *Socialist Review* 75 (76): 41–71.

———. 2000. *Striking Steel: Solidarity Remembered.* Philadelphia: Temple University Press.

Milkman, Ruth. 1987. *Gender at Work: The Dynamics of Job Segregation by Sex during World War II.* Urbana: University of Illinois Press.

———. 1993. "Union Responses to Workforce Feminization in the U.S." In *The Challenge of Restructuring: North American Labor Movements Respond,* edited by Jane Jenson and Rianne Mahon, 226–50. Philadelphia: Temple University Press.

Misa, Thomas J. 1995. *A Nation of Steel: The Making of Modern America, 1865–1925.* Baltimore: Johns Hopkins Press.

Mohanty, Chandra Talpade. 1997. "Women Workers and Capitalist Scripts: Ideologies of Domination, Common Interests, and the Politics of Solidarity." In *Feminist Geologies, Colonial Legacies, Democratic Futures,* edited by M. Jacqui Alexander and Chandra Talpade, 3–29. New York: Routledge.

Morris, Aldon D., and Carol McClurg Mueller. 1992. *Frontiers in Social Movement Theory.* New Haven: Yale University Press.

Munro, Anne. 2001. "A Feminist Trade Union Agenda? The Continued Significance of Class, Gender, and Race." *Gender, Work, and Organization* 8 (4): 454–71.

Murray, Gregor. 1998. "Steeling for Change: Organization and Organizing in Two USWA Districts in Canada." In *Organizing to Win: New Research on Union Strategies,* edited by Kate Bronfenbrenner, Sheldon Friedman, Richard W. Hurd, Rudolph A. Oswald, and Ronald L. Seeber, 320–38. Ithaca: ILR Press.

Naples, Nancy A. 1998. *Grassroots Warriors: Activist Mothering, Community Work, and the War on Poverty.* New York: Routledge.

Naples, Nancy A., and Manish Desai, eds. 2002. *Women's Activism and Globalization: Linking Local Struggles and Transnational Politics.* New York: Routledge.

Needleman, Ruth. 1990. "It's Never Too Late: Office Workers at Bethlehem Steel." *Labor Research Review* 9 (1): 81–87.

———. 1998. "Women Workers Strategies for Inclusion and Rebuilding Unionism." In *A New Labor Movement for the New Century,* ed. G. Mantsios, 175–96. New York: Garland.

———. 2000. "Women of Steel in the Calumet Region: Coalitions Create Power." Presented at North American Labor History Conference, Detroit, Michigan.

———. 2003. *Longest Struggle: Black Freedom Fighters in Steel.* Ithaca: Cornell University ILR Press.

Nelson, Bruce. 1997. "'CIO Meant One Thing for Whites and Another Thing for Us': Steelworkers and Civil Rights, 1936–1974." In *Southern Labor in*

Transition, 1940–1995, edited by Robert H. Zieger, 113–45. Knoxville: University of Tennessee Press.

———. 2001. *Divided We Stand: American Workers and the Struggle for Black Equality.* Princeton: Princeton University Press.

Nelson, William E., Jr., and Philip J. Meranto. 1977. *Electing Black Mayors: Political Action in the Black Community.* Columbus: Ohio State University Press.

Ng, Roxana. 1998. "Work Restructuring and Recolonizing Third World Women: An Example from the Garment Industry in Toronto." *Canadian Woman Studies/Les Cahiers de la Femme* 18 (1): 21–25.

Norrell, Robert J. 1986. "Caste in Steel: Jim Crow Careers in Birmingham, Alabama." *Journal of American History* 73: 669–94.

Nyden, Philip. 1983. "Evolution of Black Political Influence in American Trade Unions." *Journal of Black Studies* 13 (4): 379–98.

———. 1984. *Steelworkers Rank-and-File: The Political Economy of a Union Reform Movement.* South Hadley, Mass.: Bergin and Garvey Publishers.

O'Connor, Julia S., Ann Shola Orloff, and Shelia Shaver. 1999. *States, Markets, Families: Gender, Liberalism, and Social Policy in Australia, Canada, Great Britain, and the United States.* Cambridge: Cambridge University Press.

O'Farrell, Brigid, and Joyce L. Kornbluh. 1996. *Rocking the Boat: Union Women's Voices 1915–1975.* New Brunswick: Rutgers University Press.

Olson, Karen. 1995. "The Gendered Social World of Steelmaking: A Case Study of Bethlehem Steel's Sparrows Point Plant." Ph.D. diss., University of Maryland, College Park.

Omi, Michael, and Howard Winant. 1994. *Racial Formation in the United States: From the 1960s to the 1990s.* New York: Routledge.

Ong, Aihwa. 1999. *Flexible Citizenship: The Cultural Logics of Transnationality.* Durham: Duke University Press.

Orleck, Annelise. 1995. *Common Sense and a Little Fire: Women and Working-Class Politics in the United States, 1900–1965.* Chapel Hill: University of North Carolina Press.

Orloff, Ann Shola. 1996. "Gender and the Welfare State." *Annual Review of Sociology* 22: 51–70.

Pidgeon, Mary Elizabeth. 1947. "Women Workers and Recent Economic Change." *Monthly Labor Review* (December): 666–71.

Pierson, Ruth Roach. 1983. *Canadian Women and the Second World War.* Historical Booklet No. 37. Ottawa: Canadian Historical Association.

Pierson, Ruth Roach, and Marjorie Griffin Cohen. 1995. *Canadian Women's Issues: Twenty-five Years of Women's Activism in English Canada.* Toronto: James Lorimer and Company.

Pocock, Barbara, ed. 1997. *Strife: Sex and Politics in Labour Unions.* St. Leonards: Allen and Unwin.

Prentice, Alison, Paula Bourne, Gail Cuthbert Brandt, Beth Light, Wendy Mitchinson, and Naomi Black. 1988. *Canadian Women: A History.* Toronto: Harcourt Brace Jovanovich.

Prieto, Norma Iglesias. 1985. *Beautiful Flowers of the Maquiladora: Life Histories of Women Workers in Tijuana.* Austin: University of Texas Press.

Proceedings of the Eighteenth Constitutional Convention of the United Steelworkers of America, A.F.L.-C.I.O. 1976. Las Vegas, Nevada, August 30 to September 3. United Steelworkers Archives and Oral History Collection and Labor Archives, Pattee Library, Penn State University.

Randall, Vicky, and Georgina Waylen. 1998. *Gender, Politics and the State.* New York: Routledge.

Ray, Raka. 1999. *Fields of Protest: Women's Movements in India.* Minneapolis: University of Minnesota Press.

Reskin, Barbara, and Patricia A. Roos. 1990. *Job Queues, Gender Queues: Explaining Women's Inroads into Male Occupations.* Philadelphia: Temple University Press.

Robnett, Belinda. 1997. *How Long? How Long? African-American Women in the Struggle for Civil Rights.* New York: Oxford University Press.

Roediger, David R. 1991. *The Wages of Whiteness: Race and the Making of the American Working Class.* New York: Verso.

Rose, Jim. 1995. "'The Problem Every Supervisor Dreads': Women Workers at the U.S. Steel Duquesne Works during World War II." *Labor History* 36 (1): 23–51.

Rosen, Ruth. 2000. *The World Split Open: How the Modern Women's Movement Changed America.* New York: Viking Press.

Roth, Silke. 1997. *Political Socialization, Bridging Organizations, Social Movement Interaction: The Coalition of Labor Union Women, 1974–1996.* Ph.D. diss., University of Connecticut, Storrs.

Rowbotham, Sheila, and Stephanie Linkogle, eds. 2001. *Women Resist Globalization: Mobilizing for Livelihood and Rights.* London: Zed Books.

Rucht, Dieter. 1996. "The Impact of National Contexts on Social Movement Structures: A Cross-Movement and Cross-National Comparison." In *Comparative Perspectives on Social Movements: Political Opportunities, Mobilizing Structures, and Cultural Framings,* edited by Doug McAdam, John D. McCarthy, and Meyer N. Zald. Cambridge: Cambridge University Press.

Rupp, Leila. 1978. *Mobilizing Women for War: German and American Propaganda, 1939–1945.* Princeton: Princeton University Press.

Rupp, Leila, and Verta Taylor. 1999. "Forging Feminist Identity in an International Movement: A Collective Identity Approach to Twentieth-Century Feminism." *Signs: Journal of Women in Culture and Society* 24 (2): 363–86.

Sandoval, Chela. 2000. *Methodology of the Oppressed*. Minneapolis: University of
    Minnesota Press.

Sassen, Saskia. 1998. *Globalization and Its Discontents*. New York: New Press.

Schur, Lisa A., and Douglas L. Kruse. 1992. "Gender Differences in Attitudes
    toward Unions." *Industrial and Labor Relations Review* 46 (October): 89–102.

Seifer, Nancy. 1976. *"Nobody Speaks for Me!": Self-Portraits of American Working
    Class Women*. New York: Touchstone Press.

Serrin, William. 1993. *Homestead: The Glory and Tragedy of an American Steel
    Town*. New York: Vintage Books.

Shanley, Mary Lyndon, and Uma Narayan, eds. 1997. *Reconstructing Political
    Theory: Feminist Perspectives*. University Park: Pennsylvania State University
    Press.

Skocpol, Theda. 1992. *Protecting Soldiers and Mothers: The Political Origins of
    Social Policy in the United States*. Cambridge: Belknap Press of Harvard
    University Press.

Smith, Jackie. 1997a. "Transnational Political Processes and the Human Rights
    Movement." In *Social Movements: Perspectives and Issues*, edited by S. M.
    Buechler and F. Kurt Cylke Jr., 541–63. Mountain View, Calif.: Mayfield.

———. 1997b. "Characteristics of the Modern Transnational Social Movement
    Sector." In *Transnational Social Movements and Global Politics: Solidarity
    beyond the State*, edited by J. Smith, C. Chatfield, and R. Pagnucco, 42–58.
    Syracuse: Syracuse University Press.

Smith, Larry. 1995. *Beyond Rust*. Huron, Ohio: Bottom Dog Press.

Smith, Peggie R. 1991. "Separate Identities: Black Women, Work, and Title VII."
    Harvard Women's Law Journal 14: 21–75.

Smith, William Dale. 1959. *A Multitude of Men*. New York: Simon and Schuster.

Snow, David A., E. Burke Rochford, Steven K. Worden, and Robert D. Benford.
    1986. "Frame Alignment Processes, Micromobilization, and Movement
    Participation." *American Sociological Review* 51: 464–81.

Snow, David E., and Robert Benford. 1992. "Master Frames and Cycles of
    Protest." In *Frontiers in Social Movements Theory*, edited by Acton Morris and
    Carol McClurg Mueller. New Haven: Yale University Press.

Sobel, David, and Susan Meurer. 1994. *Working at Inglis: The Life and Death of a
    Canadian Factory*. Toronto: James Lorimer and Company.

Stein, Judith. 1998. *Running Steel, Running America: Race, Economic Policy, and
    the Decline of Liberalism*. Chapel Hill: University of North Carolina Press.

Stepan-Norris, Judith, and Maurice Zeitlin. 1996. *Talking Union*. Urbana:
    University of Illinois.

———. 2002. *Left Out: Reds and America's Industrial Unions*. Cambridge:
    Cambridge University Press.

Stevens, Michael. 1993. *Women Remember the War 1941–1945.* Madison: State Historical Society of Wisconsin.

Stewart, James B. 2001. "The Pursuit of Equality in the Steel Industry: The Committee on Civil Rights and the Civil Rights Department of the United Steelworkers of America, 1948–1970." In *African Americans, Labor, and Society: Organizing for a New Agenda,* edited by Patrick L. Mason, 165–201. Detroit: Wayne State University Press.

Stone, Katherine V. 1975. "The Origins of Job Structures in the Steel Industry." In *Labor Market Segmentation,* edited by Richard Edwards, Michael Reich, and David M. Gordon, 27–84. Lexington, Mass.: Lexington Books.

Strobel, Margaret. 1995. "Organizational Learning in the Chicago Women's Liberation Union." In *Feminist Organizations: Harvest of the New Women's Movement,* edited by Myra Marx Ferree and Patricia Yancey Martin, 145–64. Philadelphia: Temple University Press.

Sugiman, Pamela. 1994. *Labour's Dilemma: The Gender Politics of Auto Workers in Canada, 1937–1979.* Toronto: University of Toronto Press.

Tannenbaum, Penny. 1979. "United Steelworkers of America, AFL-CIO v. Weber (U.S. 1979)." *Villanova Law Review* 25: 141–59.

Tarrow, Sidney. 1992. "Mentalities, Political Cultures, and Collective Action Frames: Constructing Meanings through Action." In *Frontiers in Social Movement Theory,* edited by Aldon D. Morris and Carol McClurg Mueller, 174–202. New Haven: Yale University Press.

———. 1996. "States and Opportunities: The Political Structuring of Social Movements." In *Comparative Perspectives on Social Movements: Political Opportunities, Mobilizing Structures, and Cultural Framing,* edited by Doug McAdam, John D. McCarthy, and Mayer N. Zald, 41–61. Cambridge: Cambridge University Press.

———. 1998. *Power in Movements.* Cambridge: Cambridge University Press.

Taylor, Verta. 1996. *Rock-a-by Baby: Feminism, Self-Help and Postpartum Depression.* New York: Routledge.

———. 1999. "Gender and Social Movements: Gender Processes in Women's Self-Help Movements." *Gender and Society* 13 (1): 8–33.

Taylor, Verta, and Nancy Whittier. 1992. "Collective Identity in Social Movement Communities: Lesbian Feminist Mobilization." In *Frontiers in Social Movement Theory,* edited by Aldon D. Morris and Carol McClurg Mueller, 104–30. New Haven: Yale University Press.

———. 1995. "Analytical Approaches to Social Movement Culture: The Culture of the Women's Movement." In *Social Movements and Culture,* edited by H. Johnston and B. Klandermans, 163–87. Minneapolis: University of Minnesota Press.

Thom, Mary. 2000. "Promises to Keep: Ford Leaders Assess the International Women's Movement and the Road Ahead." *Ford Foundation Report,* Winter, 30–34.

Tilly, Charles. 1984. "Social Movements and National Politics." In *Statemaking and Social Movements,* edited by Charles Bright and Susan Harding, 297–317. Ann Arbor: University of Michigan Press.

Turner, Lowell, Harry C. Katz, and Richard W. Hurd. 2001. *Rekindling the Movement: Labor's Quest for Relevance in the 21st Century.* Ithaca: IRL Press/Cornell.

Vickers, Jill, Pauline Rankin, and Christine Appelle. 1993. *Politics as if Women Mattered: A Political Analysis of the National Action Committee on the Status of Women.* Toronto: University of Toronto Press.

Vogel, Lise. 1993. *Mothers on the Job: Maternity Policy in the U.S. Workplace.* New Brunswick: Rutgers University Press.

Waterman, Peter. 1998. *Globalization, Social Movements, and the New Internationalisms.* London: Mansell.

Weigand, Kate. 2001. *Red Feminism: American Communism and the Making of Women's Liberation.* Baltimore: Johns Hopkins University Press.

Wertheimer, Barbara Mayer. 1977. *We Were There: The Story of Working Women in America.* New York: Pantheon.

Weston, Kath. 1990. "Production as Means, Production as Metaphor: Women's Struggle to Enter the Trades." In *Uncertain Terms: Negotiating Gender in American Culture,* edited by Faye Ginsburg and Anna Lowenhaupt Tsing, 137–51. Boston: Beacon.

White, Julie. 1993. *Sister and Solidarity: Women and Unions in Canada.* Toronto: Thompson Educational Publishing.

Williams, Christine L. 1989. *Gender Differences at Work: Women and Men in Nontraditional Occupations.* Berkeley: University of California Press.

Wilson, Joseph F. 1980. *Cold Steel: The Political Economy of Black Labor and Reform in the United Steelworkers of America (USWA).* Ph.D. diss., Columbia University, New York.

Wood, Roberta. [Referred to as Wood Papers. District 31 Women's Caucus records and related materials given to the author. See end of Bibliography for list of documents.]

Young, Iris. 1994. "Gender as Seriality: Thinking About Women as a Social Collective." *Signs: Journal of Women in Culture and Society* 19 (3): 713–38.

Zald, Mayer N. 1996. "Culture, Ideology, and Strategic Framing." In *Comparative Perspectives on Social Movements: Political Opportunities, Mobilizing Structures, and Cultural Framing,* edited by Doug McAdam, John D. McCarthy, and Mayer N. Zald, 261–74. Cambridge: Cambridge University Press.

Zuckerman, Mary Ellen. 1998. *A History of Popular Women's Magazines in the United States.* Westport, Conn.: Greenwood Press.

Zukin, Sharon. 1991. *Landscapes of Power: From Detroit to Disney World.* Berkeley: University of California Press.

Union-Related Documents

For Respect for the Rights of Working Women: Authentic Labor Front and Women of Steel (n.d.).

"Gender and Solidarity" (n.d.).

"Let's Put It on the Table: United Steelworkers Guide to Violence Prevention" (Toronto: Canadian National Office of the USWA, 1997).

Los Trabajadores del Mexico de hoy frente al nuevo milenio (1998).

Report of the Organizing Task Force (1998).

"Steelworkers Humanity Fund at a Glance" (1998).

"Steelworkers Humanity Fund: Partner Profile" (1998).

The Frente Auténtico del Trabajo and the Workers' Center of Juarez (1996).

United Steelworkers of America, Harassment Policy (Toronto: Canadian National Office of the USWA, n.d.).

Racial and Sexual Harassment, and Violence Against Women: Policy and Prevention (Toronto: Canadian National Office of the USWA, n.d.).

"The Union" (membership department brochure, n.d.).

United Steelworkers of America, Women of Steel: Building Solidarity (Toronto: Canadian National Office of the USWA, n.d.).

Women an Essential Presence for Development (Centro de Organización y Desarrollo Intergral do al Mujer [CODIM], n.d.).

Women an Essential Presence for Development: National Coordination of the Women of the Frente Auténtico del Trabajo (n.d.).

XI Congreso Nacional Frente Auténtico Del Trabajo (1998).

"Economic and Political Empowerment of Poor Women in Nicaragua" (n.d.).

"Reaching Out to Build a Movement for Social Justice" (Resolution 29, 30th Constitutional Convention of the USWA, 2000).

"Globalization: Making It Work for Workers" (Resolution 31, 30th Constitutional Convention of the USWA, 2000).

"Women of Steel Go Global" (n.d.).

"Women of Steel: Building Solidarity" (n.d.).

Wood Papers: District 31 Women's Caucus records and related materials given to the author, including:

    Annual Officers Report (n.d.).

    Amicus *(Weber).*

"Reverse the Weber Decision" (Women's Committee flyer, *Gary Works,* n.d.).

Steelworkers Position Paper on Reproductive Hazards and Health in the Workplace (signed by Joseph Odorcich, vice president of administration, n.d.).

District 31 Women's Conference Resolution Against Sexual Harassment (n.d.).

Index

Mary Margaret Fonow is associate professor of women's studies at The Ohio State University. Her research interests include union feminism, feminist methodology, and social movements. She coedited (with Judith A. Cook) *Beyond Methodology: Feminist Scholarship as Lived Research,* and she is the editor of *Reading Women's Lives,* an innovative database of more than five hundred articles and pedagogical tools for teaching women's studies. She has served on the editorial boards of *Gender and Society* and the *NWSA Journal* and is a member of Scholars, Artists, and Writers for Social Justice.